CHINESE POLITICS AND THE SUCCESSION TO MAO

John Gardner

HM

Holmes & Meier Publishers
New York

First published in the United States of America 1982 by
Holmes & Meier Publishers, Inc.
30 Irving Place, New York, N.Y. 10003

Library of Congress Cataloging in Publication Data

Gardner, John 1939-
   Chinese politics and the succession to Mao.

   Bibliograpy: p.
   Includes index.
   1. China — Politics and government — 1949-
2. Heads of state — China — Succession. I. Title.
JQ1503 1982.G37   951.05   82-6174
ISBN 0-8419-0808-7   AACR2
ISBN 0-8419-0809-5 (pbk.)

Printed in Hong Kong

For my mother and the memory of my father

Contents

Acknowledgements

I wish to express my thanks to all those who have laboured in the flinty vineyards of Chinese politics and who have gone into print with their findings; to the small group of political scientists specialising on China in the United Kingdom whose conversation and writings have been a source of stimulating ideas and hard information, particularly Stuart R. Schram, Jack Gray, Gordon White, David S. G. Goodman and David Chambers; Wong, Chiu-Yin for her patience and encouragement; and to Hanne, Sara and Paul Gardner who were compelled to share the tribulations of writing. A special debt is owed to Marilyn Dunn who transformed my semi-legible scrawl into beautiful type, and who endured with fortitude and good humour the frequent and erratic switches of romanisation. Needless to say, I alone am responsible for all errors and shortcomings.

Abbreviations

CQ *The China Quarterly*, (London), the leading scholarly journal on modern and contemporary China.

FE British Broadcasting Corporation, *Summary of World Broadcasts*, Part 3, *The Far East*, (Caversham, Berkshire). This excellent service provides summaries of translations of Chinese radio broadcasts, many of them from local stations, and also reproduces reports of *Xinhua*, the official Chinese news agency.

I & S *Issues and Studies*, (Taibei, Taiwan). Although its articles are unfailingly hostile to the leaders of the People's Republic and their policies, this monthly journal is renowned for acquiring and translating confidential intra-Party documents and leadership speeches which the People's Republic of China has made publicly available.

PD *People's Daily, (Renmin Ribao)*. The national newspaper of the Communist Party of China.

PLA People's Liberation Army. The PLA includes naval and air forces.

PR/BR *Peking Review*, to December 1978, *Beijing Review* thereafter. English-language weekly published by the People's Republic of China. It contains translations of leadership speeches, Congress proceedings, policy statements, etc.

RF *Red Flag (Hongqi)*. The theoretical journal of the Central Committee of the Communist Party of China. Originally monthly, now fortnightly.

Romanisation

The People's Republic of China uses the *pinyin* system of romanisation and, since 1979, has virtually eradicated all other forms, even in the case of the most common place-names. Thus, 'Peking' is now 'Beijing', 'Tientsin' is 'Tianjin'. Western publications are rapidly following suit and I have, therefore, used *pinyin* throughout, with minor exceptions. Where a personal name is both widely known in a traditional form and is almost unrecognisable in *pinyin*, I have retained the conventional spelling: thus, 'Chiang Kai-shek' and 'Confucius'.

I have also cited books and articles by the exact title. However, when quoting from translations or texts I have taken the liberty of substituting *pinyin* for the original romanisation in which a name appeared.

The Leader and His Passing

... Comrade Mao Zedong, the esteemed and beloved great leader of our Party, our army and the people of all nationalities in our country, the great teacher of the international proletariat and the oppressed nations and oppressed peoples, Chairman of the Central Committee of the Communist Party of China, Chairman of the Military Commission of the Central Committee of the Communist Party of China, and Honorary Chaiman of the National Committee of the Chinese People's Political Consultative Conference, passed away at 00.10 hours on 9 September 1976 in Beijing as a result of the worsening of his illness ...

... Chairman Mao Zedong was the founder and wise leader of the Communist Party of China, the Chinese People's Liberation Army and the People's Republic of China ...

... Chairman Mao Zedong was the greatest Marxist of the contemporary era ...

... The passing away of Chairman Mao Zedong is an inestimable loss ...

(from the official communiqué announcing Mao's death)

One View of the Succession Problem

The historical experience of all revolutionary movements shows that the death of the great leader of a revolution always means very serious difficulties for the revolutionary classes and revolutionary movement. As for the enemies of the revolution, it is always a very good opportunity to pounce upon the revolution and strangle it by making use of these difficulties. Under this situation, it is of the utmost importance to the success or failure of the revolutionary cause whether the revolutionary classes and their political party have their successor, and whether their succeeding leader can carry on the behest of the great leader, raise high the revolutionary banner and triumph over the frenzied attacks launched by all the enemies, particularly the inside enemies.

(Xinhua News Agency, 16 December 1976)

The Successor

At this grave historical juncture, the Party Central Committee headed by Comrade Hua Guofeng, with the boldness and vision of proletarian revolutionaries, shattered at one stroke the criminal plot of the 'Gang of Four' to usurp Party and state power . . . By leading our Party from danger to safety through tempestuous storms, Comrade Hua Guofeng averted a major retrogression in Chinese history and a great disaster for our people, thereby winning the complete trust and wholehearted affection of the whole Party, the whole army and the people . . . Comrade Hua Guofeng is indeed a worthy successor selected by Chairman Mao himself, a worthy helmsman to steer Chairman Mao's cause forward, and a worthy wise leader of the Communist Party of China founded by Chairman Mao.

(from a Jiefangjun Bao [Liberation Army Daily] article, 29 October 1976, in Peking Review, no. 45, 1976, p. 5)

And yet . . .

At a meeting of the Politbureau held from late November to early December 1980, Hua offered his resignation as Party Chairman and it was agreed that this proposition should be submitted to the sixth plenum of the eleventh Central Committee.

(Zhengming [Contend], a well-informed Hong Kong journal, February 1981, pp. 7—8)

Introduction – The Problem of Political Succession

In most modern nation-states, whatever their political complexion, one individual generally has the role of what Seweryn Bialer calls the 'top leader' in the simple sense that he or she possesses a greater measure of power than anyone else.[1] In liberal democracies the top leader can easily be recognised by virtue of holding a major office of state, such as 'President' or 'Prime Minister', which invests the incumbent with a range of formal powers. Sometimes, as in the socialist states, the top leader's position normally derives from command of the ruling Communist Party, and carries the title of 'Chairman', 'First Secretary', or 'General Secretary' (the exact nomenclature differs between parties and individual parties may change their titles from time to time).

Generally speaking, the task of identifying the top leader in any state is relatively easy.[2] The top leader is usually highly visible and his or her activities attract considerable attention, as do the methods by which a top leader has achieved power and, subsequently, been replaced by another. The question of political succession is of abiding interest because of its intrinsic importance and also because of the sheer diversity of the processes by which power is transferred and the consequences for the political system concerned. This book will examine the problem as it has affected the People's Republic of China but, before doing so, it is worth making some brief points of a comparative nature.

Succession in liberal democracies is relatively easy to observe and it has, therefore, been studied in enormous depth. Liberal democracies have evolved methods of changing their top leaders which are highly institutionalised and predictable. Usually the succession process is determined by

'rules of the game' in the form of legal regulations and constitutional conventions. For example, statutes determine the
fixed or maximum terms for which a top leader may serve
without facing the electorate. The method of election is prescribed by law. Political parties have their own rules and
regulations governing the selection of candidates.

Abuses can, of course, occur. Ballots are occasionally
rigged, gerrymandering may take place, and the funds spent
on behalf of a candidate may grossly exceed the legally-
prescribed maximum. Nevertheless, because the process is one
of relatively open competition in which rival candidates and
their supporters are quick to shout 'foul!', there is a reasonable
likelihood that acts of illegality and dishonesty will be
uncovered and will rebound to the detriment of those per-
petrating them.

Hence, when a new leader emerges he or she is widely
accepted as having a legitimate title to rule. On assuming
office the top leader must similarly exercise power within
certain constitutional restraints, and attempts to exceed one's
formal authority will encounter vigorous, well-publicised
opposition. Indeed, displaced leaders or unsuccessful contenders are likely to play a major role in acting as 'watch-
dogs'. For the notion of 'loyal opposition' is enshrined in
liberal democratic systems. Failure in a leadership contest
brings hurt pride and disappointment, but leaves defeated
candidates in positions of importance from which they can
serve as critics of the administration and present themselves
as an alternative government with an eye to the next election.
Indeed, as Roger Garside has observed:

In Britain and the US, that otherwise dangerous moment
when power is transferred [has] been made one of dignity
and grace, thanks to finely honed ritual. The outgoing
American president would attend the inauguration of his
successor. A newly appointed British prime minister would
drive to Buckingham Palace to kiss the hand of the monarch,
and the outgoing premier would pause on the steps of
Number 10 Downing Street to say a few words to the press,
wishing his successor well and looking forward to spending
more time with his grandchildren.[3]

Moreover, liberal democracies and the political parties within them also have 'rules of the game' to deal with emergencies. Should a top leader die or become incapacitated there are established and well-publicised arrangements for the smooth transfer of power until such times as the 'normal' method of choosing a top leader may be resumed.

Finally, top leaders in liberal democracies possess only limited power. Apart from constitutional restraints, they function in pluralistic societies and are constantly aware of the imminence of the next election. They must, therefore, command widespread support among the electorate if they are to survive politically. This does not in itself prevent abrupt changes of policy; electorates can be volatile and can welcome them. But, generally, changes of direction are usually minor or gradual. Whatever leaders and their opponents may say, the election of a new American president or British prime minister rarely makes a radical difference to the lives of their citizens.

In the socialist states the picture is very different. Over fifty years after the Bolshevik Revolution and over thirty after the establishment of communist rule in Eastern Europe and China, the succession issue remains a problem and frequently assumes crisis proportions. In the most recent work relating to the subject in the Soviet Union, Bialer has succinctly identified the inadequacies of that political system and most of those which have followed it in ordering their own political arrangements. He observes:

No predetermined tenure of office is ascribed to the position of the top leader. Neither are the terms of the office predetermined to the extent which would make similar from one occupant to another the attributes of rights and obligations, of power and influence. Nor is the manner by which the incumbent of the top leadership position relinquishes his post in any sense standardised. Most importantly, the degree of unpredictability and uncertainty in the procedures for selecting a new leader and in the process of consolidating his position is much higher than in democratic polities or authoritarian military regimes; and this situation injects a more pronounced element of unpredictability and uncertainty into the entire Soviet political process than is characteristic of its operation in 'normal' times.[4]

Myron Rush drew similar conclusions from his wider study of all socialist states, published in 1974, in which he highlighted the importance of succession in such polities in that 'power is highly concentrated and uncontrolled at the top'. Like Bialer he noted how problematic the succession issue is. In part this is because 'the ordering of their institutions and offices remains a problem'. The relative power of Party and state organs, and the relative importance of different offices within each other is neither stable nor standardised. Moreover, Rush observed, 'while personal rule has been customary, there is no constitutional or ideological justification for it, hence no principle by which personal rule can be made legitimate. In the absence of such a principle, the authority of a personal ruler in a communist state cannot be transferred to another person by a regulated succession.'[5]

Consequently, in socialist states the succession question has regularly involved bitter factional disputes and conspiratorial dealings within the political élite. In North Korea Kim Il Sung even resorted to the dynastic principle by attempting to ensure that he should be succeeded by his son. In Eastern Europe the outcome has often been determined by the Soviet Union which has usually had the power to exercise options varying from 'influence' to outright invasion. Most recently the practice of bringing about leadership changes by invasion has moved eastwards — witness the Vietnamese invasion of Kampuchea and the Soviet invasion of Afghanistan.

Popular movements *have* played a part in bringing about changes in the top leadership in some socialist states. In July 1981, for example, Stanislaw Kania, the Polish Party leader, had to undergo a genuinely competitive election at the ninth Party Congress. Unhappily, on other occasions, as in Hungary in 1956 and Czechoslovakia in 1968, the final outcome has not necessarily been what the initiators intended.

And in the socialist states top leaders who are ousted, or contenders for supreme office who fail, face penalties which may well be far more excessive than those experienced by their counterparts in liberal democracies. The age of bloody purges may be over in the USSR and Eastern Europe but in China Liu Shaoqi died miserably in imprisonment and Lin Biao also came to an untimely end in mysterious circumstances. The two pre-invasion rulers of Afghanistan also appear to have died violently.[6] Most recently, although Mao's widow was eventually given a 'suspended' death sentence for her attempt to 'usurp' power, it is known that the Chinese leadership was divided on this matter, and that some would have preferred her to be executed.

Nearer home, the case of Dubcek of Czechoslovakia illustrates how miserable defeat can be. Accompanying and following his ousting in 1968, Dubcek was subjected to physical brutality and police harassment. He was reduced to political impotence and assigned to a job of trivial importance.

In the Soviet Union Stalin's successors fared somewhat better. In 1955 Malenkov was permitted to 'resign' and was given an office of moderate importance. In 1964 Khrushchev was ousted and 'retired' into private life. It was perhaps his outstanding achievement that he had humanised Soviet politics to such a degree that he himself could be left to live out his days in peace. Equally, it was a sad reflection on the intolerance of the Soviet system that he became almost a 'non-person' after his fall. His death was noted in an official obituary, but it was very brief, and no Soviet leader bothered to attend his funeral.

The pattern of uncertainty, instability, conflict and major policy changes, which characterises successions in virtually all the socialist states, has been most vividly illustrated in the People's Republic of China. To be sure, China was a relative late-comer in terms of facing its first succession, but when it came it was particularly explosive and dramatic. Mao Zedong, the original top leader, held power for almost twenty-seven years. Although not a record in the communist world, his tenure of office was unusually long and this in itself contributed to the massive political upheavals surrounding his death.

When the People's Republic was founded on 1 October 1949, Mao was 55 and was already Party Chairman. Although he subsequently held a number of Party and state offices it was from this post that his power derived, and he held it to the day of his death, in his eighty-third year, on 9 September 1976.

From a comparatively early stage Mao was himself very conscious of the succession problem. In the late 1950s, Liu Shaoqi emerged as the man most likely to succeed. He was, however, found wanting and in the early stages of the Cultural Revolution he was disgraced and died in imprisonment shortly thereafter. Lin Biao then emerged as the heir-apparent but died in even more dramatic circumstances in 1971.

Thereafter the problem became particularly acute. By this time Mao was old and his physical condition was poor. It is likely that his mental state had also declined. Within the top leadership factional groupings began to jockey for position. They were loosely organised and membership was fluid. One group coalesced around Zhou Enlai and Deng Xiaoping, and consisted largely of individuals who were on the Right of the Chinese political spectrum. Another formed around Jiang Qing, Mao's wife, and three political leaders from Shanghai: Zhang Chunqiao, Yao Wenyuan and Wang Hongwen. This group was Leftist in orientation.

There were, however, many leaders who did not fall neatly into this 'Left-Right' dichotomy. Of these, the most important to emerge was Hua Guofeng, a man who only became a *national* figure in the 1970s. After a particularly intense struggle from 1973 onwards, Deng Xiaoping and his supporters were vanquished in the early months of 1976. But the Left's 'victory' was both limited and temporary. In the last months of Mao's life it was Hua Guofeng who assumed a position in the hierarchy which established his formal claim to succeed. And, less than a month after Mao's death, he consolidated his position by his spectacular arrest of the 'Gang of Four' as Jiang Qing's group then became known.

Hua then attempted to establish himself as the top leader by claiming Mao's blessing, by creating something of a personality cult, and by presenting himself as the foremost opponent of the 'Gang of Four'. He was not, however, able to prevent the return of Deng Xiaoping to the political arena in 1977. Thereafter, Hua's power was eroded. His claim to be Mao's chosen successor lost some of its appeal as Mao's legend came increasingly under attack, and step by step Hua's authority was diminished, and he was deprived of the major offices on which his power was based, which passed to protégés of Deng Xiaoping.

In this book I shall attempt to describe and analyse the Chinese succession problem. Certain caveats are in order. The first is that many of the events discussed here are very recent, and interpretations of them must, of necessity, be very super-ficial. This is, therefore, a general acount intended primarily for undergraduate readers. The second is that China remains politically unstable. Many of the actors in this drama are still alive, the problems facing the present leadership, particularly those relating to the economy, are acute, and past experience teaches us that the political pendulum may well swing violently again.

And thirdly, one is dealing with 'official' sources. The Chinese élite has always been one of the most secretive in the world. Despite very welcome moves towards greater openness in recent years, the information made available to outsiders (and that includes most of the Chinese population) is limited and edited. The partial and partisan reporting of the 'Gang of Four' trial is a vivid example of this.

Generally it may be said that Chinese official sources only rarely invent, but regularly exaggerate and distort. Occasion-ally, it is possible to confirm or rebut official statements by ref-erence to alternative sources. Sometimes, as in the case of Liu Shaoqi, it has been officially admitted that earlier accounts of his 'crimes' were falsified. But there are a number of instances where there is no way a foreign observer can be satisfied that the 'facts' at his disposal constitute the whole truth. The major example of this problem here concerns the Lin Biao affair. The official version was provided in the year after his death and was repeated and enlarged upon between November 1980 and January 1981. It reads like fiction and, indeed, has already inspired at least one fictional 'thriller'.

Hence, although it is hoped that this book is broadly accurate, it has been necessary to sprinkle it liberally with such phrases as 'it was alleged' and 'he was accused of' — a technique which is stylistically unpleasant but necessary.

Even so, it is believed that the story is worth telling. For it reveals how the Chinese leadership think and behave in terms of political succession. This in itself is a subject of great importance and a study of it throws considerable light on the workings of the Chinese political system.

1

Liu Shaoqi and the Cultural Revolution: The Rise and Fall of a Chosen Successor

Mao's first successor

In the early months of the Cultural Revolution, Mao Zedong made a speech in which he explained that the Chinese Communist élite had made arrangements for the succession at a very early stage. For seventeen years, he said, the leadership had been divided into 'two fronts'. He himself had stood in the 'second front' where he 'did not take charge of daily work'. That was in the hands of other senior leaders who constituted the 'first front'.[1] In part this division no doubt reflected Mao's own distaste for regular involvement in the multifarious details of governing the Chinese state. For, as one scholar has put it, Mao chose 'at times to stand outside the political system on a high eminence where he deliberated on questions of ideology and on the grand strategy of the revolution'.[2] But there was another reason. Mao wanted to give his colleagues public exposure and experience so that their prestige might be cultivated. It was the original intention, he said, that 'when he met with God, the state would not be thrown into great convulsions'. He pointed out that the 'two fronts' had been partly inspired, or reinforced, by Chinese perceptions of 'the lessons in connection with Stalin in the Soviet Union'.

Unhappily, the arrangement did not work and the 'great convulsions' China was to suffer constitute the theme of this book. But in the pre-Cultural Revolution era there was reason to believe that China could undergo a peaceful and orderly succession, for an 'heir-apparent' had not only been formally acknowledged but had acquired considerable power. That person was Liu Shaoqi.

Like Mao, Liu was a Hunanese. Just a few years younger than the Chairman, he had a revolutionary history that was almost as long. He had joined the Communist Party in the Soviet Union where he was a student in 1921–2. On his return to China he served the revolutionary cause as a labour organiser and, in the late 1920s, became a leader of the Communist 'underground' which operated in the 'White Areas' controlled by the Nationalists. In 1945, at the seventh Party Congress, he was clearly identifiable as a leader of the highest seniority. According to one account he was recognised as Mao's successor at this time. In formal terms this may not have been the case: in the elections for the Central Committee he received the third highest total of votes, being ranked after Mao and Zhu De, the great guerrilla general. Zhu, however, appears to have had only limited talents outside of military affairs and it was Liu who seems to have acted as Mao's 'second-in-command'. Even before liberation he deputised for Mao on various occasions. His rise may well have been aided by an apparent willingness to acknowledge Mao's ideological contribution to the revolution. For Liu had popularised the concept of 'Comrade Mao Zedong's system of thought' as early as 1943.[3]

From 1945 to 1955 Liu was General Secretary of the Central Committee Secretariat in which capacity he 'seemed to act as *de facto* supervisor of the routine administration of domestic affairs. He also delivered reports introducing important legislative initiatives and began to fill certain ceremonial functions'.[4] In December 1958, it was announced that Mao did not wish to stand for a second term as the State Chairman (he did, of course, retain the *Party* chairmanship which was by far the more important office). On 20 April 1959, the second National People's Congress duly elected Liu to the state position and from then on references describing him as Mao's 'closest commander-in-arms' began to appear in the press. In 1961, any possible doubt as to his status was removed, when Mao told Lord Montgomery that the identity of his successor was not in doubt: it was Liu Shaoqi.[5]

For Liu, therefore, the 1950s were a time for strengthening the eminent position he had already achieved before liberation. His organisational and urban experience nicely complemented the 'guerrilla style' and mobilisational politics developed by Mao in the 'Red Areas' of the countryside. The move to the cities in 1949 increased Liu's authority not least because it boosted the power of the 'White Area' Communists he had led, whose skills were now at a premium. And, despite numerous Cultural Revolution allegations to the contrary, there is no reason to suppose that Mao had differences of opinion with Liu during this decade which went beyond the norms of what might be reasonably expected among senior members of any ruling élite.

That friction did develop and, ultimately, produced 'great convulsions', was really the consequence of the 'Great Leap Forward'. The Leap constituted Mao's attempt to modernise and develop his country by the application of mobilisational techniques and the creation of radically new organisational forms, most notable of which was the establishment of the communes. Implemented at high speed and with inadequate planning, the Leap caused considerable economic dislocation and widespread hardship. It also provoked a major and bitter dispute within the senior leadership when Peng Dehuai, the Minister of Defence, attacked its excessive Leftism at the Lushan plenum in July 1959.

For some time tension had been developing between the People's Liberation Army (PLA) and the Chinese Communist Party. This focused on the problem of reconciling the need for, on the one hand, a professionalised military instrument, with demands, on the other, that the PLA remain loyal to its guerrilla heritage with all that implied in terms of politicisation and involvement in a range of non-military activities. Peng had leaned towards professionalism, taking an attitude later to be labelled as the 'bourgeois military line' in opposition to Mao's 'proletarian military line'. The Leap exacerbated these tensions and, because it infuriated the Soviet Union, also put at risk the Sino-Soviet alliance. But Peng objected not only as a military man representing a sectional interest. He spoke out in his capacity as a Communist leader of thirty years' standing who was desperately worried that an excess of radicalism was losing the Party the respect and loyalty of the peasant masses who had brought it to power.

In the event Peng was defeated. Mao vigorously defended the policies of the Leap, admitting that mistakes had been made but arguing that these were in the process of being corrected. By a combination of cajolery and threat he secured the support of a majority of his colleagues at Lushan. Peng, and the few other leaders bold enough to challenge Mao openly, were branded as an 'anti-Party clique' and dismissed from office. In September 1959, Marshal Lin Biao was appointed to replace Peng as Minister of Defence. Before liberation Lin had enjoyed a military career of the utmost distinction and, as commander of the Fourth Field Army, had played a part second to none in achieving final military victory over Chiang Kai-Shek. Because of ill-health he was politically inactive for most of the 1950s but his new appointment presaged a vigorous return to political life.

The leadership after Lushan

Although Mao was successful in defeating Peng Dehuai, the Lushan plenum unleashed a chain of events which destroyed the unity of the élite and, eventually, both Liu Shaoqi and Lin Biao. After the plenum Mao withdrew from active political involvement, being motivated, no doubt, by a belief that he should adopt a low profile while senior colleagues implemented whatever policies were necessary to clean up the mess resulting from the Leap. It is possible that other leaders may have pressed this course of action upon him as their price for saving his 'face' by supporting him at Lushan.

Consequently it fell to Liu Shaoqi, aided and abetted by Deng Xiaoping, the Party's General Secretary, to take command and repair the damage. And under Liu's general guidance the 'front line' leaders of the Party and state apparatus introduced a series of policies which were decidedly conservative. In the Cultural Revolution it was to be alleged that Liu had deliberately embarked on a strategy of 'walking the capitalist road', emulating Khrushchev in the USSR and trying to lead China into 'revisionism' and, indeed, 'counter-revolution'. Numerous articles described in detail how he had *personally* been responsible for opposing Maoist principles at every stage.

Many of these charges are demonstrably exaggerated, distorted and sometimes quite untrue. Nevertheless Liu did *preside* over China in the early and mid-1960s. He was responsible for the Party and state bureaucracies and, therefore, it is reasonable to refer to a 'Liuist' approach when discussing the policies of the period. For Liu came to symbolise a political organisation which, by the early 1960s, was running out of revolutionary fervour.

It is necessary to note here that the Chinese political élite had changed considerably since 1949. True, the men at the top were, for the most part, those who had been leading revolutionaries at the time of liberation. In contrast to the Soviet élite under Stalin, very few senior Communists were purged in the 1950s and few 'new men' rose to the highest echelons. But the men themselves had changed. Obviously they were much older and, with advancing years, becoming more conservative. More important, perhaps, was the change in their 'work style'. Before liberation they had been 'many-sided hands', jacks-of-all-trades, who applied their talents to the wide variety of tasks which the exigencies of a guerrilla-war environment necessitated. After victory, however, they moved into leading positions in the continually growing Party and state apparatus, and became functional specialists. As such they developed loyalties and attachments to the departments, areas and individuals under their control. They also acquired the trappings of bureaucrats everywhere; a concern for hierarchical leadership patterns, and a liking for routinised and orderly procedures. Increasingly, they saw society as the object of management rather than mobilisation, and the dislocations of the Leap (which became even more apparent after the fall of Peng) diminished Mao's stature in their eyes. The Soviet Union's unilateral decision in 1960 to withdraw all assistance, together with the horrendous series of natural disasters which beset China in 1959, 1960, and

1961, further strengthened their desire to proceed with caution.

Moreover the rank-and-file Party membership was far from being a revolutionary shock-force by the early 1960s. In 1945 the seventh Party Congress had produced a constitution which laid down criteria governing admission to the Party, in a way which discriminated heavily in favour of persons of humble origin. In the mid-1950s, however, the inexorable demands for more and more skilled personnel meant that the doors were opened not only to peasants and workers, but also to the intellectuals, most of whom were not from the poorer classes. In 1956 the eighth Party constitution recognised their importance when it revised the criteria for admission to make membership available to anyone 'who works and does not exploit the labour of others'. Hence the 'class composition' of the Party changed as the 1950s progressed. Although the peasant component remained the major one, there was a steady decline in its percentage of the total membership, and an increase in the recruitment of people with skills.

Furthermore, and related to these changes, the Party grew considerably. By mid-1959 it had 14,000,000 members and, two years later, 17,000,000. At the end of 1961 some 80 per cent of members were persons who had joined since 1949. Therefore, while the most senior Party leaders were revolutionary veterans, most of the ordinary members were not. They had joined after nationwide victory, and it is safe to assume that many were careerists who became part of the new 'Establishment' for the rewards it could offer. Such people were not enthusiastic about Mao's style of mobilisational politics and the problems caused by the Leap were bitterly resented.

Indeed, considerable dissatisfaction with Mao and his policies was expressed in a relatively open manner by leading cultural figures who obviously enjoyed the tacit support of senior cadres. In the aftermath of Lushan some writers and dramatists complained of the glorification of Mao, the failures of the Leap, and the treatment accorded to Peng Dehuai. Many of these critics were Party members and some had senior posts under the Central Committee's Propaganda Department and the Beijing Party Committee.

A common theme in their work was that the peasants had suffered unduly because of the Leap. For example, in August 1962, one critic maintained that 'the main contradiction [was] between the socialist ideological leadership and the actual needs of the peasants', and asked fellow short-story writers to show that the Leap had caused hardship and misery. Deng Tuo, a former editor of *People's Daily* and, from 1959, director of the cultural and ideological work of the Beijing Party Committee, wrote a series of essays in the Beijing press under the title 'Evening Chats from Yanshan'. In these he used Aesop's fables to engage in oblique but biting criticism and satire of Mao, whom he condemned for refusing to listen to the views of others, and for living in a cloud-cuckoo land of unjustified optimism. In one essay he even suggested that Mao might not have been quite right in the head.

The most important works, at least in the light of later events, were written by Wu Han, a prominent historian and deputy mayor of Beijing. In June 1959 he had published the first of a number of articles on Hai Rui, a Ming dynasty official, and in 1961 he wrote a play entitled 'The Dismissal of Hai Rui'. As interpreted by Wu Han, Hai Rui was a courageous and honest governor who attempted to redress the grievances of an oppressed peasantry. In his play, Wu put the following words into his hero's mouth:

> The local officials are the great bane in Jiangnan. They appropriate the people's land by force, and make farming difficult.
> Many, many wrongful judgements need to be straightened out or reversed.
> And only if the land is returned to the people will they be at peace.[6]

But Hai's concern for the well-being of the peasants made him powerful enemies. These successfully prevailed upon the Emperor who unjustly dismissed him from office.

Wu Han, in fact, was resorting to the traditional Chinese practice of using historical allegory to criticise contemporary events. His play was a defence of Peng Dehuai and an attack on 'Emperor' Mao. Wu was not alone in using drama to make this point but, as will be discussed below, he was to be singled out as the first target for attack when the Cultural Revolution began.

The cultural assault on Mao was unprecedented. Although it died away in 1962 as the Chairman attempted to make a political comeback, it signified the extent to which opposition had developed, and had been permitted to find expression. And in the policy arena generally, changes were introduced which Mao was to find objectionable. Liu Shaoqi and his colleagues were undoubtedly successful in repairing much of the damage caused by the Leap, and the economy began to grow again at a healthy rate. But this growth was achieved by concentrating on a technocratic strategy of development. The actual policies involved have been described in detail elsewhere and a few brief examples will suffice here. Essentially, the 'Liuist' approach was to place a high premium on the services of those with skills. Such persons were given encouragement and material rewards while those of lesser ability suffered relative deprivation.

Thus, in education there was a heavy emphasis on academic excellence. Gifted students could progress through a highly competitive school system to lengthy university courses and a relatively well-paid and satisfying career. Their intellectually weaker contemporaries were shunted off to the countryside to undertake arduous and menial tasks in an inhospitable environment. In large and modern factories skilled workers enjoyed highly differentiated pay-scales, trade union membership and a variety of welfare benefits. The unskilled were poorly paid and, in many cases, lacked job security. Managers, scientists and intellectuals were accorded considerable respect and privileges. Even among the peasants, a reform of commune organisation after the Leap created new divisions, in that rewards became more closely related to ability and effort, and the reintroduction of private plots and free markets gave a stimulus to entrepreneurial talents.

The result was an increase in social stratification which negated the egalitarian tenets of Mao's philosophy. The stress on professionalism and the lack of attention given to political (and, in the widest sense, moral) considerations, caused society to divide between those who were privileged and those who were deprived. Furthermore, the system was not entirely meritocratic. Senior cadres and the urban professional classes were able to use their own talents and 'connections' to ensure that their children had greater access to educational and career opportunities than the general populace. A 'new class' was beginning to emerge.

The Maoist resurgence

In January 1962, Mao emerged once more to try and rectify the situation. In that month he made a major speech at an enlarged work conference of the Central Committee in which he observed:

> Among the old and the new Party members, especially among the new Party members, there have always been some persons of poor character and work style. They are the individualists, bureaucrats, subjectivists, and even degenerates. They are also those who display the sign-board of Communist Party membership but instead of representing the working class, they represent the bourgeoisie. *We must realise that purity does not exist within the Party; if we do not, we shall suffer the consequences.*[7]

Mao was especially critical of those Party leaders who kept all power in their own hands, and were afraid of 'discussions which will give rise to opinions different from those of the leading organs and the leaders'. Whenever discussions were started, Mao alleged, such persons 'suppress the enthusiasm of the masses and stop others from talking'. He followed up this criticism in September 1962, when he addressed the tenth plenum of the eighth Central Committee, and declared his belief that 'Right-wing opportunism in China should be renamed: it should be called Chinese revisionism'. As Schram has pointed out, what Mao was in fact saying was that 'the errors of those in the Party who opposed Mao's policies were in danger of accumulating to a point where they would make a qualitative leap from a socialist to a capitalist position, and become defenders of "bourgeois ideas" '.[8] He did not, it appears, name names on this occasion. In 1969 Lin Biao was to claim that Mao had already perceived 'the danger of a counter-revolutionary plot by Liu and his gang' as early as 1962, but this was almost certainly just a sycophantic statement in support of the Chairman's omniscience. Nevertheless, Mao's remarks clearly indicated that he was unhappy with the way the Party was moving under Liu's stewardship.

And it is certainly true that after the tenth plenum Mao began to rely very heavily on a small group of confidants who were, or at least claimed to be, as 'Left' as he was and, perhaps more important, were intimates of long standing. As he became increasingly concerned that the Party apparatus was moving away from him he turned for support to his personal clique. In this, four people were of special importance. Jiang Qing was Mao's wife, and her 'meteoric' rise to power in the 1960s was to evoke dark comparisons with certain periods of dynastic decline. Chen Boda was Mao's former secretary and Editor-in-Chief of *Red Flag*. Kang Sheng was a leading ideologue and chief of the secret police; he was an old friend of Jiang Qing and came from the same home district in Shandong. And then there was Lin Biao who, initially, was the most useful of Mao's supporters.

Following his appointment as Minister of Defence in 1959, Lin had given himself three tasks: to restore morale within the PLA, which had been greatly shaken by the Peng Dehuai affair; to reaffirm control over the army; and to resolve the 'struggle between the proletarian and bourgeois military lines' in favour of the former. Consequently, in 1960 he initiated a drive to elevate the political awareness and ideological consciousness of the army, the guidelines being laid down by a resolution of the Party's Military Commission in September, which declared that 'ideological penetration' should be based on the acceptance of four principles. The 'four firsts', as they became known, were that: in the relation between man and weapons, man was the primary factor; in that between political work and other work, political work took precedence; ideological education was more important than ordinary education; and practice was superior to 'book knowledge'.[9]

To put these ideas into effect a series of mass campaigns were launched within the PLA. Their scope was both to encourage the development of the soldiers' 'revolutionary spirit and will' and to strengthen relations between the troops and the civil population. The most celebrated campaign was that to cultivate the glorious 'three-eight working style'. The 'three' represented the three basic qualities of the good soldier: correct political orientation, a style of plain hard work, and flexibility in strategy and tactics. The 'eight' signified eight Chinese characters meaning 'unity, enthusiasm, dedication, and activism'. Other campaigns to cultivate 'five-good soldiers' and 'four-good companies' were based on analogous principles.

Lin paid particular attention to strengthening the role of the Party within the military machine. A vigorous recruitment drive brought over 200,000 soldiers into the Party in 1960 alone, and there was a proliferation of Party organisations at the lower levels. The power of political commissars and Party committees was strengthened and that of the 'professional' specialists diminished correspondingly. But it was not enough to ensure that Party members were in control of the PLA; after all, Peng and his supporters were Party members of long standing. What was essential, in Lin's view, was to ensure that the army was run by Party members of the right type, namely those loyal to Mao. Therefore a rectification of military Party organisations also took place, and there was a moderate purge of those deemed to be 'undesirable'.

The result of these changes was that the PLA turned again into a highly politicised instrument. Lin's reforms were assisted by two circumstances which made many soldiers more readily disposed to accept political control. First, the improvements in the economic situation after 1961 diminished resentment towards 'politicians', and second, the PLA was becoming a much more important organisation politically than it had been, and this offered new opportunities for increased status and career mobility.

It was not simply that more soldiers could join the Party itself; as the army was 'proletarianised' it was given increased responsibilities. This was most noticeable in the propaganda and cultural fields, where Lin built up the army's role as a disseminator of Maoism. Army men were moved into key positions in cultural work and, at the lower levels, PLA propaganda and drama groups multiplied, touring the villages to perform works of an appropriately proletarian nature. The army itself became the object of emulation, with the launching of a 'learn from the PLA' campaign; and certain PLA heroes and martyrs, such as the celebrated Lei Feng and Wang Jie, were presented to the nation's young as models of revolutionary virtue. Serving soldiers and demobilised veterans also began to enter economic enterprises where they staffed 'political departments' run on PLA lines.

Not all army leaders supported Lin's reforms. Some remained true to the ideas and practices of Peng Dehuai while others were reluctant to accept Lin's authority. But Lin undoubtedly had considerable success. When the Cultural Revolution began, most army leaders were prepared to be at least neutral, if not positively pro-Maoist.

Outside the PLA, however, Mao's ideas made little headway and he became increasingly preoccupied with the fear that 'his' revolution was in danger of dying. In connection with this Mao was particularly concerned about the attitudes of young people. For, as time passed, memories of the 'old society' were steadily fading and, of course, by the mid-1960s over half of China's population was so young as to have had no personal experience of 'past bitterness'. Conscious of the new conventional wisdom of Western observers, which took the line that just as the Soviet Union had 'softened' because of generational change, China, too, would soon produce a leadership of 'reasonable men', the question of his personal successor became inextricably linked with that of training 'revolutionary successors' in general. As an editorial in *Red Flag*, the Party's theoretical journal, put it in 1964: 'The imperialists abroad headed by the United States pin their hopes on the "peaceful evolution" of China through the degeneration of our third and fourth generations. Who can dismiss this view as entirely groundless?'[10]

It was necessary, therefore, to provide a cultural *milieu* which could, as it were, act as a substitute for 'practice', and so lead to the inculcation of ideas of a proper proletarian rectitude. An early step in this direction was taken by Jiang Qing who, after the tenth plenum, made the reform of Beijing Opera her personal mission. This extremely resilient and popular art form was, in her opinion, riddled with feudal and bourgeois themes. Her attempts to persuade opera companies in Beijing and elsewhere to rid themselves of slavish devotion to the doings of 'emperors' and 'beauties' and to produce works portraying contemporary themes based on peasants, workers and soldiers, did make their mark. But there was much opposition from the Party élite. Liu himself allegedly equivocated, arguing for the retention of the old operas as well as for developing the new. Zhou Yang, deputy Minister of Culture, was more outspoken, arguing that the old ones were harmless, and refusing to accept that 'all our ancestors were despicable swine'.[11]

In 1964 Mao's attack assumed greater dimensions. A rectification movement in literary and art circles was launched, and in a bitter comment on 27 June, Mao claimed that cultural workers had 'slid right down to the brink of revisionism'. He went on to warn that 'unless they removed themselves in real earnest, at some future date they are bound to become groups like the Hungarian Petofi Club'.

This reference to the organisation which had spawned the Hungarian uprising of 1956 was indicative of Mao's conviction that certain figures in the cultural field were actually sowing the seeds for a 'capitalist restoration', and the force of his words caused many to dive for cover by performing criticism and self-criticism. But for the most part this was highly ritualised, consisting of admissions of failure to implement Mao's ideas energetically enough. Sins of omission were acknowledged; sins of commission were not.

Later in 1964 a 'Group of Five' was set up under the Central Committee to mastermind this 'Cultural Revolution'. With the exception of Kang Sheng, its members were not close to Mao and its leader was Peng Zhen, first Party secretary and mayor of Beijing. Under his direction, the rectification of cultural life in 1965 was subject to limitations. Criticism was muted, and it was stressed that many who had made 'mistakes' in the post-Leap period were, fundamentally, good communists. In September 1965, Peng and his followers made a number of speeches to the effect that the rectification campaign had basically accomplished its objectives. But Mao begged to differ and urged that Wu Han be criticised for his work on Hai Rui. His senior colleagues had little stomach for the idea and, it seems, politely but firmly ignored it.

At this point Mao made the decision to bring his differences with his senior colleagues into the open. The venue chosen was Shanghai, where he had support among Party Leftists: the instrument was Yao Wenyuan, a Party propagandist and literary critic who was a protégé of Jiang Qing; the medium was an editorial in a Shanghai newspaper, the *Wenhui Bao*. On 10 November 1965 this newspaper published an attack by Yao on 'Hai Rui', an attack which criticised Wu Han on political grounds.

Peng was placed in a difficult position. If he ignored the attack he would be admitting that he agreed with Wu Han. On the other hand, if he instructed the Beijing media to 'bombard' his deputy mayor, it would raise very awkward questions as to why he had not done so earlier and would also demonstrate to his underlings that he was not prepared to give them support. In December Wu Han made a self-criticism in which he admitted having made historical and literary errors, but not political culpability. On 12 February 1966 Peng Zhen gave official blessing to this line in a report and criticised the *enragés* of the Left for the intemperance of their criticisms. This policy was promptly adopted by other members of the Party Establishment in propaganda and cultural work. In offices, on university campuses, and in schools, the 'Hai Rui' issue was side-tracked into officially directed and limited discussions of literary and historical criticism. By the spring of 1966 it seemed as though the Cultural Revolution was simply to fizzle out.

The fall of Liu Shaoqi

On 16 May the course of the Cultural Revolution changed dramatically with the issue of a Central Committee circular labelling Peng's February report as 'fundamentally wrong'. The report was revoked, the Group of Five dissolved, and it was announced that a new Cultural Revolution Group would be established under the direct leadership of the Standing Committee of the Politbureau. Peng Zhen was accused of having concocted the report without consulting his comrades, and of having issued it in the name of the Central Committee without Mao's approval.

Peng's aims, it was said, had been to deflect discussion of the 'Hai Rui' issue so as to avoid the 'heart of the matter', namely 'the dismissal of the Right opportunists' at the Lushan plenum in 1959 and the opposition of Wu Han and others to the Party and socialism. He had tried to change what was essentially a political struggle into an academic discussion, avoiding class analysis and preaching the view that 'everyone is equal before the truth'. Insisting that the struggle be waged 'with prudence', 'with caution', and 'with the approval of the leading bodies concerned', Peng and his colleagues had sought to prevent the masses from criticising and exposing 'bourgeois' cultural figures. Instead they had given 'free rein' to all the various 'freaks and monsters' who for many years had abounded in academic, educational and cultural work and in the media.

The circular concluded by insisting that it was essential to seize control over cultural work in the widest sense, and to expose thoroughly all 'bourgeois' ideas wherever they were to be found. Most importantly, it instructed that 'those representatives of the bourgeoisie' who had 'sneaked into the Party, the government, the army and all spheres of culture', were to be dragged out or transferred. Such people were definitely not to be entrusted with the task of leading the Cultural Revolution.

This circular was an intra-Party document, and was not published in the press until the first anniversary of its issue. But it was speedily and widely distributed among lower level Party organisations and its contents soon became common knowledge. To student radicals in middle schools and universities it came as a godsend, providing the encouragement they needed to attack those academic authorities who had been using every means at their disposal to contain and control the expression of dissent.

On 25 May a 'big character poster' appeared at Beijing University. Its principal author was Nie Yuanzi, an instructor in the Department of Philosophy who, as secretary of the Party branch, had read the '16 May circular'. The poster was an attack on leading Party members in the university administration (including Lu Ping, the university principal), who were accused of deliberately using their powers to suppress the mass movement.

Lu's response was predictable. Youth League loyalists were organised to counter-attack Nie and her supporters by interpreting their criticisms as evidence of an 'anti-Party' stance, a charge which made most students reluctant to commit themselves to her defence. But Lu's action was counter-productive, for Nie had the support of Mao himself. Whether, as some reports claim, Mao had personally instigated Nie's attack or, as seems more likely, news of it reached him a few days later, is not particularly important. He undoubtedly welcomed the poster and insisted that it be publicised on a national scale. On 1 June it was broadcast, and the following day was printed in *People's Daily*. On 3 June the morale of the radicals was raised still further with the announcement that Peng Zhen had been purged and the Beijing Party committee 'reorganised'. The new committee immediatly informed students that Lu Ping was dismissed.

These sudden changes led to an upsurge at educational institutions in Beijing, with students starting to criticize vigorously university teachers and administrators for their 'crimes'. In other cities across the nation campuses erupted. It appeared that the Cultural Revolution was to become a genuine mass movement at last, and that Mao had successfully overcome the opposition of those who wished to stifle it. The early days of June constituted an exciting period on many campuses, as students took full advantage of their newly-found freedom to engage in vigorous discussion of a host of educational and political issues, and to paste up posters wherever space was available. Within a few days, however, the heavy hand of authority was imposed once more in the shape of the 'work teams'.

What happened was this. From 1 June to 18 July Mao was absent from Beijing and Liu Shaoqi and Deng Xiaoping were in control. It appears that they, and other senior leaders in the Central Committee and Beijing municipal bureaucracy, had accepted that Peng Zhen's blatant attempts to protect his underlings had put him beyond salvation and that his purge was necessary, if only to serve as a sacrificial lamb. But this by no means implied that past divisions were healed, and that Mao had once more reasserted his authority over all his colleagues. Liu and other leaders had no wish to see 'extensive democracy' practised on the campuses or elsewhere, for fear that their own involvement in the 'bourgeois' policies now under attack might be made known. Even those whose hands were relatively clean in this matter wished to protect old friends and colleagues, and were anxious to maintain order and stability.

Consequently, many Party leaders in Beijing agreed with Liu that a limited purge would suffice, one confined primarily to bourgeois intellectuals and relatively minor Party functionaries. They insisted, therefore, on directing the movement themselves and had no intention of permitting the masses either to identify the 'targets' or to define the methods of attack and the degree to which struggle should be used. Like all mass movements before it, the Cultural Revolution was to be led from above.

The control mechanism used was the despatch of work teams. These were often extremely large (the one sent to Beijing's Qinghua University had 500 members) and were usually headed by very senior Party and state officials, including Central Committee members and State Council ministers. Most team members had little time for the masses they were supposed to assist, and often seem to have perceived their role as a policing one. Not surprisingly they easily gave offence. In early June these teams were sent into schools, universities and other 'sensitive' units, including government offices, banks and factories. From Beijing their use quickly spread to other cities, and their activities appear to have been co-ordinated from the centre. Liu himself took a close personal interest in their activities on certain campuses; at Qinghua he used his second daughter Liu Tao, a student there, and his wife, Wang Guangmei (an 'adviser' to the work team) as his intermediaries. At the middle school attached to Beijing Normal University, his daughters Tingting and Pingping were similarly utilised in assisting him to perpetrate 'fifty days of white terror'.

Of what, then, did this 'white terror' consist? The general pattern was for work teams and local Party leaders to take steps to clamp down on all signs of campus unrest. At first, when the teams arrived there was often widespread rejoicing among radical students. For in many cases the latter had specifically requested the higher levels to send them personnel to assist in the reorganisation of university and school administrations. But students quickly discovered that the teams' real purpose was to deflect their attacks and to curb opposition. First, restrictions were placed on the writing of posters; nothing could be pasted up without the approval of the teams' cadres. Students who had been prolific poster-writers found that their revolutionary ardour was sometimes channelled into manual labour, in that they were ordered to scrape the walls clean. Freedom to organise discussions and demonstrations was curtailed, students were often confined to their own individual classrooms and dormitories under the watchful eyes of team members, and campus gates were put under guard to prevent the radicals from exchanging news and views with like-minded groups at other universities. Members of the old university and school Party committees were isolated, ostensibly to put them through ideological reform, but often to protect them from their attackers. It was sometimes forbidden to subject them to mass repudiation and humiliation without the prior approval of the team (which would not be given), and some potential victims were spirited away to places of safety.

The teams did not prevent struggle altogether, but took the lead in directing it safely away from Party leaders themselves. Thus it was standard practice to select as targets intellectuals who were of bourgeois origin and demonstrably of bourgeois views. Another group who made an easy target were those intellectuals who had been branded as 'Rightists' in the past, and were now subjected to struggle again. A few Party cadres were also singled out, most of them being relatively 'small-fry' who had, for one reason or another, fallen foul of their superiors. Occasionally the teams would permit criticism of someone high in the Party hierarchy, but would defend such a person as one who had served the revolution well and who had made only a few small mistakes. For individuals of this sort, a ritual self-criticism was generally sufficient.

In most cases the work teams were able to secure the

compliance, and often the active support of, a majority of students for two reasons. First, a sizeable group, who were themselves from cadres' families, were already student leaders. They had little incentive to see the Cultural Revolution turn into an upheaval which might, quite literally, come too close to home. Second, the teams claimed to act in accordance with the highest authority. On almost every campus their response to criticism of any kind was to warn that, 'whoever attacks the work teams attacks the Party/the Central Committee/Chairman Mao'. In the circumstances it took a great deal of courage for a student, especially if his own class background was less 'pure' than it might be, to question the high-ranking cadres and often, as Liu was to confess subsequently, the teams had little difficulty in ensuring that 'the wings of the proletariat had been clipped'. Indeed, what is astonishing is not the fact that most students were easily persuaded to behave themselves, but that a small and vociferous minority persisted in opposing the teams despite great psychological and physical pressure.

There were a handful of rebels on most campuses — arrogant, self-righteous and doctrinaire, much given to quotations from the appropriate Marxist scriptures, and possessed of considerable audacity. Most students, however, feared that giving them support would have serious consequences, and they were right. For in the last resort the teams were able to invoke the sanction of 'labelling'. Team cadres attended meetings or used informers to find out what was going on — lists of names were compiled and reports made to higher levels. On this basis students on many campuses were assigned to specific categories. Those who supported established authority and the work teams were 'revolutionary'; those who obeyed but without much enthusiasm were 'middle of the road'; those who opposed were 'counter-revolutionary' or 'reactionary'. 'Labelling' was not merely name-calling, it had a far deeper significance. For people who acquired a 'bad' label knew that this could seriously affect their future. It would restrict entry to desirable occupations, serve as a barrier to promotion, and even result in a certain degree of social ostracism. The 'white terror' was undoubtedly a serious matter.

On 18 July Mao returned to Beijing, having demonstrated

by his well-publicised swim in the Yangtse two days earlier that he was indeed in excellent health. The minority of loyal Maoists in the capital had informed him of Liu's activities, and he immediately moved to rectify the situation. A prompt investigation of various campuses was undertaken by Chen Boda, Kang Sheng, Zhou Enlai and Jiang Qing. Their conclusions were unanimous: the teams must be withdrawn. On 28 July a directive was issued calling for their withdrawal from all schools and universities in Beijing. In the provinces, however, some teams continued to operate, or were disbanded but later restored.

There then followed a stormy meeting of China's leaders at the eleventh plenum of the eighth Central Committee, which met in Beijing from 1 to 13 August. This was the first plenum to be held in four years — a clear indication of the bitter divisions among the leadership — and it seems to have been attended by a number of people who were not Central Committee members. As it proved to be a qualified success for Mao it is reasonable to assume that it was 'packed' with his own supporters.

During the meeting Mao himself posted a 'big character poster' on 5 August. This attacked 'certain leading comrades' who 'exercise bourgeois dictatorship, put down the vigorous movement of the proletariat for [the] Great Cultural Revolution, confound right and wrong and black and white, launch concerted attacks on the revolutionaries from all sides, repress dissident views and impose a white terror.'[12]

On 8 August the plenum passed a major decision on the Cultural Revolution which became known as the 'Sixteen Points'.[13] This document defined the Cultural Revolution as a revolution 'that touches people to their very souls', one which represented 'a more intensive and extensive new stage in the development of socialist revolution' in China. Although, the document acknowledged, the bourgeoisie had been overthrown, the old ideas, culture, customs, and habits of the exploiting classes remained 'to corrupt the mind of man and capture his heart', and it was essential therefore that the proletariat contest these forces with its own ideas, culture, customs and habits.

What was needed, then, was a mobilisation of the broad

masses, for 'it is the masses who must liberate themselves. We cannot do the things for them which they must do themselves'. The young especially were to participate, so as 'to temper themselves, to gain experience and learn lessons, to know that the road of revolution is tortuous and not smooth and straight'. Party organisations were urged to cast aside 'fear', to forget about rules, regulations and conventions, and to 'mobilise' the masses with a free hand.

The document criticised those officials who had deliberately distorted the 'focus' of the movement, which, it unequivocally stated, was 'the purge of those power holders within the Party who take the capitalist road'. This was not to argue that a majority of Party cadres were bad. The majority were described as being 'good' or 'comparatively good', and even the minority were divided into two groups: those who had made serious mistakes but were not anti-Party and anti-socialist elements, and the small number who were. Even the last category, although they were to be 'fully exposed and knocked down', 'should be given a chance to start again'.

Indeed, on the subject of struggle, the document could be construed as a relatively moderate one, for it preached the need to distinguish carefully between 'antagonistic' and 'non-antagonistic' contradictions, and stressed the importance of relying on debates, meetings, and big character posters, rather than fists. Organisationally, it called for the creation of cultural revolution groups, committees and congresses, the members of which were to be elected on Paris Commune lines. That is, they would be delegates subject to instant replacement should the masses find them unsatisfactory. As it was envisaged that the Cultural Revolution would last a long time these organisations were to be viewed as permanent rather than temporary, and were to be set up in factories and government organs as well as in schools and universities. Finally, the decision emphasised the need for mass study of Mao's thought, which it defined as 'a compass to the Cultural Revolution'.

The Sixteen Points resulted in widespread demonstrations and the formation of hosts of 'revolutionary' organisations, particularly among students. It was in August that the term 'Red Guard' began to be used extensively. It became extremely popular with student groups, especially after 18 August when Mao reviewed a march past of one million students in Tiananmen and accepted a Red Guard armband.

The eleventh plenum had major implications for the succession question. For Liu Shaoqi it marked the beginning of the end. Mao's growing resentment of Liu's conduct of affairs was brought to a head when Liu tried to restrict the scope of the Cultural Revolution and, with Mao's public expression of disapproval, Liu's fall was inevitable. At the plenum he was demoted from second to eighth place in the Politbureau. Initially it appeared that he was not to suffer unduly. He continued to appear in public throughout the remainder of 1966 and, although he was criticised by Mao and other leaders, and was required to perform self-criticism, steps were taken to discourage 'the masses' from attacking him in wallposters.[14]

In 1967, however, his position worsened dramatically. By this stage the Cultural Revolution had developed as a violent mass movement and various Red Guard groups, hysterically anxious to take revenge on those who had opposed their beloved Chairman Mao, vented their rage on 'China's Khrushchev'. They were encouraged in so doing by Mao's leading supporters who were anxious to strengthen their own positions by ensuring that Liu could never return to active political life. At the eleventh plenum Lin Biao was appointed sole Vice-Chairman of the Party and Mao's new successor. He bolstered his position by taking Mao's personality cult to absurd lengths, creating an atmosphere in which anyone who disagreed with the Chairman in the slightest was held to be guilty of sacrilege. Chen Boda, Jiang Qing and Kang Sheng, as leading members of the new Cultural Revolution Group, also viciously attacked Liu. From the beginning of 1967 his residence was ransacked and he was subjected to harassment by Red Guards, although they were not permitted to drag him out of Zhongnanhai, the heavily-guarded quarter of Beijing where senior leaders live. His wife and children were also subjected to intimidation and violence.

In May 1967, a 'group for inquiring into the special case of Liu Shaoqi and Wang Guangmei' was established under the leadership of Jiang Qing which spent a year in collecting evidence of all Liu's 'crimes' stretching back to the 1920s. The group allegedly used torture to force Liu's staff and associates to produce suitable denunciations.[15] On the basis of these activities Liu's 'case' was considered by the twelfth plenum of the eighth Central Committee which met in October 1968. He was formally stripped of all his offices and cast on 'the garbage heap of history'. By this time he was under house arrest and a sick man. In November 1969, he died.[16]

The Sixteen Points also brought violence and tragedy to millions of others. For calls to rebel against 'capitalist-roaders' resulted in the factionalisation of Chinese politics. Those who were deprived, socially and economically, together with those who were genuinely Leftist ideologically, gleefully turned on 'power holders' at all levels. Similarly, those who benefited from the status quo fought vigorously to defend themselves from being 'dragged out'. And the 'power holders', being senior and skilled politicians, were initially highly successful in 'deflecting the spearheads' of the Cultural Revolution away from themselves. Until the end of 1966 few senior members of the Party and state élite had actually been dismissed.

The rise of the PLA: January 1967 – September 1968

At the turn of the year Mao and his colleagues in the Cultural Revolution Group took new initiatives in an attempt to improve the situation. First, they changed the nature of the struggle by turning it from one in which the masses were organised to attack *individuals* within key institutions to one in which they were encouraged to seize control of the *institutions* themselves. Thus, in December, Jiang Qing gave her approval to the seizure of various organisations in Beijing which had proved reluctant to support the Maoist cause and, in some instances, had actively opposed it. Second, they tacitly acknowledged that they had been mistaken in expecting the masses to 'liberate themselves' as the Sixteen Points had urged. Assistance was required, and on 23 January 1967 Mao called on the People's Liberation Army to intervene in order to 'support the Left'. Until that time the role of the military had been limited. Lin Biao, of course, had been actively sycophantic. The *Liberation Army Daily* had served as a powerful propaganda tool in support of Mao's policies. But *physical* intervention had been strictly limited. In late 1966 the PLA had done little more than to help to cope with the influx of Red Guards into Beijing and other cities and, on occasions, to prod them gently into obeying the orders of the Cultural Revolution Group. Mao's initial insistence on maximising the participation of the masses meant that only benevolent neutrality was required of the military, and many PLA leaders were happy to remain uninvolved.

But these two policy departures did not bring the Cultural Revolution to a speedy and successful close, for their actual effect was to widen the conflict. Military intervention obviously increased greatly the number of people taking part in the movement, and the call to 'seize power' added new dimensions to the issues over which the conflict was waged. This was because it called into question the very nature of those organisational forms through which China was governed. In 1966 the Cultural Revolution was concerned in the main with the rectification of existing institutions, but their relevance and value were not seriously challenged. After January 1967, however, the debate broadened as people at all levels began to ask whether specific organisations were worth preserving and, if not, with what should they be replaced. Not only did the machinery of state come under scrutiny, but the position of the Chinese Communist Party also. The Cultural Revolution Group itself was obviously divided over many of these issues, and individual leaders changed their minds in the light of events. The result was that 1967 was a year of even greater violence than 1966, and it was not until late in 1968 that the period of major convulsions could be said to have ended.

What happened in January was that the call to 'seize power' sparked off a wave of take-overs and attempted take-overs in many cities and provinces as groups of Leftists and/or PLA forces began to seize control of public security bureaux, newspapers, radio stations, factories, educational institutions, and governmental and Party headquarters. The most important of the early power seizures was in Shanghai where the 'January Storm' led to the take-over of the municipality by rebel mass organisations. But having seized it, the masses had then to decide what to do with it. On 5 February, they gave the answer when they proclaimed the establishment of the Shanghai 'Commune', based on the Paris model of 1871.

The influence of the Paris Commune on the Cultural Revolution is both important and intriguing. As described by Marx, through whose writings it was popularised in China, it was a highly egalitarian and democratic organisation. Commune officials were elected and were completely dependent on the will of their constituents in that they were liable to instant dismissal and replacement should they fail to maintain popular support. They possessed no bureaucratic perquisites and were paid no more than the average working-man. The Commune was also noteworthy in that it functioned without a standing army, relying instead on a civilian 'national guard'.

From the spring of 1966 the Paris Commune was the subject of a number of favourable pronouncements delivered by Mao and his supporters. In March 1966 a *Red Flag* editorial commemorated its ninety-fifth anniversary, commenting on its role in 'preventing the transformation of the proletarian state organs from the servants of society into the masters of society', and observing that the masses had enjoyed widespread discussion and participation in it. As already noted, the Commune was mentioned in the Sixteen Points as a suitable model for Cultural Revolution organisations. In January 1967 it was referred to by Chen Boda when he publicly urged that 'within the municipality [of Beijing] the power should be seized after the manner of the Paris Commune', and *Red Flag* once more discussed it.

There is no doubt that these references evoked a warm response among Leftist organisations. In late January and early February reports that Communes had been, or were about to be, set up emanated from several cities. It was in Shanghai, however, that the notion found most favour. But the Commune lasted for only eighteen days, its sole recorded act being the issue of a resolution on municipal sanitation. And the man who killed it was Mao.

Within a week of its proclamation, Zhang Chunqiao and other leaders of the Shanghai Commune were summoned to Beijing. Mao asked them what would happen if Communes on the Paris model were to be established throughout the country. Would it be necessary to change the name 'People's Republic of China' and, if so, would China be recognised by other powers? At first sight this might be taken to indicate that Mao had developed a perplexing preoccupation with the niceties of diplomatic protocol. But, it may be suggested, Mao's question was directed at a really fundamental matter — the very survival of the Chinese state. By this stage, Mao was well aware of the centrifugal forces at work in Chinese society. The Commune of 1871 had operated in Paris alone and questions of national organisation were unimportant. Consequently, it could not serve as a model on a national scale. A vast conglomeration of self-governing Communes with no overriding authority implied that the Chinese state would cease to exist.

Connected with this basic issue were two others. First, what of the Communist Party? Despite Mao's great reservations about the Party, he was not prepared to destroy it entirely, for a mixture of emotional, ideological and practical reasons. The Commune would have made the Party superfluous. Similarly, there was the question of the PLA. The idea of dispensing with a standing army was hardly consistent with a situation in which the military had just been ordered to assume a major political role.

Furthermore, the electoral aspects of the Paris model presented problems. It was reasonable enough to operate through democratic elections in an area under full revolutionary control, but this was not the case in much of China in early 1967. Mao himself conceded that in many areas the Leftists were a minority. Democratic elections, therefore, could well be a disaster for the revolutionary forces. For those reasons, then, Mao was unwilling to see the Commune emerge as the new organisational form of the revolution.

Shanghai duly fell into line as did those other localities in which the term had been used. Instead, a new organisational form appeared, the 'Revolutionary Committee'.

The first of these was established on 31 January in the Manchurian province of Heilongjiang, where a coalition of Leftist groups and garrison troops had overthrown the provincial Party Committee. In February similar power seizures took place in Shandong and Guizhou, and the Shanghai

Commune obediently changed its name. The Revolutionary Committee idea was given official approval in March and, by a series of fits and starts, they were set up in China's remaining provincial-level units of administration during the course of the next eighteen months. The last to appear was in the sensitive border and minority province of Tibet, where it made its debut on 5 September 1968.

At provincial level the Revolutionary Committees combined all pre-existing functions of both the state and Party machinery. In composition they were 'three-in-one alliances', drawing their membership from representatives not only from the mass organisations, but also the PLA and 'revolutionary cadres'. Theoretically, they were supposed to be coalitions of true revolutionaries, loyal to Chairman Mao and the ideals of the Cultural Revolution. But, in practice, membership varied enormously from province to province, both in terms of the proportion of places allotted to each of the three component groups, and in terms of the political 'standpoint' of those gaining positions. In a majority of provinces it was the PLA which took the initiative in seizing power and establishing Revolutionary Committees, and in a number of others it played a strong supporting role. In very few areas was the military of little importance. Details of the rise in the army's political influence will be discussed in the next chapter. Suffice it to say at this point that the PLA reaped the greatest rewards.

This is not to argue, however, that the armed forces either functioned as a cohesive entity or that they encountered little opposition. In the twenty months from January 1967 to September 1968, the PLA was under enormous pressure. It was ordered to 'support the Left', but given no precise guidelines as to whom the 'Left' in a given area might be. It was told to impose discipline on warring factions, and almost simultaneously denied the right to use force. It was encouraged by central leaders and yet a number of its commanders were purged. In some provinces it was attacked by the Left; in others by the Right. Some army units found themselves fighting against each other in support of rival factions.

Even when fundamentally loyal to Mao, many commanders were unsure of whom to support. This was partly due to the introduction in February 1967 of a policy of leniency for erring cadres. Introduced by the Maoists as a tactic to weaken the conservatives, and to win some of them over, it in fact contributed to an 'adverse current' in that many senior officials felt emboldened to resist still further, which they often did by means of a 'fake seizure of power'.

This stratagem was simply a refinement of those earlier techniques of 'deflecting the spearhead' which we have already encountered, and was quite beautiful in its simplicity. A senior official would organise his loyal subordinates to don revolutionary garb by forming 'rebel' organisations with names of suitable Maoist militancy, whereupon they 'took control' of their chief's department, and then duly reinstated him as their 'revolutionary' leader. As an added refinement they might brand genuine Leftists as 'counter-revolutionaries' and have them arrested. In the short term at least, this technique was extremely effective and made the PLA's task even more difficult.

Another problem besetting army leaders was the Maoists' insistence that they protect production, and supervise the spring planting. This was interpreted by some PLA leaders as justification for cracking down on all factionalism with a very heavy hand, so that all mass organisations found themselves 'suppressed'. As a result of these factors the drive to establish Revolutionary Committees began to lose momentum, and Leftist resentment towards the PLA began to grow, until in the summer of 1967, demands were made that 'the handful' of capitalist roaders in the army should themselves be 'dragged out'.

The men primarily responsible for the attack on the PLA were members of the '16 May group' taking their name from Mao's circular of 1966, which was published nationally on 18 May 1967. As J. B. Starr has aptly observed, their leaders were the 'literati' of the Cultural Revolution Group, all of them holding important posts in Mao's propaganda network. Wang Li, Qi Benyu and Guan Feng were editors of *Red Flag*, and other members of the group worked for the *Liberation Army Daily*, *Guangming Daily*, and various other leading newspapers and journals. They had been active participants in the 'Hai Rui' affair and were closely connected with the most Left-wing student factions in Beijing.

A certain amount of editorial sniping at the PLA took place in the first six months of 1967, but this swelled to a crescendo in late July, when a magnificent opportunity arose in the shape of the 'Wuhan Incident'.

Wuhan had suffered from a particularly turbulent and violent period, which resulted in Chen Caidao, the local commander, throwing his support behind mass organisations which the Maoists regarded as 'reactionary'. A high-level delegation, including Zhou Enlai, Wang Li, and Xie Fuzhi, Minister of Public Security, was sent from Beijing but failed to persuade Chen to change his mind. Indeed, it seems likely that the arrogant behaviour of the delegation, particularly Wang Li, contributed to a hardening of attitudes, and infuriated a number of Chen's supporters who believed they had been following the correct revolutionary line. In the event, after Zhou Enlai had left Wuhan, Wang and Xie were seized by Chen's followers and subjected to rough treatment (which was subsequently much exaggerated by their supporters). It was necessary for Mao to use naval and air force units to bring Wuhan under control, and the incident was seen as constituting the most open defiance of the Maoists since the Cultural Revolution began. Following the hostages' release, Wang Li returned to Beijing and mobilised his colleagues to instigate a vicious propaganda barrage against capitalist roaders in the PLA. Wang's 'sufferings' made him the subject of much student adulation and he organised militant Red Guards to attack various regional military commanders, and to seize files in order to build up dossiers of their 'crimes'.

By the end of July the situation had escalated danger-ously.[17] In Beijing senior PLA men were attacked, and in the provinces there were pitched battles between Leftist factions and army units considered to be guilty of suppressing them. A particularly ugly dimension was added to the conflict by mass seizures of arms from warehouses, militia depots and army installations. Even consignments destined for Vietnam were ransacked. By August *armed* struggles were taking place in virtually every province.

Not content with attacking the PLA, the '16 May group' also turned their attention to the state bureaucracy, where their main target was Zhou Enlai. They disliked Zhou for his relatively moderate role in the Cultural Revolution, and they especially accused him of having protected senior state officials from attack. It is undeniable that Zhou, as the man primarily responsible for the running of state affairs, did indeed speak out on behalf of a number of his ministers, and kept the Red Guards at bay so as to protect economic work.

But the '16 May group' had gone too far and by the early autumn of 1967 most of them had been purged, and the details given above suggest the obvious reasons why. Despite their close identification with him earlier, Mao at this stage certainly had no wish to see conflict erupt into full civil war, which was the logic of the '16 May group's' position.

From September, then, the emphasis was on restoring discipline by quelling the ranks of both Right and Left. In the provinces army corps were ordered to become active and in some localities took over from regional military forces. Squabbling factions were hammered into submission and the PLA was allowed to use more force than previously. The creation of provincial Revolutionary Committees began to speed up, and the mass organisations now had less influence on them than before. Red Guards and rebels found that restrictions were once more imposed. Orders to return to their schools and universities, which had begun to appear in February, assumed a greater urgency, and the PLA was used to bring the 'little generals' into line. This was a long and uphill struggle as many Red Guards had lost all sense of respect for authority and order, and had little desire to return to their units to 'make revolution in the classroom'. Many factions, which had long since forgotten the cause of their original quarrels, continued to engage in bitter and murderous battles on the campuses until the latter part of 1968.

The year of 1968 also saw the resumption of a drive to send 'educated youth' to the countryside. Measures were taken to make it impossible for them to obtain employment and, for that matter, basic rations as long as they stayed in the cities. Many Red Guards in schools and universities found themselves summarily 'graduated' and ordered to the villages also. Public order was restored.

In September 1968 Tibet became the last provincial-level unit of administration to establish a Revolutionary Committee. The Cultural Revolution, far from ushering in an era of mass democracy had greatly strengthened the power of the army. And the chief beneficiary was Lin Biao.

2

The Fall of Lin Biao

The ninth Party Congress, April 1969

In April 1969, the ninth Party Congress met in Beijing. It gave formal recognition to the tumultuous changes of the previous three years by adopting a *Report* on the history of the Party as construed from the vantage point of the Cultural Revolution, producing a new Constitution to replace that of 1956, and electing a new Central Committee. Lin Biao had reasons to be happy with all three actions.

For although Mao addressed the Congress, Lin was the focus of everyone's attention because the occasion appeared to formalise his position as the inheritor of the Chairman's revolutionary mantle. On 1 April it was Lin who delivered the official *Report* and in it he had the pleasure of consigning to the dustbin of history the man who had preceded him in the role of 'Crown Prince'. It had, he said, been proved:

... that as far back as the First Revolutionary Civil War period Liu Shaoqi betrayed the Party, capitulated to the enemy and became a hidden traitor and scab, that he was a crime-steeped lackey of the imperialists, modern revisionists and Guomindang reactionaries and that he was the arch-representative of the persons in power taking the capitalist road. He had a political line by which he vainly attempted to restore capitalism in China and turn her into an imperialist and revisionist colony. In addition, he had an organisational line to serve his counter-revolutionary political line. For many years, recruiting deserters and turncoats, Liu Shaoqi gathered together a gang of renegades, enemy agents, and capitalist roaders in power.[1]

In contrast to the anathema pronounced on Liu, the Congress bestowed upon Lin the 'apostolic succession'. For the ninth Constitution declared him to be not only Mao's 'close comrade in arms' but also his successor as Party chairman![2] This was a development without precedent in the history of Chinese Communism and, as Stuart Schram has wryly observed, constituted an apostolic 'laying on of hands'.[3] Whatever constitutional niceties Leninist parties may have ignored, they remained firmly wedded to the principle that 'the Party', as a collective entity, had the right to choose a new leader when the previous incumbent had passed away or become incapacitated. At the ninth Congress, however, Mao and his supporters were powerful enough to ignore such constraints and attempted to legislate for the situation after the Chairman's death.

The election of a Central Committee dominated by military men was further reason to suppose that the elevation of Lin (who retained his post of Minister of Defence) was not just a paper victory. For of the 170 full members of the ninth Central Committee as many as 87 were military men (about 51 per cent) in contrast to only 53 who were veteran cadres and a mere 29 who represented mass organisations. At Politbureau level, at least ten of the twenty-one full members and two of the four alternates could be regarded as having a 'primary identification' with the PLA.[4]

This dramatic increase in military representation at the highest levels of the Party gave the PLA formidable power, for it had already come to dominate the state apparatus through its control of the provincial Revolutionary Committees. The process of establishing Revolutionary Committees was, of course, one in which the army had played a major part. By September 1968, Revolutionary Committees had been set up in all twenty-nine provincial-level units of administration and in twenty-two of them the chairman was either a military commander or a political commissar. Each Revolutionary Committee had a Standing Committee to carry out executive functions. Of the 479 Standing Committee members almost half were soldiers.[5]

Furthermore, the army presence did not stop at provincial level. Army representation was found throughout society: in local administration, in industrial enterprises, and in educational institutions. It appeared then that the army controlled China, that Lin Biao controlled the army and that Mao had given his blessing to a new successor. Yet, as events were to show, Lin's position was far less secure than it appeared. Indeed, the ninth Congress marked the summit of his career and, even as it met, developments were taking place which were, speedily, to reduce his power.

One of these concerned the familiar oscillation of the Chinese political process between phases of mass mobilisation and bureaucratic routinisation. Lin's star had risen with the Cultural Revolution, the most violent upheaval since the early 1950s. Although probably more of an opportunist than a committed ideologue,[6] Lin had chosen to identify himself as a man with a *forte* for promoting radical change. But the turmoil of the Cultural Revolution had, by 1969, produced its own corrective in the form of a manifest need to restore order, allow passions to cool, and concentrate on the possibly mundane but vital tasks of managing and developing an economy badly dislocated by a long spell of near-anarchy. Inevitably this placed a premium on the services of those with administrative skills and a talent for conciliation and, in particular, strengthened the position of Zhou Enlai. After the ninth Congress the premier quickly began to bring back to their desks a number of veteran cadres disgraced, humiliated and mistreated during the Cultural Revolution, and these people could have had little love for Lin Biao, its principal beneficiary.

Moreover, the PLA was no monolith in 1969. Lin had used the Cultural Revolution to favour his own military followers, particularly those whose ties to him could be traced back to service in the Fourth Field Army under his command. According to one account he had replaced more than three hundred senior military officials with his own men, thus causing resentment among other military factions which saw their own influence reduced.[7] The Cultural Revolution had also exacerbated tensions between the central organs of the army and the regional commands, and had stimulated inter-service rivalries as well as divisions based on ideological differences. A number of the military men on the ninth Central Committee

had come under attack from the Red Guards and believed
either that Lin Biao had done little to protect them or, in
some cases, had actually been responsible. Forced to participate in the Cultural Revolution against their will, they
had ultimately responded by assuming positions of political
power, but they were not automatically disposed to use it in
the interests of their Minister of Defence. Some regional
commanders in particular were amenable to the prospect of
allying with veteran civilian cadres against Lin.

Most importantly, from late 1969 onwards Mao began to
turn against Lin Biao. At least three factors were responsible
for this, one of which concerned the psychological dimension.
Once again Mao found himself torn between a desire to ensure
the succession by grooming one man to replace him as
supreme leader and an intense resentment when that leader
actually showed signs of exercising independently the power
bestowed upon him. As with Liu Shaoqi, Lin Biao was to
some extent the victim of his own success.

Secondly, at the institutional level, having ordered the
PLA to intervene in the political arena, Mao became concerned
at the extent to which 'the gun' had come to command the
Party, in practice if not in theory. Thirdly, he determined to
root out any vestiges of that 'ultra-Leftism' which had brought
China to the brink of civil war in 1967.

At the end of 1969 an investigation was launched into the
'16 May Group'.[8] It is quite likely that this investigation not
only revealed that Chen Boda, an associate of Lin's who had
headed the Cultural Revolution Group, was implicated but
may also have raised the possibility of Lin's own involvement.

A propaganda campaign directed against the army's 'arro-
gance and complacency' was also instituted.[9] In this context
Mao chose to bolster the power of civilian leaders at the
expense of the military. This measure not only benefited
Zhou Enlai and the veteran administrators, it also benefited
civilian Leftists like Zhang Chunqiao and Yao Wenyuan. In
November 1980, when the 'Gang of Four' were put on trial
alongside the survivors of the 'Lin Biao clique' every effort
was made to demonstrate linkages between them. However,
the intra-Party documents on the Lin Biao affair which were
circulated in 1972 tell a rather different story. They reveal

quite clearly that by 1970—71 Lin and his associates were desperately worried about Mao's patronage of Zhang Chunquiao, and that both Zhang and Yao were identified as primary targets in Lin's proposals for a coup.[10] However close the earlier connections between Lin and the Shanghai radicals may have been, Mao had successfully driven a wedge between them by the beginning of 1971. It is likely that his move away from Lin was accompanied by a new strategy of alternatively giving support to rival factions within the civil leadership.

The Lushan plenum, August 1970

The rift between Mao and his 'chosen successor' widened considerably in the late summer of 1970. In March that year, as a further step towards normalisation, Mao had proposed that a fourth National People's Congress be held and that the State Constitution of 1954, which had ceased to function in any meaningful way after 1966, should be revised. The Central Committee duly made preparations and, on 12 July, established a committee to carry out revision. This body in turn produced a draft which was submitted to the second plenum of the ninth Central Committee which convened at Lushan on 23 August.

At this meeting, one particular constitutional issue was definitely not on the agenda: the question of the office of Chairman of the People's Republic. In March Mao had 'recommended' that this should not be revived. He had repeated his objection on several occasions, and the Central Committee had already agreed to follow his wishes.[11] In part Mao may have been motivated by the painful memories of what he regarded as Liu Shaoqi's abuse of the office to 'walk the capitalist road'. But his principal objection was what he now perceived to be the danger of giving too much power to Lin Biao. Without a state chairman, Zhou Enlai's position as premier made him the leading figure in the state machine and a powerful counterweight to Lin.

Lin, however, was aware of the potential threat. At a 'secret meeting' in July, his wife and one of his principal supporters, Wu Faxian, asked: 'If no Head of State is instituted, what would happen to Lin Biao? What position would Lin Biao be in?' Accordingly, on 23 August, Lin brushed aside other speakers and reopened the issue, urging that the office be restored. He was supported in this by Ye Qun, his wife, and by his leading followers in the PLA.

These were Huang Yongsheng, whom Lin had had appointed Chief of the General Staff in 1968; Wu Faxian, Deputy Chief of the General Staff and Commander of the Air Force; Li Zuopeng, Deputy Chief of the General Staff and First Political Commissar of the Navy; and Qiu Huizuo, Deputy Chief of the General Staff and Director of the General Logistics Department. All four were Politbureau members. Chen Boda, a member of the Standing Committee of the Politbureau, also supported Lin on this issue and addressed the plenum on the subject of Mao's 'genius', a theme on which Lin Biao had also waxed eloquent in the Cultural Revolution. Although the evidence is not absolutely clear on this point it appears that Lin and his colleagues wanted Mao to assume this post, becoming once more the supreme leader of both Party and state as befitted his 'genius'. The logic behind their actions was that this would legitimate a subsequent monopolisation of Party and state power by Lin after Mao's death. As his 'constitutional' successor as Party leader and the 'best student' of the 'genius', Lin's assumption of both offices could be presented as a perfectly natural development.

In fact the attempt badly misfired because it infuriated Mao. He later observed that he had said: 'Do not establish a state chairman and I will not be a state chairman — I said this six times'.[12] It also seems likely, although details are vague, that Mao also took issue with Lin and Chen over various policy matters. On 25 August he criticized Chen Boda for his 'fallacies' at an enlarged meeting of the Politbureau and also summoned Lin Biao 'for a talk'. Zhou Enlai similarly had 'private talks' with Lin's military supporters and ordered them to make self-criticisms before the Central Committee. The Lushan plenum concluded on 6 September with a decision that Chen Boda should be 'investigated' and a campaign directed against him began shortly thereafter.[13]

The 'conspiratorial' activities of Lin and Chen at Lushan badly unsettled Mao and strengthened him in his resolve to diminish Lin's power although, at that stage, it seems possible that he had not determined to disgrace Lin altogether. Over the winter of 1970–71, however, Lin's perception of threat grew. In December 1970 an enlarged Politbureau meeting was held at Beidaihe at which senior military leaders were ordered to participate in the repudiation of Chen Boda.[14] That month, Mao received his old friend Edgar Snow and, in the course of their conversation, complained that the 'cult of personality' built up around him had been taken too far:[15] a remark which had clear implications for Lin who, after all, had been the man mainly responsible. Then, in January 1971, the leadership of the Beijing Military Region was reshuffled. Lin's supporters, Zheng Weishan and Li Xuefeng, were removed from their respective posts as commander and second political commissar and were demoted to jobs of relative obscurity.[16] It seemed that Mao was suspicious enough of Lin to ensure that the capital was not under his military control.

Another issue which assumed great importance concerned foreign policy. In 1969 and 1970 Mao and Zhou Enlai became increasingly alarmed at the Soviet threat. Sino-Soviet relations had worsened considerably during the Cultural Revolution which the Soviet Union had seen, rightly, as a most un-Leninist development. The Soviet invasion of Czechoslovakia in 1968, and the violent incidents on the Sino-Soviet border in 1969, together with indications that some Soviet 'hawks' were contemplating a nuclear attack, vividly demonstrated the dangers inherent in China's isolationist stance. Conversely, the election of President Nixon in 1968 opened the possibility of reaching some form of rapprochement with the United States.

Whereas Mao and Zhou were prepared to be flexible, and to work for a 'diplomatic revolution', Lin was much more rigid. It was later to be claimed that he was pro-Soviet and it is possible that he advocated reaching some accommodation with the Soviet Union. It seems more likely, however, that he obstinately held to a strategy of resisting both superpowers simultaneously, a view which other leaders now found to be unacceptably dangerous. Either way he was opposed to 'building bridges' to the United States, and this question further poisoned his relations with Mao.[17] By February 1971 Lin had apparently come to the conclusion that Mao was opposed to him and that he should take steps to safeguard his position.

The Lin Biao plot

It should be emphasised that Lin Biao may well have been predisposed to over-react. Even if Mao intended to do nothing more than limit Lin's power and to promote a more 'collective' leadership, there is reason to believe that Lin may have interpreted the march of events since the ninth Party Congress as a threat to his very survival politically and, perhaps, literally. His personal experience of Mao's capacity for ruthlessness did, after all, go back a long way. On one celebrated occasion, for example, he had unwittingly provoked Mao to speak exultingly of this.

The occasion was the second session of the eighth Party Congress when, on 8 May 1958, Mao made a speech in which he praised Qin Shi Huang, the tyrannical emperor who had ruled China from 221–209 BC, for his 'progressive' attitude of respecting the present and having contempt for the past. Lin Biao interrupted Mao's remarks to interject the traditional condemnation of the much hated first emperor, that he had 'burned the books and buried alive the Confucian scholars'. Mao's reply had been chilling: 'We needn't reckon much to Qin Shi Huang. He only buried 400 Confucian scholars, we [the Communist Party] buried 40,000'. Mao was referring to 'counter-revolutionary intellectuals' and, he reminded his listeners, when certain democratic personages had compared his regime to that of the first emperor he had blithely assured them that they were incorrect: 'We surpass Qin Shi Huang one hundred times over'.[18] Mao in fact deliberately chose to identify with the man who, for over two millenniums, had been regarded as China's most ruthless ruler.

Moreover, as the documents produced by Lin and his fellow conspirators showed, the Cultural Revolution had left him with no illusions about the Chairman's ability to sacrifice without qualms those erstwhile comrades whom he deemed to have failed him. Although it was not to be publicly revealed until 1980, Lin would certainly have known that Liu Shaoqi had died miserably in 1969. And having himself contributed to the purges of the Cultural Revolution, which had filled the prisons and labour camps, and not a few graves, with cadres who had earlier enjoyed the highest seniority he could have had little reason to assume that his own fall from grace would receive more lenient treatment.

In addition there is evidence which shows that Lin's perception of the world around him bordered on the paranoic. This was clearly revealed in a remarkable speech he made to an enlarged meeting of the Politbureau on 18 May 1966. The subject was political power which he defined as being, in essence, 'the power to suppress'. He observed then that:

> Generally speaking, change of political power results from either people's revolution, which starts from below. . . or counter-revolutionary coups d'état, which include court coups d'état, internal coups d'état, collusion of the high and the low, collusion with the subversive activities of foreign enemies or with armed invasion, and combination with natural calamities. *This has been so historically, and it is true in the present.*[19]

He went on to quote 'incomplete statistics' which showed that there had been sixty-one coups in the capitalist countries of Asia, Africa and Latin America since 1960, of which fifty-six were successful. 'Eight chiefs of state were beheaded, seven were kept on as puppets, and eleven were deposed.'

He then examined the succession problem throughout Chinese history in these terms, pointing out that there were 'many examples of political power being lost through coups d'état before a dynasty was in existence for ten, twenty, thirty or fifty years'. Surveying leadership changes from the 'Spring and Autumn' period to the Republican era, Lin painted a picture of 'subversion', 'treachery', 'assassination' and 'merciless killing'. Sons killed fathers, brothers massacred brothers, and intrigue and violent death were the norms by which leaders were changed.

Lin observed that this bloody legacy 'should have terrified us and heightened our vigilance', and he presented a view of the world which permitted no compromise: 'Struggle is life —

if you don't struggle against them, they will struggle against you; if you don't fight against them, they will fight against you; and if you don't kill them, they will kill you.'

It is scarcely surprising that a man who saw politics in terms like these (even allowing for the fact that the speech was made on the eve of the Cultural Revolution) should have been willing to contemplate violence against other leaders in order to safeguard his own position. Immediately after the Lushan plenum he told Wu Faxian, 'when civilised ways fail, we resort to force'. A few weeks later, his son Lin Liguo told two members of his father's faction that 'it seems that this struggle is going to be long drawn out' and 'we must grasp the army units and prepare for action'.[20]

Lin Liguo was, in fact, to be the principal organiser of his father's plot, and he was a classic example of the way in which young people of little proven merit were occasionally catapulted into senior positions during the Cultural Revolution as a result of their personal connections or their usefulness to the purposes of a particular faction. Lin Liguo had joined the Air Force in 1967 and, although not even a Party member at the time, was assigned to be Secretary of the General Office of the Party Committee at Air Force Headquarters. In 1968 he joined the Party, with Wu Faxian as his sponsor. Then, in October 1969, Wu appointed him as Deputy Director of the General Office of the Air Force Headquarters and Deputy Head of its Operations Department. At the time Wu ordered that 'Everything about the Air Force must be reported to Comrade Liguo, and all movements and commands are under Comrade Liguo.' At the time Lin Liguo was twenty-five years old.[21]

Thereafter Lin Liguo began to build up his own factional support and, by the beginning of 1971, had gathered round him a group which chose to call itself the 'joint fleet'. This title derived from their alleged enthusiasm for watching old Japanese war films, such as 'Admiral Yamamoto' and 'Our Navy', and their desire to emulate the 'Edajima spirit', the fanatical warrior code of the Imperial Japanese Naval Academy. In actual fact, naval representation in the 'joint fleet' was minimal. Its principal members were drawn from the Air Force (particularly from its Headquarters organisation in Beijing), together with a sprinkling of political commissars and officials in civil aviation.

In February 1971 Lin Biao warned his wife and son of the threat to his position, and Lin Liguo was entrusted to prepare measures to defend him. Lin Liguo duly held secret meetings with members of his 'joint fleet' in Shanghai in late March at which he expressed concern over his father's prospects. There were, he said, three possibilities:

> The first is to take over by a peaceful transition which will take five or six years. There may be some major changes in these five or six years. It is hard to say whether the leader [Lin Biao] will still be able to maintain his position. The second is that somebody else may grab the opportunity to take over and our leader may be forced to step down. The third is to take over ahead of time by eliminating B-52 [a code name for Mao] and launching an armed uprising.[22]

In discussion Lin Liguo made it clear that he regarded a 'peaceful transition' as the 'ideal thing' but he had doubts as to its likelihood. Zhou Yuchi, a fellow Deputy Director of the General Office of the Air Force Headquarters, suggested that Lin Biao was unlikely to be ousted in the foreseeable future. To which Lin Liguo replied, 'Nothing is predictable. The Chairman commands such high prestige that he need only utter one sentence to remove anybody he chooses.' When another colleague observed that 'the chief has been chosen by the Chairman himself', Lin Liguo similarly pointed out that 'Liu Shaoqi was also his own choice'. He further observed of Mao that 'he always uses one faction at one time and another at another time, in order to strike a balance'. In this context he remarked that Mao had chosen to build up Zhang Chunqiao at Lin Biao's expense.[23]

Lin Liguo therefore recommended that contingency plans be drawn up and these were given the code name of the 'Outline for Project "571"'. This unlikely title was chosen because '571' in Chinese has a similar sound to characters meaning 'armed uprising'. The 'Outline', in fact, was a series of jottings, many of which are opaque and sometimes quite unintelligible. In one section the authors painted a picture of

'B-52' and his supporters which would have fitted nicely into Lin Biao's 1966 speech on coups d'état. In part this read:

Today he uses this force to attack that force; tomorrow he uses sweet words and honeyed talk to those whom he entices, and tomorrow he puts them to death for some fabricated crimes. Those who are his guests today will be his prisoners tomorrow.

Looking back at the history of the last few decades, [do you see] anyone whom he has supported initially who has not finally been handed a political death sentence?[24]

The document warned that contradictions were intensifying and that 'both we and the enemy are riding a tiger from which it is difficult to dismount'. It reviewed Lin's strength in the military, identified general grievances in society which could be exploited, and even listed slogans which might be used to mobilise the masses.

What it did not do, however, was provide an absolutely clear indication as to the plotters' intentions. The 'Outline' seems to suggest that the actual assassination of Mao was only to be considered if other measures failed. Thus it refers to 'surrounding' him and having the Chairman 'in our hands'. The most likely interpretation is that Lin Liguo and his followers planned some sort of pre-emptive strike against civilian leaders such as Zhang Chunqiao and Yao Wenyuan with the object of leaving Mao as their puppet.

In any event Lin Liguo began to organise a network of support to defend his father from an anticipated attack by Mao and senior civilian cadres of both radical and moderate persuasion. This involved giving some members of the 'joint fleet' command positions. Wang Weiguo, Political Commissar of PLA Unit 7341 (the élite body with special responsibility for guarding senior Party leaders) was put in charge of Shanghai. Chen Liyun, Political Commissar of PLA Unit 7350 was made responsible for Hangzhou and Zhou Jianping, Deputy Air Force Commander of PLA Units in Nanjing was made responsible for that city. Jiang Tengjiao was appointed 'frontline commander' to liaise with the others. Jiang had originally been Political Commissar of the PLA units in

Nanjing but had been dismissed as a trouble-maker in 1968.[25]

These men, and other members of Lin Biao's faction, began to prepare for a show-down. Their activities included providing specialised training for the men under their command, and creating an extensive intelligence and communications network. Members of the 'joint fleet' also travelled to various cities to canvass support.

Meanwhile, relations between Mao and Lin worsened steadily. In March a press campaign was instituted to criticize Chen Boda as a 'sham Marxist', although he was not actually identified by name. The following month Zhou Enlai presided over a meeting of ninety-nine central and regional leaders which criticized those who had opposed Mao at Lushan.[26] What drove the plotters to desperation, however, was the realisation that Mao had gained at least an inkling of their conspiratorial activities.

This became apparent in August 1971, when Mao left Beijing in a special train for an extended tour of central, southern and eastern China. As became immediately obvious, his aim was to strengthen his own support among leaders in those areas, especially military ones, and to precipitate a show-down before Lin's supporters were properly organised.

On 10 August Mao arrived in Wuhan where he stayed for ten days, holding conversations with the senior Party, Governmental and military leaders of Henan and Hubei. In the course of discussions Mao issued an instruction to his listeners which became one of his most celebrated utterances: 'Practise Marxism and not revisionism; unite and don't split; be open and above board, and don't intrigue and conspire'. He observed that in the history of the Party there had been 'ten big struggles over line', during which people had attempted to split the Party. The last of these, he revealed, had taken place at the 1970 Lushan conference. There, said Mao, the 'big generals' (whom he named) had 'maintained airtight secrecy and suddenly launched a surprise attack. Their coup did not just last a day-and-a-half, but went on for two-and-a-half days . . . ' Their attack was, in Mao's opinion, 'planned, organised, and programmed'. The reason behind it was that 'a certain person was very anxious to become state Chairman, to split the Party, and to seize power'.

Mao went on to warn that 'the Lushan incident is not over and has yet to be resolved' and that 'someone is behind Chen Boda'. He urged the army to be careful, saying that it must be unified and 'put in order'. In a clear indication that he was fully aware that some sort of military conspiracy was in the offing he observed that, 'I do not believe Huang Yongsheng is able to direct the PLA to rebel'.

Mao did give some slight indication that he had not finally decided how far Lin Biao was personally involved in conspiratorial activities. Thus he said 'we still want to protect Lin' and he quoted his old adage 'cure the disease and save the patient'. He announced that on his return to Beijing he would seek out the 'big generals' and talk things over. It was possible, he opined, that some could be 'saved'. On the other hand, he admitted that it was very difficult to reform and noted that none of the anti-Party elements in earlier struggles, the last of whom was Liu Shaoqi, had managed to do so. Hence the prognosis for Lin and his followers was obviously poor. Moreover, Mao also spoke scathingly of Lin's elevation of his wife to a position of great power, and of the cult of personality developing round Lin Liguo.[27]

Mao then left Wuhan and, between 27 August and 2 September, repeated the exercise in Changsha and Nanchang where he met leaders from Guangdong, Hunan, Guangxi, Jiangsu, Jiangxi and Fujian, and on these occasions he began to taunt Lin Biao's followers quite openly and with obvious relish. Thus he asked Ding Sheng and Liu Xingyuan, who were respectively the Commander and Political Commissar of the PLA units in Guangzhou, 'since you have maintained close contacts with Huang Yongsheng, will you not be in trouble if Huang Yongsheng falls?'[28]

On 3 September he moved on to Hangzhou, where 'many working personnel' came to see him and 'gave him some information about the situation'. In Hangzhou, Chen Liyun 'held garrison power' and had direct command over the residence in which Mao stayed. By going there Mao was obviously daring Lin's followers to take action against him, presumably in the certain knowledge that their conspiracy was not sufficiently advanced. He took particular delight in revealing to Chen Liyun that he knew what was afoot, questioning Chen about his 'personal history' face to face: 'How about your relations with Wu Faxian? Wu Faxian found a number of right people in Lushan, including Shanghai's Wang Weiguo, someone in the navy and you. What have you done?'[29]

The death of Lin Biao

The final act of the drama was the most bizarre episode in the history of the People's Republic. For if Mao's objective in the summer of 1971 was to force Lin Biao's hand he was eminently successful. At the time of Mao's southern tour Lin and his wife were in the north Chinese coastal resort of Beidaihe but their intelligence network was active. On 5 September Yu Yexin, Deputy Department Chief of the Air Force Headquarters, telephoned Gu Tongzhou, Chief of Staff of the PLA Guangzhou Air Force units, to inquire about Mao's talks in Changsha. Gu duly sent a text to Lin and Ye Qun. The following day Li Zuopeng, who happened to be in Wuhan, was briefed on Mao's talks there by the Political Commissar of the PLA Wuhan units. He returned immediately to Beijing and informed Huang Yongsheng, who in turn telephoned Ye Qun.

By the evening of 6 September Lin was fully informed of what Mao had said, and his understandable reaction was to panic. He and his wife decided that there was no alternative to assassinating the Chairman, and on 7 September they instructed Lin Liguo to put the 'joint fleet' on 'red-alert' combat readiness. The following day Lin Liguo returned to Beijing where he and Zhou Yuchi went to a 'secret stronghold' at the airport in the western suburbs and held a meeting of their supporters. Lin Liguo told them: 'Time is pressing, and we are determined to take action in Shanghai' (the next stop on Mao's itinerary). He also said that three methods of assassination were being considered: 'Using flamethrowers and 40-mm bazookas to attack B-52's train, or using reassembled 100-mm artillery to shoot the train, or alternatively having Wang Weiguo carry out the murder with a pistol while being received by B-52 on the train.'[30] It was agreed that as soon as action was taken in Shanghai, 'joint fleet' members in Beijing would lead the garrison battalion directly under the control of the Air Force to attack Diaoyutai, a residential and work complex used by senior leaders. Huang Yongsheng and Wu Faxian were kept informed of these proposals.

Further discussions took place on 9 September, when members of the 'joint fleet' examined the practicalities of assassination. Jiang Tengjiao suggested that if Mao's train were to stop near Hongqiao airport in Shanghai, the plotters should blow up a nearby oil depot and 'enter the train to get rid of him' in the ensuing commotion of fighting the fire. It was also said that 'if things go well and petrol flows near the train, we shall be able to wipe out the train with him on board'. The possibility of blowing up a railway bridge as the train passed over was also entertained.

In addition, arrangements were made to have planes placed at the disposal of the plotters, who apparently had two strategies in mind should the assassination attempt be un-successful. One was for Lin and his senior associates to fly to south China to establish a separatist regime. The other was to flee to the Soviet Union. Thus on 10 September Lin Biao ordered his supporters in Air Force Headquarters to obtain maps showing the deployment of radar units in north-east, northern and north-west China, frequency tables of radio stations in neighbouring countries which could be used for navigational purposes; maps showing air lanes from Beijing to Ulaan Baatar and Irkutsk, and the location of their air-ports, call signs and radio frequency tables; and information concerning airports in the Guangzhou and Fuzhou areas.

Interestingly, the official condemnations of the conspira-tors which, unfortunately, are our only source of information for this remarkable story, made little attempt to suggest that Mao remained in blissful ignorance of these developments. On the contrary, they clearly imply that he knew exactly what was going on, and that he was deriving a certain grim satisfaction out of outwitting his opponents by the simple method of changing his travel arrangements without warning. For example, in Hangzhou on 8 September, 'just when everyone had finished a midnight snack', Mao suddenly ordered that his special train should be moved. Then, two days later, 'Chairman Mao suddenly said again: "Now turn the train back. We shall leave right away!" ' This order was implemented so quickly that 'Chen Liyun did not know what had happened'.

On 10 September Mao's train entered Shanghai and stopped near Hongqiao airport. Lin Biao's men in the city sent a coded message signalling its arrival to Beijing, where Lin Liguo and his fellow conspirators assumed that Mao would remain in Shanghai for several days as, apparently, had been originally intended, and that the plot to assassinate him could be operationalised. However, as they made their final arrangements, Wang Weiguo telephoned to inform them that Mao had already left Shanghai, having spent one day there. During his stop Mao had summoned General Xu Shiyou from Nanjing for discussions. Xu was one of China's most senior military commanders and was renowned for both his toughness and his loyalty. His discussions presumably concerned the Lin Biao conspiracy. Significantly, Wang Weiguo was not allowed to board Mao's train which, it would seem, is a further indication that the Chairman was aware of the danger.

Thereafter Mao's train headed back to Beijing, speeding through the areas where the 'joint fleet' had contemplated attacking it. On Mao's instructions it failed to make anticipated stops until it reached the vicinity of Beijing, when Mao summoned leaders of the Beijing military units and Beijing municipality for discussions. On 12 September the train finally arrived at Beijing station.

The news of Mao's unexpected return caused consternation among the conspirators and Lin Biao determined to fly to Guangzhou. On 12 September Lin Liguo briefed the 'joint fleet' about his father's intentions:

After arriving in Guangzhou, the chief wants to call an emergency meeting of cadres at and above divisional levels, establish another Party Central Committee and set up a separatist regime by force, thereby bringing about a south-north confrontation. He will then set the conditions for negotiation with Beijing. He will establish diplomatic relations with the Soviet Union and other countries and, by force of arms and in alliance with the Soviet Union, attack Beijing from north and south . . . [31]

It was arranged that Huang Yongsheng, Wu Faxian, Li Zuopeng and Qiu Huizuo would fly to Guangzhou from Beijing the following morning. Lin Liguo then boarded a Trident jet and flew to Shanhaiguan near Beidaihe. The idea was that this plane would take Lin Biao and his entourage to Guangzhou the following morning.

In fact, even these arrangements fell through. On the evening of 12 September the guard unit at Beidaihe learned that Lin was planning to flee and promptly reported to Zhou Enlai in Beijing. The premier began to make enquiries and, having ascertained that an Air Force Trident was indeed at Shanhaiguan airport, he instructed that it must not take off without an order signed, inter alia, by himself. At the last minute, therefore, Lin Biao abandoned his plan to fly south and decided to head for Irkutsk in the Soviet Union.

If the official accounts are to be believed, what then followed was worthy of a Hollywood film. Lin, with his wife and son, jumped into a 'high-class, bullet-proof Red Flag saloon' and set off for the airport at high speed, hotly pursued by the Beidaihe guard unit. They boarded the waiting Trident in great haste and demanded that it take off immediately, even though the co-pilot, navigator and radio operator had not arrived. The plane left shortly before one o'clock in the morning on 13 September and headed north, tracked by Chinese radar stations. It left Chinese airspace and, at 2.30 a.m. crashed near Ondorhaan in Mongolia. The bodies of Lin Biao, Ye Qun, Lin Liguo and others were subsequently identified by staff from the Chinese Embassy in Ulaan Baatar.

Lin's death was extremely fortuitous for the Chinese leadership. There is no reason to suppose that the Soviet Union had been actively involved in his plot at any stage, but the Soviet authorities would obviously have relished the prospect of giving him sanctuary. Not only would this have been of major value as propaganda, but it would have given them a unique source of intelligence covering China's most important military and political secrets. Not surprisingly, therefore, there has been considerable speculation ever since that his death was simply due to a flying accident. This question, like so many concerning the Lin Biao affair, is one for which the true answer will probably never be known.

Another intriguing question is how Mao was so well-informed of Lin's intentions, especially in the final days of his life. Here, another strand can be woven into the plot. On 18 September 1971 the Central Committee issued an intra-Party communiqué giving brief details of Lin's plan to assassinate Mao and his subsequent flight and death. This claimed that Lin Doudou, Lin Biao's daughter, had 'placed national interest above filial piety by refusing to escape with Lin Biao' and had, moreover, 'reported the situation to the premier in time, which led to the foiling of her father's monstrous conspiracy'.[32] The communiqué made no reference to the time at which she informed on her father. But it raises the possibility that Mao and Zhou had their own spy in Lin's household.[33]

After Lin's death, Huang Yongsheng, Wu Faxian, Li Zuopeng and Qiu Huizuo were arrested and were subjected to 'investigation'. Their fate remained unknown until they were put on trial in November 1980. Yu Xinye, Zhou Yuchi and Chen Liyun attempted to escape from China by helicopter but were forced down. Yu and Zhou committed suicide but Chen was captured and subsequently confessed. Other members of the 'joint fleet' were also arrested. A purge of Lin's close associates in the PLA was instituted which, according to one estimate, removed at least 130 military leaders at various levels from active duty.[34] This is not, of course, to suggest that all were implicated in his conspiracy. It is reasonable to suppose that the Chinese penchant for 'guilt by association' may well have resulted in the dismissal or demotion of perfectly blameless soldiers who simply had had connections with Lin, particularly through the Fourth Field Army.

After Lin's death the Chinese leadership was faced with the unenviable task of explaining to the Chinese people and the outside world just how it was that, yet again, Mao's chosen successor had proven himself unworthy (and, in this instance, in the most spectacular way imaginable). One measure adopted was to distribute throughout the Party, in September 1972, a letter supposedly written by Mao to Jiang Qing on 8 July 1966. In this Mao referred to Lin Biao's speech on coups d'état stating that he 'was quite uneasy at some of his [Lin's] thinking'. Mao complained particularly that Lin Biao had exaggerated Mao's own achievements and the supremacy of his 'thought', stating, 'I have never believed that the several booklets I wrote would have such supernatural power'. Mao informed his wife that, although he objected, he felt obliged to stay silent for the time being as he had no wish to pour cold water on the Leftists just as the Cultural Revolution was being launched.[35] Hence the message was that Mao already had reservations about Lin even at that early stage.

By the time Mao's letter was circulated, a campaign to vilify Lin Biao was well-advanced. Indeed, even as early as November 1971 the press had begun to publish articles attacking 'political swindlers like Liu Shaoqi', a nice device to link Lin with his predecessor. From late 1971 to the end of 1973 a series of Central Committee documents catalogued Lin's crimes and came complete with confessions of Lin's supporters and photocopies of incriminating documents. This material outlined Lin's plot as described above, attributing to him the most base of motives throughout.

Then, at the tenth Party Congress in August 1973, Zhou Enlai delivered the *Report* in which he anathematised Lin just as Lin had condemned Liu a little over four years previously. Zhou said:

Lin Biao, this bourgeois careerist, conspirator and double-dealer, engaged in machinations within our Party not just for one decade but for several decades ... At important junctures of the revolution he invariably committed Right opportunist errors and invariably played double-faced tricks, putting up a false front to deceive the Party and the people. However, as the Chinese Revolution developed further and especially when it turned socialist in nature and became more and more thoroughgoing, aiming at the complete overthrow of the bourgeoisie and all other exploiting classes, the establishment of the dictatorship of the proletariat in place of the dictatorship of the bourgeoisie and the triumph of socialism over capitalism, Lin Biao and his like, who were capitalist-roaders in power working only for the interests of the minority and whose ambition grew with the rise of their positions, over-estimating their own strength and underestimating the strength of the people, could no longer remain under cover and therefore sprang out for a trial of strength with the proletariat.[36]

So Lin, too, had become a capitalist-roader. And the tenth Congress similarly reversed other decisions taken at the ninth. Needless to say the question of identifying a 'chosen successor' did not arise. Whereas Lin had been sole Vice-Chairman of the Party in 1969, there was now a more collective leadership with the appointment of five Vice-Chairmen. Similarly, there was a significant decline in the military presence at the highest levels. Military representation in the Politbureau fell to only 20 per cent. In the Central Committee only 29 per cent of full members and 23 per cent of alternates were from the PLA. Seventy-six per cent of the military elected to the ninth Central Committee failed to secure election to the tenth. The decline in the political fortunes of the men who had worked in Lin Biao's Fourth Field Army was particularly notable. Forty-one of them had been elected in 1969; only twenty-seven were in 1973.[37]

Mao's second attempt to groom a successor had failed even more disastrously than his first. The tenth Congress formally disposed of the Lin Biao affair but it brought China no closer to the goal of peacefully replacing the top leader, for new factional groupings emerged.

On the left of the political spectrum was the group later to be labelled as the 'Gang of Four', all of whom had greatly improved their political fortunes as a result of the Cultural Revolution and, therefore, had a vested interest in defending its 'achievements'. Three of these we have already met. They were Jiang Qing, Mao's wife, Zhang Chunqiao, the Party leader of Shanghai, and Yao Wenyuan, his fellow Shanghainese whose pen had actually 'started' the Cultural Revolution. The fourth was Wang Hongwen, also from Shanghai. Wang had been an unknown security guard in the no. 17 Textile Mill in Shanghai when the Cultural Revolution began. He threw himself into the violent political struggles which convulsed that city and mobilised workers in support of Zhang Chunqiao. Of all the 'mass representatives' thrown up in the Cultural Revolution he was by far the most successful. By 1972 he had become Vice-Chairman of the Shanghai Revolutionary Committee, political commissar of its military garrison and leader of its trade union federation. In 1973 he was appointed as a Vice-Chairman of the Party Central Committee of the tenth Congress. At the time he was only in his mid-thirties.

With the exception of Wang, the 'Gang's' members were particularly skilled polemicists and propagandists and much of their strength came from control of the media, where many of their supporters had been moved into key positions. Shortly after the tenth Congress they launched, in Shanghai, their own theoretical journal, *Study and Criticism*, the better to promote their policies and attack their enemies. And enemies they did have. For, as we shall see in the next chapter, Right-wing leaders mounted a formidable challenge. From 1973 onwards another bitter struggle developed as Left and Right fought over policy issues with the question of the succession very much in mind.

From the 'Four Modernisations' to the 'Three Poisonous Weeds': Deng Xiaoping and the 'Gang of Four'

The first return of Deng Xiaoping

Four months before the tenth Congress, China-watchers were surprised at an event which took place in Beijing. The occasion was a state banquet for Prince Sihanouk of Cambodia on 12 April 1973, which in itself was a matter of no great significance. What did attract attention, however, was the sight of a cadre of the Ministry of Foreign Affairs approaching a small man who stood diffidently by the door as if unsure whether he was welcome to enter. Taking him by the arm the cadre led him into the throng in the banqueting hall. The cadre was Wang Hairong, Mao Zedong's niece. The man was Deng Xiaoping, and Miss Wang's action symbolised that 'Vice-Premier Deng', as he was once again styled, had not only come in from the cold, but had done so with Mao's blessing.[1] And at the tenth Congress, over which Mao presided, Deng was by far the most senior of the pre-Cultural Revolution leaders to be rehabilitated.

The following year he was regularly to be seen seated on Mao's right at receptions for distinguished foreign visitors, a position previously reserved for Zhou Enlai himself. In January 1975 Deng was promoted to be a Vice-Chairman of the Central Committee and was listed first among the Vice-Premiers appointed by the National People's Congress, pushing Zhang Chunqiao into second place. Immediately thereafter he was appointed Chief of the General Staff. In 1977 it was to be claimed that Deng's elevation to all these positions was proposed by Mao and that, at an unspecified date in the first half of 1975, Mao had also 'entrusted him with the responsibility of presiding over the day-to-day work of the Central Committee during Premier Zhou's grave illness'.[2]

For a man who had been so thoroughly discredited in the Cultural Revolution and who had disappeared completely from public life, Deng's return was indeed spectacular. But with the benefit of hindsight it was perfectly understandable. First, it may be noted, he was one of China's most distinguished and experienced leaders. A Party member since 1924, Deng had made the Long March and subsequently served as a political commissar in the Eighth Route Army. Elected to the Central Committee in 1945 he had gone on to play a major part in the defeat of the Nationalists and, at the time of liberation, was engaged in pacifying the south-west, the most difficult area in China proper. From there he had gone to Beijing and, after his election as General Secretary of the Party in 1956, spent the ensuing decade as a key member of the Chinese élite, with extensive influence in both domestic and foreign affairs.

Deng's abilities were undoubtedly recognised by Mao who, on one occasion, had pointed him out to Khrushchev, saying: 'See that little man there? He's highly intelligent and has a great future ahead of him.'[3] On the eve of the Cultural Revolution few foreign analysts would have denied that he was a strong contender to succeed one of the existing triumvirate of Mao, Zhou and Liu Shaoqi. And yet, in 1967 he was condemned to political oblivion and was not to emerge for six years.

His disgrace in the Cultural Revolution was due to two factors. As alleged at the time, he had chosen to disagree with Mao over a number of policy issues which arose after the Great Leap Forward. Whereas Mao became increasingly concerned at the prospect of the death of the revolution to which he had dedicated his life and called upon his colleagues to re-commit themselves to its goals, Deng had leaned the

other way, his attitude being exemplified in a famous statement in 1961 when, to encourage professionalism, he asserted
that 'it doesn't matter if a cat is black or white; if it catches
mice, it's a good cat'.[4]

In the 1960s, therefore, Deng had come to 'walk the
capitalist road', taking good care that Mao had limited
opportunities to interfere. Thus, as the Chairman was to com-
plain, 'Deng Xiaoping is deaf, but at meetings he has not
reported to me about his work . . . Deng Xiaoping respects
me but prefers to stay away from me'.[5] Consequently, when
Mao's exasperation with his erstwhile colleagues caused him
to unleash the Cultural Revolution, Deng was one of its most
prominent victims and was branded in the Red Guard press as
'China's Second Khrushchev'.

Nevertheless, there is evidence to suggest that Mao was
unwilling to subject Deng to the full rigours of Red Guard
'justice'. On 24 October 1966 he asserted that 'it's bad to
paste up big-character posters about Liu and Deng in the
streets'. Unlike Peng Dehuai and other of his opponents, 'Liu
and Deng acted openly' and, Mao argued, 'the essential thing
is that they should reform, that their ideas should conform,
and that they should unite with us'.[6]

That matters did not end here, and that Deng was subsequently subjected to the humiliation of mass criticism
followed by six years of menial work in Jiangxi province,
suggests the second factor responsible for his disgrace: it was
partly due to Lin Biao who wanted to rid himself of a potential rival as he used the Cultural Revolution as a vehicle to
supreme power. In 1975 Deng told a foreign correspondent
of his years in the wilderness that 'This question cannot be
separated from the Lin Biao affair.'[7] In October 1966 Lin
had, in fact, implied that Deng might have been involved in a
plot against Mao, and Lin was a principal supporter of the
Red Guards in their attacks on power-holders. Although Mao
did not question Deng's integrity, his belief that the Left had
to be encouraged in the early stages of the Cultural Revolution
may well have prevented him from stopping, or at least
limiting, Deng's disgrace.

Conversely, in 1973 there were good reasons to bring Deng
back. It should be emphasised that these did not include any

convincing evidence that he had sincerely repented, promised to mend his ways and return to office committed to the principles and policies of the Cultural Revolution. In 1976 the 'Gang of Four' were to claim that his rehabilitation had been due to Mao's kindly decision to give him a 'second chance' and that the 'unrepentant capitalist-roader' had betrayed Mao's trust yet again.

It is, of course, possible that Deng produced an appropriate 'form of words' before coming back in 1973. But it is straining credulity to imagine that Mao could have believed that Deng was a reformed character. Had his return been arranged on the promise of 'good behaviour', Deng would hardly have thrown himself so whole-heartedly into masterminding the drive to 'reverse verdicts' on the Cultural Revolution which will be discussed below. The reality, rather, was that the times had changed, and Mao with them.

For whatever achievements had been gained in the Cultural Revolution, the cost was far greater than Mao had originally envisaged when he launched it. Violence had been widespread, conditions of near-anarchy had arisen in some areas, and many of Mao's self-proclaimed supporters had revealed themselves to be either self-seeking careerists or unyielding and intolerant dogmatists seeking Utopian solutions. The early leaders of the radical students had fallen into the sins of 'ultra-Leftism'; so too had the younger members of the Cultural Revolution Group, the Marxist literati of *Red Flag* and other journals who had constituted the '16 May group', purged for conspiratorial activity in 1967. Chen Boda had been disgraced in 1970. And, above all, there was the Lin Biao affair.

In the circumstances there can be little doubt that by 1973 Mao was somewhat disillusioned with those who claimed most vociferously to be his loyal followers. Not only had they betrayed him but they had also grossly exceeded his instructions in the viciousness of their attacks upon veteran cadres. In the process they had seriously damaged the administrative and economic structures of the Chinese state, and had contributed to China's dangerous isolation in international affairs.

Mao was unwilling to jettison the Left entirely, and the

power exerted by the 'Gang' after 1972 amply testifies to this, but it was essential to restore the balance after the untimely demise of Lin Biao. In the context of the need to restore order, re-build the Party and state administration, develop the economy and continue to improve relations with the United States, Deng's return was simply the logical culmination of the process whereby, since the upheavals of the late 1960s, Zhou Enlai had quietly brought back to their desks many of the senior cadres purged in those years.

There was, however, a new element in the equation. In 1972 it became known that Zhou was suffering from cancer.[8] Despite his legendary ability to work incredibly long hours and to take an active personal interest in not only the highest affairs of state but in a host of relatively minor matters also, the Premier was clearly becoming incapacitated and needed to groom his own successor. Deng was one of the few leaders who possessed the experience and ability to take over Zhou's burden and who, moreover, was in tune with his thinking on policy issues. Moreover, as was later to become evident, Deng commanded widespread support among cadres and masses alike.

In the eighteen months following his return, Deng's status was publicly bolstered. He regularly 'filled in' for Zhou by receiving and entertaining foreign dignitaries, a function which may have had little importance internationally, but which ensured that his face and name regularly appeared in the Chinese media. In April 1974 he led the Chinese delegation to a Special Session of the United Nations General Assembly in New York, thus becoming the most senior Chinese leader to visit the West since the Cultural Revolution. Because of his long absence from public affairs, he no doubt needed considerable time to plan policy initiatives, and it was also necessary to 'establish' him as a senior leader once more in the eyes of the masses. By the end of 1974, however, he and Zhou were preparing policy departures to be announced at the fourth National People's Congress.

Deng and the 'Four Modernisations'

The fourth Congress met in January 1975. In addition to

appointing a new slate of Government ministers and adopting a new state Constitution to replace that of 1954 (which had ceased to exist for all practical purposes), the Congress received Zhou's 'Report on the Work of the Government', the first he had delivered since the Cultural Revolution began. Although the Premier paid lip-service to that movement, Zhou's main emphasis was on stability and unity, and on the need for a high rate of economic growth. Thus he talked of the unity of workers and peasants and 'the many intellectuals' and stated that 'we should unite over 75 per cent of our cadres and the masses and unite with all the forces that can be united in a joint effort to build our great socialist motherland'. It was essential, he said, to 'work hard to increase production and speed up socialist construction so that our socialist system will have a more solid material formation'.

In a key passage of his 'Report', Zhou referred back to 1964, when

> On Chairman Mao's instructions, it was suggested in the report on the work of the Government to the third National People's Congress that we might envisage the development of our national economy in two stages beginning from the Third Five-Year Plan: the first stage is to build an independent relatively comprehensive industrial and economic system in fifteen years, that is before 1980; the second stage is to accomplish the comprehensive modernisation of agriculture, industry, national defence and science and technology before the end of the century, so that our national economy will be advancing in the front ranks of the world.[9]

In fact, when Zhou had first called for the 'Four Modernisations' in 1964, he had not claimed Mao's authority for it. Now he did. And he called on all organisations from ministries to grass roots units to 'arouse the masses to work out their plans through full discussion and strive to attain our splendid goal ahead of time'.

Suitably emboldened by the power base he had now established in Party, state and army bureaucracies, Deng promptly turned his attention to implementing Zhou's call for the 'Four Modernisations'. A series of conferences was held which resulted in the production of three major policy documents, which were put through several drafts in the summer and autumn of 1975. After the fall of the 'Gang' it was to be claimed that many of China's leaders, and most notably Hua Guofeng, had been actively involved, but there is no doubt that Deng was the driving force. It was he who was singled out for attack when the 'Gang' declared the documents to be 'three poisonous weeds' in 1976, and it was he who was praised when, in 1977, it was officially announced that the documents were 'fragrant flowers' after all.

Although full texts of the documents have never been published, we have access to partial versions of various drafts, together with records of meetings at which they were discussed. One of the texts, 'On the General Programme of Work for the Whole Party and the Whole Nation', was a general analysis of what was wrong with Chinese society and what needed to be done. The second, 'Some Problems in Accelerating Industrial Development', had a specifically economic focus. The third, 'On Some Problems in the Field of Science and Technology', emphasised the vital importance of such work to China's modernisation drive, and called for drastic changes to be introduced.[10]

These documents (and possibly others which either never reached completion or have received little publicity[11]) presented a devastating critique of the harm done by excesses arising from the Cultural Revolution, and contrasted markedly with the picture of sweetness and light presented to foreign visitors and in the official press. They set out, in considerable detail, how matters should be put right. The documents contain much repetition as to the problems China faced and the solutions advocated and, therefore, rather than summarise them in turn it is more convenient to concentrate on the main themes running through all the texts.

To begin, then, with what was wrong. In general terms the problems besetting China were blamed on 'anti-Marxist class enemies'. Deng was astute enough to employ some of the rhetoric of the Cultural Revolution and was particularly careful to criticise capitalist-roaders like Liu Shaoqi. But he left little doubt that the people causing most damage in 1975 were 'Lin Biao's successors'. It was the Left who caused 'ideological confusion' and 'disorder'; they 'split the Party, the working class and the ranks of the masses'. These trouble-makers, it was argued,

> ... are not a bit sorry when the socialist construction suffers losses and are not a bit moved when the socialist system is undermined. They have a mania for 'creating mountain strongholds' and engaging in factional fights. They are permanently entangled in the struggle between this faction and that faction, between the so-called rebel-lious faction and conservative faction, between the so-called new and old cadres, and between the so-called 'Confucian school' and 'Legalist school'.[12]

Following Lin Biao's evil example they 'completely dicho-tomised politics and economics and distorted the leading role of politics to mean politics can combat everything'. They put a 'hat' on those who dared to take an interest in economic work and accused them of revisionism. Good cadres and model workers were often attacked and 'pulled down'; scientists and technologists who tried to carry out theoretical research were criticised for being 'divorced from production, divorced from politics, and divorced from the workers and peasants'. The Left regarded 'the masses' as the fount of all wisdom, and expertise in any field was treated with contempt.

The result was widespread intimidation and demoralisation. According to Deng, many cadres had come to believe that 'grasping revolution is good insurance, while grasping produc-tion is dangerous'; 'revolution is extremely important, but production is not'; 'he who grasps revolution has it made, he who grasps production has had it'. In a 'substantial number' of industrial enterprises, Deng claimed, 'management is in chaos, work productivity is low, product quality is poor, maintenance is expensive, costs are high and breakdowns are frequent, causing serious loss to the country and the people'. Industrial discipline was lax.

Similar problems abounded in scientific research. Deng's investigations revealed that many research institutes had actually been closed down completely and highly-qualified personnel had been transferred to the countryside and the factories to undertake menial jobs. Those institutes which continued to function had often been forbidden to recruit new staff, as a consequence of which the average age of researchers was in the forties. (As is well-known, a disproportionate number of scientific breakthroughs are made by very young scientists, hence this failure to recruit and train people at an age when their scientific creativity was at its height was particularly damaging.)

Deng, then, painted a picture of demoralisation, incompetence, and mismanagement. China would not modernise in such circumstances, and a change of course was essential. First, it was necessary to downgrade the importance of 'struggle', which had become virtually a way of life to many following the breakdown of controls in the 1960s. Therefore Deng urged people to 'say and do things which will promote unity; and don't say and do things which will harm unity'. He reminded his readers that Mao himself had pointed out during the Cultural Revolution that there was 'no reason whatsoever for the working class to split into two big irreconcilable groups'. Instead people should be much more critical of their own shortcomings and more tolerant of those of others.

Furthermore, it was incumbent upon all good citizens to scrutinise carefully the words and deeds of those who mouthed revolutionary slogans. For example, when faced with a call to 'rebellion' one should not immediately experience a Pavlovian reaction but should, rather, ask which class was being rebelled against and which was doing the rebelling. Similarly with the concept of 'going against the tide', that Leftist principle enshrined in the tenth Party Constitution, and which had been used to justify numerous attacks on established authority from 1973 onwards. Here, one should ask, is it a correct tide or an incorrect one, Marxist or revisionist? Beware, Deng said, of naïvely assuming that methods popularised in the Cultural Revolution were the sole preserve of true revolutionaries. Such tactics as 'speaking out freely', putting up wallposters and organising 'great debates' could be utilised by 'sham Marxist political swindlers' as well as by the politically virtuous. As far as Deng was concerned, 'struggle' could well be the last refuge of the scoundrel.

In particular, a correct attitude to economic work was required for, as he crushingly pointed out:

> It is purely nonsense to say that a certain place or work unit is carrying out revolution very well when production is fouled up. The view that once revolution is grasped, production will increase naturally and without spending any effort is believed only by those who believe in fairy tales.[13]

He was equally scathing about those who thought that scientific work should only concern itself with the practical and immediate, and that it was safe to ignore long-term and theoretical work. This, he said, was as absurd as waiting until one felt thirsty before beginning to dig a well. If long-term research were neglected Chinese industry would suffer the consequences decades hence.

Whereas the Left, throughout the Cultural Revolution era, had tended to present the central task of revolution as the liberation of Man from various real or imagined forms of oppression and exploitation, Deng emphasised the need to 'liberate' the forces of production also. And in contrast to those who believed that 'the masses' were the people best equipped to do this, he advocated a centralised and orderly process of development under the guidance of the Communist Party. It was the Party's bounden duty to reassert its control over all other units in society and, moreover, over its own individual members. Discipline was to be restored, especially in economic units, and he enlisted the support of Engels to refute tendencies towards 'anarchism', quoting to telling effect the latter's assertion that 'wanting to abolish authority in large-scale industry is tantamount to wanting to abolish industry itself, to destroy a power loom in order to return to the spinning wheel'.

There was, then, no room for latter-day Luddites in Deng's economic thought. For him a modern economy could only thrive on the basis of strict adherence to rules and regulations. This was just as true for socialist as for capitalist societies and, he observed, would still hold true under full communism. Indeed, Deng insisted that China must learn from *all* advanced industrial societies, whatever their political complexion. He encouraged scientists to keep abreast of developments elsewhere so that they might not only learn from others' success but, equally important in a country with limited time and resources, from their failures also. The import of foreign technology, as well as 'know-how', was also advocated as a means of enabling China to catch up, the high costs of such a venture being met by the export of coal, oil and other resources.

Indigenous expertise was not, of course, to be despised. Although stressing the importance of Party control over experts, Deng carefully distinguished this from undue interference by 'the masses' in matters which he believed were best left to professionals. Thus in terms of scientific research he even went to the extent of praising 'white' experts, intellectuals whose commitment to Marxism was less than wholehearted. Provided their work was in the national interest, he argued, they were to be preferred to political appointees who, as he crudely put it, 'occupy the privy but can't shit'. It was necessary to ensure that the Academy of Sciences was 'an Academy of Sciences, not an Academy of Cabbage'. Distinguished scientists like Huang Kun, a leading authority in semi-conductor research who had been sent off to do menial work in a factory, were to be allowed to return to their specialisms.

Deng did not stop at calling for improved status for those with expertise; they were further to be encouraged by material incentives. He rejected demands for the rapid destruction of 'bourgeois right' on the grounds that 'an egalitarian distribution that does not distinguish between differences in the intensity of work, standards of ability, and magnitude of contribution, is not conducive to the mobilisation of the masses for building socialism'.

His approach, then, was to advocate a modernisation strategy in which the Party would favour and direct those who were expert, skilled and hard-working, and would place less emphasis on the contribution of politics and 'the masses'. Although he made some attempt to couch his arguments in the jargon of the Cultural Revolution, his impatience with revolutionary phraseology was readily apparent in the way he dealt with 'three important instructions' Mao had issued in late 1974 (calling somewhat ambiguously for unity, pushing the economy forward, and studying the dictatorship of the proletariat), in that he attempted to subordinate them to the dictates of rapid economic growth. Thus although the 'General Programme' stated that Mao's call for 'study of the dictatorship of the proletariat' occupied the 'foremost' position among the directives, it was subsequently asserted that all three were an 'interconnected and inseparable entity' and that they must be taken together to constitute 'the key link'. The whole tenor of Deng's documents was to stress stability and economic growth and to imply that the goal of the dictatorship of the proletariat was not so much to foment class struggles as to 'safeguard everybody so that they can work in peace, so that our country can be built into a socialist country with modern industry, agriculture, science and culture'.

As the documents were being put through various drafts, Hu Qiaomu, a distinguished propagandist in Deng's entourage, was deployed to embellish them with phraseology appropriate to the Cultural Revolution era. Even so, some of Deng's colleagues expressed misgivings as to the reactions these hard-hitting reports were likely to provoke. Thus at one meeting it was pointed out that the texts contained 'many pigtails', an allusion to the Chinese expression 'to pull the pigtail', meaning to criticise. Deng, however, confidently rejected the suggestion that he and his colleagues were giving too many hostages to fortune. Replying in similar vein he compared himself to a 'a Uighur girl with many pigtails'.[14] It was the custom for Uighur maidens to braid their hair into one pigtail for each year of their age, and Deng was encouraging the faint-hearted to follow his example in speaking out, regardless of the consequences.

Even before the policy documents were completed Deng had been active in taking practical steps to curb Leftist excesses. For example, he had vigorously opposed certain aspects of the campaign to restrict 'bourgeois right' when, in the spring of 1975, an attempt had been made to change the 'eight-grade wage system' for factory workers. The Left wished to reduce differentials by raising the lower grade and lowering the highest, but Deng had sharply criticised such 'egalitarianism', apparently with considerable success.[15]

He also stood on Leftist corns by his handling of the 'Hangzhou question'. Since 1974 Hangzhou in particular, and Zhejiang province in general, had been beset by appalling factionalism which resulted in considerable violence, labour unrest, drastic losses of production and the appearance of a considerable amount of 'free enterprise' and, indeed, black marketeering. Matters were so bad that Hangzhou was closed to foreigners in the winter of 1974–5. In 1975 Wang Hongwen was sent to Hangzhou but was unable to solve the problems there, and in the summer Deng sent in the PLA to restore discipline and to arrest Weng Senhe, the leading Leftist, who was held to be the man responsible for the trouble. The picture of economic chaos painted in the policy documents appears to have owed much to Deng's personal experience in Hangzhou.[16]

Furthermore, in the late spring and early summer, the Politbureau, 'with Comrade Deng Xiaoping in charge, severely criticised the "Gang of Four" '. This was, allegedly, 'in accordance with Chairman Mao's instructions', and may have been directly related to the Hangzhou situation.[17] Similarly, as Deng's investigations revealed an appalling drop in standards in scientific and educational work, steps were taken to dismiss or demote a number of the Leftists deemed responsible.

Until well into the summer, then, Deng was on the offensive and the 'Gang' were faring badly. And yet, after the submission of the policy documents to Mao and the highest echelons in the autumn, it was the 'Gang' who went on to attack. Unfortunately, the pattern of developments between August and November 1975 is less clear than it might be, but the following factors would appear to be relevant.

First, Zhou's illness worsened as the autumn progressed and it must have been apparent to all that he had little time to live. On the one hand this deprived Mao of the moderate counsel of his oldest and most distinguished colleague, and made him more susceptible to advice from the Left. On the other, it deprived Deng and those who thought like him of the protection which Zhou had always afforded to his subordinates.

Secondly, Deng's policy documents did demand substantive reversals of the settlements imposed by the Cultural Revolution. Despite Hu Qiaomu's embellishments, the texts could certainly be viewed as 'revisionist' and they were far more outspokenly Right-wing than Zhou's carefully balanced remarks to the fourth Congress. At the best of times Mao may well have found fault with their contents.

Thirdly, it is highly likely that Mao's judgement was affected due to his own deteriorating health. His failure to attend Zhou's memorial service on 15 January 1976 is difficult to explain except on the grounds of severe illness. At best he was physically enfeebled and was probably highly dependent on information 'filtered' to him by his immediate entourage. He may well have been given a highly distorted picture of what Deng was attempting to do. He may also have declined mentally and may have been happy to agree to any thoughts put into his mind by the 'Gang of Four'. This is not to argue that, from the autumn of 1975, he was incapable of making rational decisions; like many very elderly and sick people, he no doubt had 'good days' and 'bad days'. But the possibility that he was, from time to time, subject to unscrupulous manipulation must be taken seriously, and there have been official hints to this effect.[18] In any event, the 'Gang' were able to turn on Deng and to claim Mao's blessing for so doing. It is also highly probable that Mao would have objected to Deng's proposed policies even without their prompting.

Opposition to the 'Right Deviationist Wind'

The 'Gang's' counter-offensive actually began in the field of education. In January 1975 the fourth National People's Congress had re-established the Ministry of Education which had simply ceased to function in the early stages of the Cultural Revolution. Zhou Rongxin, a rehabilitated veteran cadre and long-time associate of the Premier, was appointed Minister.

Acting in concert with Deng, the new Minister sought to

correct failings in the educational system, a sector which had been particularly subjected to radical reorganisation since 1966. At a series of meetings Zhou Rongxin complained of the decline in academic standards at all levels, and of the excessive attention given to political education and practical work. He called for a new emphasis on formal study, more respect for intellectuals, and greater discipline in schools, and he attacked 'ultra-Leftists' for their intimidation and interference.

The Minister was a less formidable opponent than Deng and, happily for the 'Gang', he made a protocol visit to Africa in November. During his absence a wallposter campaign began at Qinghua, which called on students to 'beat back the Right Deviationist Wind to reverse previous verdicts'. Instigated by Chi Qun and Xie Jingyi, the leading Leftists in educational circles, the campaign was initially directed against Zhou Rongxin and his colleagues in the educational sector. In December the criticisms made in the wallposters were given wider circulation. A *People's Daily* editorial of 4 December, entitled 'The Revolution in Education Must Not Be Tampered With', was the first of many media attacks which gradually began to refer to themes running through Deng's reports, although not at that time specifically associating them with Deng.

Thus the New Year editorial, published jointly by *Red Flag* and the national newspapers on 1 January 1976, alluded positively to the 'socialist new-born things' emanating from the Cultural Revolution. It referred to the 'Right Deviationist Wind' as a 'conspicuous manifestation of the revisionist line that stands against the proletariat on behalf of the bourgeoisie'. The editorial contained a new quotation from Mao: 'Stability and unity do not mean writing off the class struggle; class struggle is the key link and everything else hinges on it.' For those familiar with the 1975 documents it was now apparent that Deng was under attack.

On 8 January Zhou Enlai died. Although his passing was marked with official obituaries and mass mourning, the 'Gang' used their control of the media to hide the widespread affection and esteem he had obviously enjoyed. Thus Yao Wenyuan saw to it that press and television coverage of the mourning service was kept to a minimum. He had the bier containing Zhou's body placed in a small room so that the television cameras covering the ceremony were unable to 'pan' from side to side without revealing the cramped surroundings. He also refused to allow *People's Daily* to publish letters mourning Zhou's death, and on the eve of the memorial service ordered the front page to be devoted to a lengthy article on the 'Revolution in Education' at Qinghua.[19] *Study and Criticism* did not even publish a single article paying tribute to the Premier, although it found space to praise the memory of Kang Sheng, who had died a little earlier.

Both Zhou Rongxin and Deng Xiaoping were prominent mourners at the memorial service, Deng reading the oration. For the Minister this was his last public appearance: he was to die three months later at the age of 59, although that fact was not to be officially announced until September 1977. Deng, too, made no further public appearances until July 1977. To the astonishment of foreign observers, it was Hua Guofeng who was appointed Acting Premier at the beginning of February.

Thereafter the anti-Deng campaign intensified. On 6 February *People's Daily* attributed the 'Right Deviationist Wind' to 'those capitalist-roaders who were subjected to criticism during the Great Proletarian Cultural Revolution but who had refused to show any repentance'. These people had either only repented 'in the heat of the moment but started to reverse verdicts immediately afterwards' or had 'never given in'. The article claimed to detect a 'complete set of revisionist programmes and lines' hidden behind the 'Four Modernisations', which were purportedly designed to 'clear the way for capitalist restoration'.

On 10 February wallposters criticising Deng were put up at Beijing University. He was not named but was clearly identified by references to his 'white cat, black cat' remark.[20] On the 13th *People's Daily* declared that the 'capitalist-roaders' had 'started to negate and revise the principle of taking class struggle as the key link' and had 'blatantly opposed what they termed the ultra-Left'. By the end of the month the 'white cat, black cat' identification was being used in the press, Deng's name was appearing in wallposters, and the campaign was being developed powerfully in Shanghai and other cities, as well as Beijing.

Throughout March Deng was attacked for pushing his 'capitalistic' modernisation programme, and for opposing such other 'socialist new-born things' as Jiang Qing's beloved revolutionary operas. On 10 March *People's Daily* produced two 'very recent' sayings of Mao's to support its attack on Deng. One was a simple statement that 'It is contrary to the will of the people to reverse previous verdicts'. The other was more substantial:

The socialist revolution has fallen on the heads of the people within the Party who opposed the formation of agricultural co-operatives and resent criticism of bourgeois right. You are making the socialist revolution without knowing where the bourgeoisie are. They are in the Communist Party — the Party leaders who have taken the capitalist road. They are still following the same road.

A further saying of Mao's was published on 28 March, firmly linking him with the criticism of Deng:

Chairman Mao pointed out recently: 'This person does not grasp class struggle; he has never referred to this key link. Still his theme of white cat, black cat, making no distinction between imperialism and Marxism'.

In March the 'Gang of Four' also directed their attention towards Zhou Enlai. On 5 March the *Xinhua News Agency* transmitted a report on how PLA units in Shenyang were 'learning from Lei Feng', the young soldier whose legendary loyalty to Maoist precepts had led to his posthumous recognition as a 'model' in the mid-1960s. The report contained an inscription which Zhou Enlai had written on this paragon of virtue. *Wenhui Bao*, the major Shanghai newspaper under the 'Gang's' control, relegated this report to an inside page and, moreover, shortened it by excising Zhou's inscription. This minor insult to the Premier's memory was followed by an actual attack. For on 25 March the paper carried on its front page an article in which Zhou was identified as 'that capitalist-roader in the Party' who had wanted 'to reinstate in power the capitalist-roader who had been overthrown and is unrepentant to this day'.[21]

The Tiananmen Incident

Although the *Wenhui Bao* article apparently aroused resentment in Shanghai, protests against it began in Nanjing, a seven-hour train journey away. In Nanjing there was considerable support for Deng and some people were prepared to demonstrate against the dishonouring of Zhou's memory. On 29 March wallposters appeared which claimed that 'the anti-Party articles in the *Wenhui Bao* are the signals for usurping Party leadership and seizing state power' and asserting that 'we will never give up until the sinister behind-the-scenes boss of the *Wenhui Bao* is ferreted out'. Some people marched to a memorial at Yuhuatai hill and laid wreaths to Zhou. When a Beijing-bound train pulled into Nanjing station, people painted slogans on the sides of the carriages and news of the incident quickly reached the capital.[22]

At the time China was preparing to celebrate the *Qingming* festival, the traditional day for sweeping the graves of ancestors which, under the People's Republic, had been transformed into an occasion to honour the 'people's martyrs'. On 30 March a group of Beijing trade unionists put up a eulogy to Zhou on the face of the Martyrs' Memorial, a large obelisk in the centre of Tiananmen Square. Wreaths and poems began to appear round the memorial and by 3 April there were several thousands. Most were signed by the names of the work units presenting them. Ministries and the Academy of Sciences were well represented, but so were army units, schools, universities and factories.

On *Qingming* itself, 4 April, hundreds of thousands of people flocked to Tiananmen and the square became the scene of the most astonishing tribute to Zhou's memory.[23] The memorial was piled high with wreaths, and daring young men vied with one another to scale the mound and place their wreaths on top. Gigantic placards proclaiming 'revered Premier Zhou, we cherish your memory forever' were hung from flagpoles, and ropes were strung from tree to tree to carry 'galleries' of poems praising his memory. A typical eulogy went thus:

> He left no inheritance, he had no children, he has no grave, he left no remains. It seems he left us nothing, but he shall live for all time in our hearts. The whole land is his. He has hundreds of millions of children and grandchildren. All China's soil is his tomb. He left us everything. He shall live in our hearts for all time. Who is he? Who is he? He is our Premier![24]

One young man earned the adulation of the crowd by displaying a 'letter of determination' to Zhou written in his own blood — a traditional and highly-respected method of political expression. Others gave short speeches or shouted slogans. For many, the presentation of wreaths and poems was a mark of love and respect, and nothing more. But even before 4 April there was evidence that some people were consciously demonstrating against Jiang Qing and her colleagues. Thus one poem read:

> The 'reversed verdicts' game is up, its poisoned
> barb exposed;
> A towering crime in attacking Premier Zhou.
> Murky demons flit about the shaky bridge
> On the Blue River.
> Put down the tyrannical river demons, and we'll see
> the Red sunrise.[25]

In English translation the poem appears somewhat vague and mysterious, its meaning not entirely clear. In Chinese, however, its targets were easily identifiable. For the Chinese language is characterised by its relative phonetic poverty which results in an abundance of homonyms, and Chinese delight in the opportunities for literary puns which these provide. In this instance 'shaky bridge' (*yao qiao*) refers to *Yao* Wenyuan and Zhang Chun*qiao*, and 'Blue River' refers to Jiang Qing.

On the monument itself a poem entitled 'Call to Arms at Qingming Festival' was even more direct:

Today we respect our dear departed, but those people
are worse than ever.
They declare themselves against outmoded customs,
but they are really up to mischief.
We are informed by telephone of their slanders and
falsehoods,
As though those 'seen from afar' [*yao* and *qiao* again]
are innocent while the Premier is tarnished.
All who have eyes can see these things.
When you get to the root,
Its the cliques of Shanghai and Liaoning,
Overwhelmed by fame-seeking and avarice, burning to
set up their own dynasty.
Adulate the emperor to lead all the others,
'Better Left than Right', just like Lin Biao's clique.[26]

Jiang Qing was singled out for special mention. The slogan
'Down with the Dowager Empress' was popular, and was
particularly insulting, comparing Mao's wife to the most
notorious and detested woman in China's recent history.
Equally offensive, though less direct, were wreaths and
eulogies mourning the passing of Yang Kaihui, Mao's first
wife, who had been executed by the Guomindang in 1930.

The mood of the crowd, then, was anti-Left. Indeed
students at Beijing University, who might be popularly viewed
as Leftists, were warned by the university authorities to keep
clear.[27] But the atmosphere was generally peaceful, and
slogans and speeches included favourable references to Mao
and the Cultural Revolution. Deng Xiaoping's name was not
mentioned.

The 'Gang of Four' nevertheless had ample cause for concern at these expressions of mass sentiment, and they branded
them as subversive from the outset. On 30 March Yao Wenyuan
told an underling on *People's Daily* that 'the Nanjing Incident
is aimed in substance at the Central Committee' and 'they
have put up big character posters in order to shape public
opinion for a counter-revolutionary restoration'. On 2 April
Yao indicated that he felt the movement was not spontaneous
but seemed 'to be directed from some headquarters'. On
Qingming itself he branded the events in Tiananmen as

'counter-revolution', despite the fact that no real violence had taken place at that stage.

The 'Gang's' initial response was to resort to undercover police activity. Wang Hongwen allegedly called a supporter in the Ministry of Public Security, saying:

> Are you still in bed? I've just been to Tiananmen Square. Have you had the reactionary poems there photographed? If not, how can you round these people up when all the cases are dealt with later? You should send your men to the Square to photograph the poems . . . [28]

Zhang Chunqiao urged the despatch of plainclothes policemen to mingle with the crowds, and the Director of the Beijing Municipal Public Security Bureau sent them to Tiananmen as early as 31 March, where they 'mixed with the crowd, noting down everything that happened, recording the poems and posters and reporting back'. On 2 April the Director called three emergency meetings at which 3,000 'reserves' were mobilised to track down all suspects and to arrest some on the spot and some outside the Square. On 3 and 4 April twenty-six people were arrested, and arrangements were made to prepare places of detention and have lorries standing by in readiness.

Yao also sought to use the excuse that it was the first anniversary of Chiang Kai-shek's death to claim that the demonstrations were really pro-Guomindang in character, and that the laying of wreaths should be stopped. Accordingly, the Director ordered that the wreaths should be removed and, on the night of 4–5 April 200 lorries were sent to clear them away.

On 5 April the Tiananmen riot took place. By its very nature such activity is extremely difficult to describe and in this instance two 'official' accounts have been published. That of the 'Gang' appeared two days later; that of their opponents in November 1978. Both are remarkably consistent in chronicling the actual chain of events. They are, of course, diametrically opposed in apportioning blame, attributing motive, and describing the physical violence committed by both sides. Fortunately, many of the events were witnessed by foreign journalists and diplomats and their accounts provide a valuable corrective to the exaggerations and distortions in the two official records. Obviously, the total accuracy of the following account cannot be vouchsafed, but it is believed to be basically correct.

Early in the morning of 5 April visitors to Tiananmen found that the wreaths had been removed, the posters torn down, and the poems and memorial scrolls had disappeared. The memorial was ringed by guards and anyone trying to approach it was told that it had to be repaired and that no wreaths could be laid. The frustration of the relatively small crowd led to one or two scuffles in which an individual, foolish enough to make disparaging remarks about 'capitalist-roaders', was beaten up and a couple of policemen who tried to intervene were chased away.

A crowd of 10,000 people then gathered outside the eastern entrance to the Great Hall of the People, which flanked one side of the square, in the apparent belief that the wreaths had been hidden away inside. They began to shout loudly for their return. At this point the 'joint command post', situated in the corner of the square, became involved. The post was responsible for security matters in the area of the square and, it would appear, controlled or liaised with units of the workers' militia and the PLA as well as Public Security personnel. Cadres in the post telephoned for a Public Security loudspeaker van which duly began to cruise up and down outside the Great Hall, broadcasting messages to the effect that *Qingming* was over, the crowd should disperse, and should guard 'against sabotage by a handful of class enemies'.

The van's broadcasts had an inflationary effect; it was overturned and its loudspeaker smashed. For the next three hours the crowd continued to mass outside the Great Hall, demanding the return of the wreaths and praising Zhou. There were further incidents of physical violence directed against individuals who were supposed to be Leftists and against militia sent to guard the Great Hall.

Then, at eleven o'clock, a youth with a loudhailer drew the crowd's attention to the joint command post, claiming that it was responsible for the removal of the wreaths and also for making arrests the day before. A group of mass 'representatives' entered the building but were unable to find anyone willing to admit they were in charge. Nevertheless, they did discover that a 'Shanghai' sedan parked outside was reserved for the 'chieftain' of the post and, at one o'clock, it was set on fire. Their appetite suitably whetted, the rioters then proceeded to wreck a fire engine which arrived to put out the blaze and, later in the afternoon, set fire to two jeeps at the post and a minibus which came with food for the militiamen on duty. Finally, at five o'clock, rioters entered the command post, smashed it up, and set it on fire also.

During this day of steadily mounting violence there was a certain amount of fighting between rioters on the one hand and police, militia and soldiers on the other. But it was not until the evening that determined efforts were made to clear the square. At half-past six Wu De, Chairman of the Beijing Municipal Revolutionary Committee, broadcast to the crowd. He claimed that a handful of bad elements had deliberately created a political incident, 'directing the spearhead at Chairman Mao and the Party Central Committee in a vain attempt to change the general orientation of the struggle to criticise the unrepentant capitalist-roader Deng Xiaoping's revisionist line and beat back the Right Deviationist attempt'. He ordered the 'revolutionary masses' to 'leave the square at once' and not be duped by the bad elements.[29] Most people drifted away but some remained and, as the night wore on, over two hundred were arrested by militiamen, police and soldiers, who used considerable violence in the process.

The following day passed with little incident in Beijing. The square and its approaches were surrounded by soldiers with fixed bayonets, workers' militia with truncheons, and police. On 7 April water carts moved backwards and forwards across Tiananmen carrying out a cleaning operation which was, at least in part, a ritual purification. Workers could be seen painting the command post and repairing the damage. The riot was over.[30]

In other cities, including Zhengzhou, Shanghai, Guangzhou and Kunming, similar incidents took place around the time of *Qingming*, leading some scholars to assume that these events were premeditated and co-ordinated.[31] This may be true up to a point: it would only be natural for those opposed to the 'Gang', and denied access to the media, to try and mobilise friends and colleagues to demonstrate the strength of their opinions by utilising the relatively 'low-risk' technique of commemorating Zhou Enlai, and using the Premier as a surrogate for Deng Xiaoping. But the circumstances were such that much of what happened can be explained perfectly satisfactorily in terms of what might be called 'imitative spontaneity' rather than co-ordination. Thus, as we have seen, news of events in Nanjing were carried by train to Beijing and duplicated there on a much larger scale. Beijing's day of violence on 5 April was followed by similar scenes in Zhengzhou the day after, and so on.

As for the violence, in Beijing at least this was entirely due to the removal of the wreaths. It may be that the 'Gang' believed this action would, by removing the rallying-point for popular discontent, defuse the situation; in which case they miscalculated badly. Or they may have deliberately sought to drive their opponents to the point where they could clearly be seen to be overstepping the mark. Whatever the truth may be, there was definite provocation. And once the riot had begun, why was it allowed to continue for so long? It is difficult to believe that the authorities could not have deployed sufficient force in Tiananmen Square to bring the situation speedily under control had they wished to do so. Instead the riot lasted for nine hours in full view of the world's press. And the immediate outcome was so beneficial to the 'Gang' that one is reluctant to accept this was entirely fortuitous.

On 7 April foreigners in central Beijing noticed a flurry of limousines in the neighbourhood of Tiananmen: the Politbureau was in session. That evening, Beijing Radio announced that two important resolutions had been passed 'unanimously' and 'on the proposal of our great leader Chairman Mao'.[32] The first of these concerned Hua Guofeng, who was not only appointed as Premier but, even more important, was made 'First Vice-Chairman' of the Central Committee.

The second resolution concerned Deng Xiaoping and stated: 'Having discussed the counter-revolutionary incident which took place at Tiananmen Square and Deng Xiaoping's latest behaviour, the Politbureau . . . holds that the nature of the Deng Xiaoping problem has passed into one of antagonistic contradiction.' Accordingly, he was dismissed from all his posts both inside and outside the Party, but was allowed to retain his Party membership 'so as to see how he will behave in the future'. Thus Deng's disgrace was less than total. It was not claimed that *he* was a counter-revolutionary, nor that he had personally instigated the riots. The reference to his 'latest behaviour' suggested that he might simply have refused to carry out self-criticism.

Within hours of the announcement, guests at the Beijing Hotel were aroused from their slumbers by the sound of heavy drumming as phalanxes of hotel staff marched off to 'celebrate' the two resolutions. For the remainder of the week the centre of Beijing was the scene of massive processions as people marched in work units, bearing banners to identify themselves. Each unit was preceded by 'cheer-leaders' in the shape of drummers and cymbalists. Smaller organisations might only boast a tympani, mounted perilously on a tri-shaw. Larger units were preceded by a lorry-load of percussion instruments. Generally, the mood of the marchers was sub-dued and, in the case of cadres from the central organs, it was apparent that their demonstration was purely ritualistic; there was silent resignation or sullen acceptance, but little evidence of real enthusiasm.

'Those who play with fire will certainly get burned'

The demonstrations and violence in Tiananmen and elsewhere were skilfully exploited by the 'Gang' through the newspapers, journals and campus militants under their control. From April until October a vituperative campaign was waged against all who disagreed with their particular goals, and distortions, half-truths and lies were used with gay abandon. By use of classic smear techniques the 'Gang' sought to present a picture of 'the enemy'. Beginning with the 'scum' responsible for disorder, the 'Gang' branded Deng Xiaoping as the instigator. And, for good measure, he was held to represent not only 'the bourgeoisie within the Party', but also the bourgeoisie outside it, both at home and abroad. 'Old' counter-revolution-aries were lumped together with 'new-born' ones, and with 'revisionists' both domestic and foreign, as saboteurs, actual and potential, of the Chinese revolution. The themes in the

'Gang's' attack did not appear in a single article: hundreds of 'revolutionary' (and usually pseudonymous) writers contributed to the building of a elaborate mosaic of accusation and innuendo, the cumulative effect of which was to suggest that the Battle of Armageddon had finally arrived.

In the first instance, the aim was to 'reach' the 'opinion-makers', that select band of cadres who received information officially denied to 'the masses' they claimed to represent. China has long possessed various journals and news-sheets which purvey news to specialised, high-level and restricted readerships. One such was *Confidential Information*, a bulletin produced by *People's Daily* for those cadres deemed worthy of richer fare than that newspaper provided. Between 1 and 6 April over a dozen issues of this bulletin were produced by *People's Daily* journalists assigned to cover the events in Tiananmen. After preliminary selection and 'polishing', the reporters concerned sent their 'copy' to Yao Wenyuan, who personally 'edited' it in such a manner that the coverage of the events in question was distorted to show the demonstrators in a particularly bad light.

Yao's technique was simple but effective. For example, one worker had posted up a statement saying that 'empty words about communism cannot satisfy the people's wishes', the emphasis being that it was 'empty words' to which he objected. Under Yao's practised hand, *Confidential Information* reported that someone had 'openly put forth the counter-revolutionary slogan: "oppose empty words of communism" ', the implication being that it was communism per se which the writer opposed.[33] The suggestion that the demonstrators had moved completely beyond the boundaries of opposition within a Marxist framework (subsequently embellished by comparisons between Deng and Imre Nagy, the leader of the Hungarian Revolt of 1956) was presumably designed to mute those voices in the higher councils of the Party which might otherwise, at this crucial juncture, have opposed Deng's disgrace.

After Deng's dismissal on 7 April Yao lost no time in deploying his dubious talents in the national press, and his doctoring of two *Qingming* poems to produce a 'counter-revolutionary' declaration of intent illustrates the ease with which meaning could be changed. The first poem ran to only four lines and was written in classical style. It mourned the passing of a hero, expressed great anger at the forces of evil which had delighted in the event, and pledged that the hero's followers would 'unsheath their swords' to defend his memory.

The second was a much longer piece, entitled 'Cherish the Memory of Premier Zhou at *Qingming*', and was a moving tribute to his 'meritorious deeds'. It noted that 'every inch of the revolutionary road bears [his] footprints' and that 'the heavens echo with [his] voice'.

But, the poem observed, the people had not been allowed to express their grief and, although no-one was actually named, it went on to make it abundantly clear that Jiang Qing and her followers were responsible for this.

Thus, the poem attacked those who 'talk glibly' and 'carry their mistress's train'. They were a 'bunch of monkeys' who were trying to 'crown themselves', 'mayflies' who 'lightly plot to topple the giant tree'. Nevertheless, it continued, these evil-doers would fail. People were 'no longer wrapped in utter ignorance' and, it was implied, the ruthless suppression of 'Qin Shi Huang's feudal society' was no longer possible. China wanted real Marxism-Leninism and those 'scholars' who emasculated it would not be tolerated. The people would carry out Zhou's behest and achieve the 'Four Modernisations'.

This second poem was, then, absolutely clear. It praised Zhou Enlai and identified the 'Four Modernisations' as his policy. Equally, it condemned the 'Gang of Four'. It did not, however, contain any explicit criticism of Mao. Indeed, as if to allay any suspicions that passages directed against the 'Gang' were meant to include the Chairman also, the author(s) deliberately evoked memories of one of the most famous and glorious episodes in Mao's life. For the determination to rise in defence of Zhou and his policies was described as 'climbing Jinggang mountains again', a reference to Mao's establishment of his first guerrilla base in those mountains.

In Yao's skilled hands, a 'poisonous weed' was evolved without difficulty. What he did was to take the last part of the second poem, delete certain lines from it, and append what remained to the first poem. The finished product was then published in the press, as one poem, which proved the despicable intentions of the Tiananmen activists. Yao's version follows.[34]

The devil howls as we pour out our grief,
We weep but the wolves laugh,
We spill our blood in memory of the hero,
Raising our heads, we unsheath our swords.

> First poem in in its entirety

China is no longer the China of yore,
And the people are no longer wrapped in utter ignorance,
Gone for good is Qin Shi Huang's feudal society,
We believe in Marxism-Leninism,
To hell with scholars who emasculate Marxism-Leninism!
What we want is genuine Marxism-Leninism.
For the sake of genuine Marxism-Leninism,
We don't fear to shed our blood or lay down our lives,
And we will not hesitate to climb Jinggang mountains again to rise in rebellion.
We will carry forward Premier Zhou's behest.
The day modernisation in four fields is realised,
We will come back to offer our libation and sacrifices.
Rest well our respected and beloved Premier Zhou.

> Latter part of second poem. The italicised lines do not appear in Yao's version.

It can readily be seen that Yao's composite effort successfully altered the meaning of the two originals in terms both of the object of praise and the object of attack. Zhou Enlai's name had disappeared completely. So had all obvious references to Jiang Qing and her 'mayflies'. As it now stood, the poem would be easily interpreted as a cry of anguish at the declining fortunes of Deng and as a declaration of intent to use violent means to support him and *his* 'Four Modernisations' policy. Similarly, the deletion of the 'positive' reference to Mao in the shape of the 'Jinggang mountains' image was paralleled by the retention of 'Qin Shi Huang' as the only easily recognisable symbol in the poem. The identification of Mao with China's first unifier, which had been repeatedly reinforced in the anti-Confucian campaign, made it appear that *he* was the target, and was the principal scholar who emasculated Marxism-Leninism. In short, a message which had been pro-Zhou and anti-'Gang' had been transmogrified into one which was pro-Deng, anti-Mao. On the basis of the version presented to them, Chinese readers could certainly agree with Yao's claims that the poem was directed against Mao, was reminiscent of Lin Biao's '571' document, and that it praised Deng's 'counter-revolutionary revisionist line'.

And, of course, the newspapers and journals under the 'Gang's' control were quick to bring to the public's attention their own version of Deng's policy statements of 1975, now condemned as the 'three poisonous weeds'. *Study and Criticism*, in its issue of 14 April 1976, pointed the way for the rest of the media when it alleged that 'taking the three directives as the key link' was simply Deng's method of 'changing the Party's ultimate goal from realisation of communism to "Four Modernisations" and ascribing all the tasks of the Party during the entire historical period of socialism to production and construction'.[35]

In like manner the journal refuted Deng's strictures on 'factionalists'. Why, it asked, had Deng been so reluctant to mention 'all the persons in power within the Party taking the capitalist road' when listing 'anti-Marxist class enemies'? 'Capitalist-roaders' were excoriated as 'the principal target of the socialist revolution, and the most dangerous enemies under the dictatorship of the proletariat'. What was wrong with ousting them? Moreover, said the journal, the struggles of the Cultural Revolution had benefited many. Far from hurting experienced old cadres, it had 'enabled many of them to generate greater revolutionary youthfulness'.

Deng's proposals for improving the economy were derisively dismissed as manifestations of his belief that 'good production is good politics', and it was claimed that he wanted to create systems of industrial organisation on the lines of the capitalist world and the Soviet Union. The 'Gang' waxed eloquent in defending the democratisation of management which had resulted from the Cultural Revolution and alleged that Deng wanted 'to reduce the workers of socialist China to slavery again' by imposing 'bourgeois dictatorship in the form of "control, checks and coercion" '. His case for adequate incentives was contemptuously dismissed as 'putting bank-notes in command', while his willingness to 'make foreign things serve China' was the product of a *comprador* mentality.

The 'Gang' also sought to establish that Deng was somehow *personally* responsible for the demonstrations and violence in Tiananmen and elsewhere. Thus on 18 May *People's Daily* produced a class analysis of the Tiananmen rioters, describing them as 'those new-born counter-revolutionaries and the old-brand counter-revolutionaries, as well as desperadoes of all descriptions and the scum of society'. But, the article continued, they were not without assistance, for: 'The trash they peddled was not of their own invention but was borrowed from Deng Xiaoping. They worked hand-in-glove with Deng Xiaoping.' In like manner, after a 'revolutionary' had been beaten to death in Zhengzhou on 6 April, it was claimed that the instigator of that incident had openly boasted of being Deng's 'black ace general'.[36]

In 1978 it was officially claimed that Deng had been 'completely isolated'[37] at the time, and there is no reason to dispute this as the Chinese political system is not noted for its willingness to permit leaders in trouble to appeal directly to the general public for support. Certainly, foreign observers rarely, if ever, witnessed demonstrations invoking his name and, although this may occasionally have happened, the claim that Deng had personally instigated the trouble was undoubtedly far-fetched.[38]

Moreover, the 'Gang' were not content to argue that Deng alone was responsible: the root went far deeper than that. For, in the weeks following the Tiananmen Incident, a drive to 'track down the sources of counter-revolutionary sabotage' developed, and in the course of this much attention was given to discrediting veteran cadres who supported him or were, at least, sympathetic to some of his ideas.

The immediate roots of this campaign went back to the end of 1975 when the assault on the 'Right Deviationist

Wind' had begun, and the 'Gang' were faced with the thorny problem of explaining just why it was that senior leaders with revolutionary credentials going back as much as fifty years should no longer be accorded loyalty and respect. Their answer was a 'theory' which was simplicity itself, and went as follows.

The veterans had indeed been 'progressive' when they joined the revolution, and consequently had assumed and retained leadership positions. But they had joined the movement at a time when its aims were limited to opposing feudalism and foreign aggression. These objectives having been accomplished, the revolution had moved on through higher and higher stages and, as it inexorably progressed, many veterans found themselves unable to adapt to the changed circumstances and, alas, had in some instances become 'reactionary'. They had been good 'democrats' in their day, but were unwilling to transform themselves into good communists. Thus Jiang Qing asserted that '75 per cent of the veteran cadres are democrats', and went on to deduce that 'it is an objective law that democrats will inevitably develop into capitalist-roaders'.[39]

Consequently, said the 'Gang', no-one should be unduly impressed by a senior cadre's achievements before 1949. As Wang Hongwen reportedly remarked on a number of occasions, 'the revolutionary experience we are talking about now is the experience of the great Cultural Revolution. What is the use of those things in the past?'. It was natural that the 'Gang' should take such a line. Jiang Qing and Zhang Chunqiao could hardly claim that their contribution to the early revolutionary struggle was on a par with Zhou's and Deng's, and Wang was only a young boy at the time of liberation. Their youthful 'constituency' was, no doubt, pleased to hear that their participation in student factionalism in the late 1960s was deemed to be the contemporary equivalent of having endured and survived the rigours of the Long March and the Sino-Japanese War. But the 'Gang's' argument did not stop at suggesting that many old leaders were simply a bunch of rheumy-eyed veterans fit only to march, in be-medalled splendour, in 'Armistice Day' parades. For, unlike most of their Western counterparts, China's veterans had power. As Chi Qun, a Leftist, told cadres in the Ministry of Education on 7 April (by which time he had effectively replaced Zhou Rongxin as Minister), the problem went deeper:

> The veteran cadres and the old intellectuals especially emphasise experience. But class analysis must be made on the meaning of experience. *To them, experience is the experience of restoration and retrogression.* To say the least, it is the experience of the bourgeois revolution, which no longer has relevance. Now we are practising socialist revolution, there is no use for such things.[40]

Echoing Jiang Qing, Chi also added: 'The capitalist-roaders are not just a couple of persons but a stratum of persons.' Accordingly, after Tiananmen the 'Gang' increasingly focused on the 'bourgeoisie in the Party' and, moreover, emphasised that such people were even more dangerous than those outside. In Henan, provincial Party leaders told a rally that:

> ... capitalist-roaders in the Party like Deng Xiaoping are the main target of the socialist revolution. Since he wore the cloak of a 'veteran revolutionary'; and had very great power and used legal forms to pursue a revisionist line and restore capitalism, he could play a role which could not be played by the bourgeoisie in society. Therefore he was more deceptive and dangerous than the bourgeoisie in society.[41]

In May *Study and Criticism* published a vicious attack 'On Capitalist Roaders' which neatly lumped together all internal and external enemies. The article noted that revisionism, like capitalism, was international in character and that the bourgeoisie both inside and outside the Party, together with counter-revolutionaries, would 'invariably collaborate with international imperialism, revisionism and reaction'. In support of this allegation it rhetorically asked: 'Haven't people like Brezhnev described Lin Biao, Deng Xiaoping and their like as "the healthy forces that represent China's real interests"?' Without actually establishing any significant connections this article succeeded in identifying Deng and those who supported him with both the greatest traitor in the history of Chinese communism and the greatest foreign arch-enemy.

And so the campaign to repudiate Deng continued. By September it was being claimed that he was a faithful disciple of the 'revisionist' Bernstein, and that his 'bourgeois demo-cratic world outlook had never been remoulded'. Incapable of improvement, he clung to the old birthmarks that exist in a socialist society 'like a fly attracted to dirt'.[42]

Deng was not, however, 'dragged out' to face struggle sessions of the sort used in the Cultural Revolution. His allies in the leadership were apparently powerful enough to ensure that he was spared such humiliation. There are some indications that he fought back against his detractors and, ultimately, withdrew to a resort in Guangdong, where he enjoyed the protection of General Xu Shiyou, a formidable opponent of the 'Gang'.

Lesser figures were not so fortunate. On 13 April Zhou Rongxin died of a heart attack, allegedly hounded to death by Leftists. And many thousands of others were arrested, the 'Gang's' attitude being neatly summarised in a wallposter at Zhongshan University in Guangzhou: 'Those who play with fire will certainly get burned.'[43]

The instruments they used were primarily units of the workers' militia and the Public Security system. Both organi-sations were highly praised after the Tiananmen Incident and embarked on a policy of mass arrests which went far further than rounding up the 'handful' of offenders responsible for violence. In both organisations the 'Gang' had their followers, especially in the militias of Shanghai, Beijing and Liaoning. But it is reasonable to assume also that many security per-sonnel, professionally trained to maintain public order, were exceedingly zealous in carrying out their duties.

In June a 'National Conference of Heads of Public Security Bureaux' was held in Beijing. Two of the 'Gang's' supporters, who headed the 'Party core group' in the Ministry of Public Security, produced a 'Discussion Draft' for this forum which took the 'Gang's' arguments on capitalist-roaders to their logical conclusion. According to this:

In the wake of the continued development in depth of the

socialist revolution, new changes have occurred in class relations. The capitalist-roaders in the Party have become a class in sharp opposition to the working class and the poor and lower-middle peasants . . . Therefore, the class enemies at home and abroad have placed more and more hope for a restoration in the capitalist-roaders in the Party. We public security organs must adapt ourselves to the new situation, not only paying attention to the old class enemy in society, but more so to the new-born counter-revolutionaries, to their contacts with the bourgeoisie in the Party and to the uprooting of the backstage bosses in order to detect significant clues and report them in time to the Party committees.[44]

The militia were also mobilised. In Liaoning alone it was publicly announced on 18 June that '130,000 worker-militiamen have taken up the task of patrolling the streets',[45] and it was later claimed that they were not solely concerned with the prevention of 'ordinary' crime. For as a secretary of the provincial Party committee told them: 'The current revolutionary task is to eliminate the bourgeoisie. The bourgeoisie is right in the Party; that's where the militia should have its tasks changed.' He also told local Public Security men to study the question of 'exercising dictatorship over the bourgeoisie in the Party'.[46]

Hua Guofeng's attitude to the wave of arrests remains one of the great enigmas of 1976. Although Minister of Public Security it is possible that, as a result of his elevation on 7 April, he retained the post in name only and was at first unaware of the excesses being perpetrated by Leftist subordinates. However, it is likely that he may have tolerated, or even encouraged, the arrests as part of a cynical balancing act designed to weaken both Left and Right and to strengthen his own 'centrist' position. Undoubtedly, the charge that he did not have clean hands over this matter was to be made against him in 1980. But by the end of June, if not earlier, he realised that the Left was going too far. At the National Security Conference he denounced the extremism of the 'Discussion Draft' and declared that only a few capitalist-roaders could be regarded as irreconcilable class enemies.[47]

Probably as a response to this, Zhang Chunqiao made a

speech on 28 June in which he denounced 'ultra-Leftism', argued that a 'chaotic bombardment' was counter-productive, and that 'no-one is to be executed, while the majority [of capitalist-roaders] are not to be arrested'. However, as he went on to reveal, Zhang's 'moderation' may in part have reflected the fact that the capitalist-roaders had already suffered massive persecution:

This time, Beijing has arrested a few too many persons. At the beginning no-one opened fire and the policy was upheld; afterwards things were less than desirable. In Beijing alone 40,000 to 50,000 persons were put under arrest. Every unit engaged itself in arresting and dragging out this or that person. A couple of lives were sacrificed also, while some [people] were wronged.[48]

Beijing was probably an exceptional case, and not only because of the heavy concentration in the bureaucratic network of the capital of cadres who had little love for the 'Gang of Four'. The presence of so many foreigners there must have encouraged the authorities to take a particularly harsh line towards those who had, in their eyes, damaged China's prestige, and to ensure that there was no possibility of a repetition. Moreover, although one official account declared that 'counter-revolutionary activities' had taken place in as many as one hundred cities and towns at the time of *Qingming*,[49] most of these were probably on a relatively small scale. Nevertheless, across the nation the number of arrests must have been considerable and those arrested were not, for the most part, traditional 'bad elements'; they were members of the political élite.

According to statistics on 'recently discovered active counter-revolutionaries' which were quoted at the National Security Conference in June, 'more than 95 per cent [were] new-born counter-revolutionaries, with a heavy proportion of Party and League members, cadres, functionaries, and children of cadres'. Among them, it was claimed, were persons who harboured 'bone-deep' hatred of the Cultural Revolution.[50]

In addition to those arrested, many cadres were dismissed

from their posts or demoted. In May, Wang Hongwen told the seventh Ministry of Machine-Building to 'ferret out those plotters who are hidden deep behind the scene' and warned against being 'soft-hearted'. By September the 'Gang' had 'reorganised 80 per cent of the leadership squads in the [Ministry's] plants and shops located in the capital, and usurped leadership power'. In July Yao Wenyuan started an investigation into the relationship between 'the bourgeoisie in the Party and the work of natural sciences' to root out those who had supported Deng's 'Outline Report'. Liu Zhongyang, the 'Gang's' principal spokesman in the Academy of Sciences, subsequently branded 70 per cent of the Party 'core group' in the Academy as being the 'bourgeoisie in the Party' and 'capitalist-roaders'. Similar re-shuffles took place in the Ministry of Railways, the Ministry of Metallurgical Industry, the Ministry of Culture, and many others.[51]

In summary, then, the Right-wing offensive which had developed so promisingly in 1975 had, by the summer of 1976, suffered major defeat. But, as the next chapter will discuss, the pendulum was to swing violently again.

4

Hua Guofeng and the Arrest of the 'Gang'

The end of an era

As the summer of 1976 progressed, the Left continued its campaign against Deng Xiaoping and his supporters. Considerable resistance to this in many provinces resulted in widespread disorders and contributed to the growth of a mood of gloomy uncertainty as rival factions manoeuvred and battled for supremacy. The succession crisis loomed larger with the announcement, in mid-June, of Mao's effective retirement on health grounds.[1] Shortly thereafter, on 6 July, Zhu De died, removing yet one more link with the heroic days of guerrilla communism.

Natural disasters also heralded the end of an era. In May severe earthquakes occurred in Yunnan and these were followed, on 28 July, by the virtual destruction of the northeastern Chinese city of Tangshan. According to one report 655,000 people lost their lives and one million were made homeless.[2] Economic devastation was widespread. The superstitious could be forgiven for seeing in this calamity the traditional portents of dynastic collapse. And on 9 September Mao Zedong passed away at the age of 82. Official reports of his death did not specify the precise cause other than to state that it was due to the 'worsening of his illness'.[3] He had made no major public appearance since 1971.

The succession crisis had finally arrived, for Mao's death left China with a leadership that was bitterly divided. Although Hua Guofeng was now pre-eminent in terms of the offices he held, there were reasons to doubt his actual power. His

elevation to the Premiership and First Vice-Chairmanship of
the Central Committee appeared to have been due to the
somewhat negative factor that he was a relative newcomer to
the 'palace politics' of Beijing. Virtually all other central
leaders had either enjoyed eminence before 1966 or had risen
rapidly immediately thereafter as a result of the Cultural
Revolution. Hua, by contrast, had played no real part in the
bitter factional fighting which convulsed Beijing and was not
really brought on to the national stage until after the death
of Lin Biao. His 'strength' seemed to be that he had had less
opportunity to make enemies than other contenders, rather
than that he had succeeded in building up positive support. It
is true, of course, that his promotion in April 1976 had had
the ostensible approval of Mao. But, as the case of Malenkov
in the Soviet Union had shown, the blessing of the previous
supreme leader was no automatic guarantee of political
survival.

Yet Hua speedily confounded those foreign analysts (and,
no doubt, many Chinese ones) who saw him as a compromise
candidate who would quickly be pushed aside. For on the
night of 6–7 October, Jiang Qing, Zhang Chunqiao, Yao
Wenyuan and Wang Hongwen, together with some thirty of
their principal supporters, were arrested on his instructions.[4]
In itself the political demise of the Leftists was not entirely
unexpected. It was widely believed, in China and without,
that their influence depended in large measure on their
claims to be close to Mao and to speak in his name. If, after
a decent interval, a leadership reshuffle had shunted Jiang
Qing and her colleagues into positions of limited importance
or even into honourable 'retirement' this would not have been
especially newsworthy. But for Mao's widow to be arrested
less than one month after his death was certainly not predicted.

And neither was the extent to which Hua concentrated
power into his own hands. Following the arrests Hua was
formally appointed to succeed Mao both as Chairman of the
Party's Central Committee and as Chairman of its Military
Commission. Moreover, he became in effect the custodian
of Mao's works, a position of far more than symbolic importance in a state where all policy had to be legitimated in
ideological terms.[5] In addition, Hua retained the premier-

ship. Thus he was not only Mao's successor but also Zhou Enlai's.

Almost overnight Hua had revealed a talent for ruthlessness and audacity, and initially there can be no doubt that these dramatic moves were extremely popular. Numerous foreign observers testified to the sheer spontaneity of the mass rejoicing which greeted the news of the arrests, and which contrasted so markedly with the highly organised but nevertheless glum 'celebrations' of Deng's dismissal earlier in the year. Yet explanations were obviously called for. It was essential to tell the Chinese people just why the 'Gang of Four', as Jiang Qing and her colleagues were now labelled, had been arrested. It was also necessary to establish the credentials of the new chairman, who was still something of an unknown quantity. And, related to both tasks was the position of Mao. As mentioned earlier, Mao's role in the events of the mid-1970s was particularly enigmatic. It was now time to illuminate and legitimate the changes of early October in terms of his wishes.

The 'Gang's' attempt to usurp power

The first account of the 'Gang's' wrongdoings was given in a series of reports which Hua, Ye Jianying and Wang Dongxing delivered to a Politbureau meeting on 7 October.[6] Then, on 16 October, a Central Committee document was issued for circulation within the Party as a basis for informing the general public. By the beginning of November this was being used as a briefing document even for foreigners working in the provinces.[7] In December, a much longer Central Committee document provided further evidence and additional collections of material were produced and circulated by the Central Committee in 1977.[8] These later compilations included confessions from the 'Gang's' followers, evidence provided by their staff, and photographs of relevant documents discovered among their personal effects. These sources provided the bulk of information for countless reports which began to appear in the media from October 1976 onwards. Ultimately, after over four years of vilification of an intensity unprecedented even by the standards of Chinese communism, the 'Gang' were put on trial in November 1980, when further evidence was produced.

Nothing was too remote to be included. Some allegations related to Jiang Qing's and Zhang Chunqiao's nefarious doings as far back as the 1930s. Others were relatively trivial. Thus, individual members of the 'Gang' were accused of luxurious living, of showing a lack of concern for Mao in his final illness, of protecting their children from being 'sent down' to the countryside, and of being arrogant to their staff and 'the masses'. Such accusations are of interest as part of the general process of character assassination but really lie beyond the scope of this book. Other charges held the 'Gang' to be responsible for the radical excesses of the 1970s and, with the ultimate rejection of the Cultural Revolution, for the horrors of the late 1960s as well. These will be examined later.

But in the autumn of 1976 the overriding concern was to show why Hua had found it necessary to arrest four extremely prominent members of the tenth Central Committee, including Mao's wife of forty years' standing, in what looked remarkably like a coup d'état. The solution to the problem was to demonstrate that it was *they* who had been attempting to seize power, and that Hua Guofeng had acted to prevent them.

The 'Gang' were alleged to have acted as a faction which sought to usurp Party and state power by means of pursuing improper policies and by attacking in a conspiratorial and unscrupulous manner others in senior leadership positions. In view of the shaky institutional structure of China in the early 1970s, charges were often presented in terms of their opposition to the one unquestioned source of authority: the principles, policies and wishes of Mao himself. Hence details of their wrongdoing were to a considerable extent explained in terms of their relations with Mao, and a constant theme of the accusations was to demonstrate that Mao had opposed them at every turn. To this end the case made against them was replete with previously unpublished statements supposedly emanating from Mao in the last years of his life.

Although the charges of usurpation concentrate on the period from 1974 onwards, they also deal with earlier episodes 'exposing' Jiang Qing's naked ambitions. One particularly intriguing example relates to the summer of 1972 when Jiang gave interviews to Roxane Witke, an American historian. According to the allegations she did so in order to extol herself, hoping that Witke would 'write a book based on their talks, a book which would establish her personal authority and which would serve as advanced preparation for usurping Party and state power'. Jiang supposedly believed that only a book written by an American author and published in the United States would 'carry weight'. She did not obtain permission from Mao or the Central Committee and gave Witke many important Party and state secrets, seriously violating Party regulations and doing harm to the interests of Party and state. It is claimed that Mao became ill on hearing of the contents of their talks.[9]

Professor Witke's study of Jiang Qing was published in 1977, after the subject's fall. In the 'Prologue' the author reveals that the interviews quite clearly did cause concern among some Chinese leaders. After her first interview with Jiang she received an official transcript which had been edited 'for accuracy and discretion' by Zhou Enlai, Yao Wenyuan and 'some other leading comrades'. Following her return to the United States, promised transcripts of her subsequent conversations were not forthcoming and attempts were made, including financial inducements, to prevent her from publishing a full biographical account.[10]

Professor Witke acknowledges the substance of the charge that Jiang was guilty of seeking personal publicity. In the 1930s and 1940s leading communists had given versions of their lives to foreign journalists, the most famous example being Mao's conversations with Edgar Snow. But after liberation this practice ended, and not even Snow was able to achieve anything approximating to his original 'scoop'. Witke describes her book as 'evidence of [Jiang's] bid for historical recognition, of her attempt to record her own past as she alone [knew] it, and to be remembered in the future for her beliefs and accomplishments'.[11] Whether this amounts to evidence of her attempt to 'usurp' power is a matter of conjecture. Suffice it to say that in the context of Chinese politics it could certainly be interpreted as a step in that direction.

It is also evident that Jiang Qing was indiscreet. Witke herself refers to 'some shocking remarks' about Lin Biao which were deleted from the one transcript she received and which, at Jiang's request, she did not include in the book. It might be stretching matters to claim that Jiang revealed secrets which, in a more open society, would be regarded as affecting, national security. But her conversations did include much that could be construed as embarrassing to a leadership which was notoriously reticent on personal and political matters. Nowhere was this shown more clearly than in the image she presented of herself. As Witke observed, the interviews showed 'the ambivalence of her personal insecurity and the firm front with which she faced the public, the paradox of her stance as a persistent adversary in a community of supposed comrades, and her ruthlessness in the service of a faith in the revolution's ultimate beneficence'.[12]

Another example of Jiang's willingness to act on personal initiative also aroused Mao's ire. The incident itself was trivial enough, consisting of her sending messages and study material to various army units in her own name. As she was not entitled to do this by virtue of her official position, Mao angrily issued an order that such individual initiatives were strictly forbidden.

It was in 1974, however, that Mao found that Jiang Qing and her colleagues were really overstepping the mark by ignoring his instructions and beginning to attack other leaders, most notably Zhou Enlai. In January of that year they allegedly 'shot three arrows at the same time'. What happened was that Chi Qun and Xie Jingyi, a leading Leftist, made speeches at rallies of military and central government cadres, on the instructions of the 'Gang', at which they urged that a campaign directed against 'going through the backdoor' be integrated with a general movement to criticise Lin Biao and Confucius. The 'backdoor' referred to a practice whereby senior cadres, particularly in the army, had used personal influence to have their children admitted to university.

The 'Gang's' aim, apparently, was to exaggerate the extent of such nepotism and, by linking it with the vilification of

Lin and Confucius, to cause serious embarrassment to Zhou Enlai who, of course, represented the senior cadres' 'constituency'. Jiang supposedly gleefully declared that she had 'Zhou in a fix and he doesn't know what to do'. Mao, however, took exception. On 15 February he declared that 'metaphysics is rampant', meaning extreme one-sidedness, and complained that the major campaign designed to destroy for ever the influence of Lin and Confucius might be diluted if its focus were to be directed to the more mundane level of 'going through the backdoor'.[13]

On 24 March Mao replied to a letter of Jiang's in which he expressed his displeasure with her, writing:

It would be better not to come to see me. In years past you failed to do many of the things I discussed with you. What good are more visits? There are books by Marx and Lenin and ones by me as well; you just don't study. I'm 81 years old and seriously ill, but you don't care. You have special privileges. What will you do after my death? You are also one of those who do not discuss great matters but send daily information about trivial matters. Think it over, please.[14]

The 'Gang', however, refused to fall into line and, in the summer of 1974 increased their attacks on Zhou Enlai, under the guise of publishing articles attacking 'Confucians' in the journals under their control. It was probably this that led Mao to criticise them openly at a Politbureau meeting on 17 July. He warned his wife to 'watch out', and to be aware that other leaders disliked her even though reluctant to say so to her face. He expressed particular disapproval of her willingness to 'label' others and to force them to 'wear dunces' caps'. And, he urged Jiang and her supporters, 'don't form a Gang of Four'. He also said of Jiang 'she doesn't represent me, she represents herself'.[15]

In the autumn, however, plans were afoot to prepare for the fourth National People's Congress. Wary of the growing strength of Zhou Enlai and Deng Xiaoping, the 'Gang of Four' met in Beijing and Wang Hongwen was deputed to visit Mao, then in Changsha, to attempt to poison the chairman's mind against the Right wing. In October Wang went to Hunan several times and told Mao that it seemed 'that a second Lushan conference [was] in the making'. He claimed that, despite the premier's illness, Zhou was holding regular talks with Deng and such veteran leaders as Ye Jianying and Li Xiannian, the implication being that they were conspiring along the lines of Lin Biao and the generals as the Lushan conference of 1970. Wang also retailed tittle-tattle concerning disagreements Jiang had had with Deng.

By this time Mao had become exasperated with the Left and had presumably been convinced of the need to support those who advocated the 'Four Modernisations'. He duly ordered that the 'Gang' should resolve disputes with their opponents openly and that Wang should consult Zhou Enlai on his return to Beijing.[16]

The 'Gang' continued to press their case, however. Jiang wrote to her husband on 19 November complaining that she had had little to do since the ninth Party Congress. A little later she urged Mao to have Wang Hongwen appointed as Vice-Chairman of the Standing Committee of the National People's Congress but Mao refused, told her not to make so many public appearances, and not to 'form a cabinet' round herself. By the end of the year he was commenting unfavourably on Jiang's ambitions and warning her that anyone who formed a faction would 'fall down'.

In the event the 'Gang' were disappointed with the ministers chosen by the fourth National People's Congress. Zhang Chunqiao did become a Vice-Premier but no other member of the 'Gang' was given an office within the central state structure. Indeed, three-quarters of the membership of the new State Council consisted of veteran cadres and army men, and ten of the new ministers were people who had suffered severely in the Cultural Revolution.[17] After the Congress Jiang attacked many of the new leaders and asked that her views be conveyed to Mao. He commented that few people met with her approval and that she did not respect even him. He forecast: 'She'll have disputes in the future. Today, although people get along with her, their relations are not sincere. After I die, she'll make trouble.'[18]

His strictures appear to have had the effect of making the

'Gang' drop their claims for immediate official preferment and, the official accusations reveal, both Wang Hongwen and Zhang Chunqiao privately acknowledged that they should give heed to his injunctions not to form a 'Shanghai faction'. In practice, this simply meant that they reverted to attacking their rivals in a slightly less direct manner.

One opportunity to do this arose as a result of an instruction issued by Mao on 26 December 1974, calling on everyone to 'study the theory of the dictatorship of the proletariat'. His aim was to institute a general ideological campaign to oppose 'revisionism', that disease to which Marxist systems are notoriously prone. The 'Gang', however, deliberately chose to narrow the focus of the movement so that it attacked simply 'empiricism'. In the early months of 1975 they developed a powerful propaganda drive in which they claimed 'empiricism is the main danger', their intention being to brand as pragmatists those like Zhou Enlai and Deng Xiaoping who were willing to temper their revolutionary zeal with practical considerations.

Yet again Mao took exception to the views of the Leftists. Commenting on a report of Yao Wenyuan's, he observed:

It appears that the proposal should be to oppose revisionism, which would include opposing empiricism *and dogmatism*, because they both revise Marxism-Leninism. You don't just mention one half and let the other go ... There are not many in our Party who really understand Marxism-Leninism. Some think they do, but actually they do not fully understand even though they think they are right and are always lecturing others.[19]

On 3 May 1975 he spoke out against the 'Gang' at a Politbureau meeting, saying 'you hate empiricism while not hating dogmatism'. On this occasion he repeated the 'three do's and three don'ts' slogan he had formulated in August 1971, in response to Lin Biao's conspiracy, and followed it by again condemning the Leftists for forming a 'Gang of Four'. He urged them to unite with the rest of the Central Committee and suggested, in a somewhat cryptic remark, that the 'problem' of the four would have to be solved in the not-too-distant future.

As a result Jiang Qing made a self-criticism on 27 April and a further one on 28 June. In the second she claimed that 'the understanding that there is a "Gang of Four" helps me to realise that this reality may give rise to sectarianism which may cause splits in the Central Committee and helps me understand why the Chairman has talked about this three or four times last year'. Nevertheless, her mood of humility did not last long. In September she disregarded her husband's wishes and delivered an address to the Dazhai conference which was 'not in accordance' with 'Mao Zedong Thought'. The speech was not published but the director of the *Xinhua News Agency* sent a copy to Mao who expressed his displeasure in no uncertain terms. For her part, Jiang subsequently took her revenge by persecuting the director, having him sent to reform himself through menial work on the Qinghua campus.[20]

Although Mao's criticisms of the 'Gang' in 1975 were later published by their enemies as evidence of a complete break, this was not the case. His remarks were delivered with characteristic bluntness and, in all probability, the versions available have been deliberately taken out of context to exaggerate the differences between himself and the 'Gang'. Moreover, as we have seen in the last chapter, in the autumn of 1975 Mao became increasingly angry with Deng Xiaoping. The 'Gang's' success in mounting the campaign which led to Deng's second overthrow in April 1976 would have been impossible had Mao unequivocally rejected them. Equally, Mao's approval of the elevation of Hua Guofeng in the early months of 1976 demonstrated that he recognised that the 'Gang' were too intolerant and divisive a force to be entrusted with power by themselves.

By April, then, Mao had apparently settled on Hua as a leader who occupied the 'middle ground' and who might be able to reconcile the bitterly opposed forces of Left and Right. And at the end of that month he indicated satisfaction with Hua's work. This move came when Hua accompanied Premier Muldoon of New Zealand when he visited Mao. After the meeting Hua remained behind to report on the situation concerning the move to criticise Deng and repel the 'Right Deviationist Wind'. Mao, who by that time was not able to speak properly, wrote a note to Hua which made three points. Hua was to 'carry out the work slowly, not in haste', and was to 'act according to past principles'. It concluded with the endorsement 'with you in charge, I'm at ease'.[21]

Later, as we shall see, Hua was to present this endorsement as conclusive proof that Mao had indeed anointed him as his own successor. This may well have been an exaggeration of a comment intended to do no more than show that Mao was happy with Hua's conduct of affairs at that stage. Even that less generous interpretation, however, could only strengthen Hua's position at a time when Mao had been throwing brick-bats at, rather than bestowing laurels on, other contenders for the leadership.

And, inevitably, it made Hua the obvious target for the 'Gang'. Even before he became Premier Hua had apparently clashed with the 'Gang of Four'. He had played some part in Deng's plans to develop scientific work in 1975 and had pursued a different line from Jiang Qing at the Dazhai conference in September of that year. In January 1976, when it became known that Mao had 'personally proposed' he should become acting premier, wallposters appeared in Shanghai urging that Zhang Chunqiao be given the post, allegedly at the 'Gang's' instigation. And when the announcement of his formal appointment was made in February, Zhang Chunqiao expressed his annoyance in a poem (later discovered among his private papers). In part this read:

Moving up so fast and so menacingly spells a downfall
that will be just as rapid.
An erroneous line gets nowhere.
He may have his own way for a while as if the whole
country belongs to him and a new 'era' has begun.
They always overestimate their own strength.[22]

The 'They' in the last line presumably referred to the 'capitalist-roaders' with whom Hua was now to be identified in the 'Gang's' eyes. Indeed, at about this time, Yao Wenyuan actually mentioned Hua by name (along with Ye Jianying) in some 'reference materials' concerning persons involved in the 'Right Deviationist Wind'. Yao also used his control of the media to restrict the coverage given to Hua, particularly after the Tangshan earthquake when Hua was extremely active in organising relief measures. Similarly, in late July, when a national planning conference was held in Beijing, two of the 'Gang's' supporters allegedly attacked Hua, although not by name. Thus on 20 July Yang Qunfu, a secretary of the Party committee of Liaoning rhetorically asked: 'Do genuine Marxists hold the leadership of the state apparatus in their grip? My answer is no.'[23]

Support for these allegations can also be drawn from articles published in the journals controlled by the 'Gang'. For example, in May 1976 *Study and Criticism* published an article entitled 'Sima Guang's Year on Stage'. Ostensibly this told the story of events which had taken place in the late eleventh century when Wang Anshi, a 'progressive' statesman had masterminded and implemented an impressive series of major and radical reforms. However, with the death of the emperor whose patronage Wang had enjoyed, a conservative backlash took place. Sima Guang led reactionary ministers to dismantle, at great speed, the reforms of Wang Anshi. The parallels between that 'reform era' and the Cultural Revolution were obvious, with Mao doubling for the emperor and Wang. Coming a few weeks after Hua's formal appointment as Premier and First Vice-Chairman, it was obviously being suggested that he was another Sima Guang.[24]

At the time of Mao's death *Study and Criticism* went even further by publishing an article in the September issue which dealt with the need to 'Continue to Purge the Revolutionary Ranks of 'Termites''. 'Termites' were those opportunists who pretended to be revolutionary and usurped leadership positions. They were swindlers who deceived real revolutionaries and altered the true revolutionary line. The 'termites' listed in the article ended with Deng Xiaoping but it was made clear that the problem still existed, and the implication was clearly that Hua fell into that category. Readers were instructed to get 'well prepared mentally for protracted struggle'.

Apart from waging a propaganda battle, the 'Gang' allegedly

took steps in 1976 to strengthen their support organisations, encouraging lower echelons to report to them directly rather than through the appropriate bureaucratic channels of the Party and state apparatus. It was not until Mao's death, however, that matters came to a head. The events from 9 September to 6 October 1976 are especially obscure and in all probability will never be fully revealed. In so far as the 'Gang' were guilty of attempted 'usurpation' the charges related to their activities in this crucial month are essentially two-fold. On the one hand they sought by underhand methods, most notably forgery, to establish that Mao had wanted them to assume considerable, if not absolute, power. On the other, they attempted an armed coup d'état.

The first accusation claims that Jiang Qing went to the General Office of the Central Committee shortly after Mao's death and brow-beat Zhang Yufeng, Mao's secretary, to allow her to remove some of her late husband's papers. This was reported to Wang Dongxing, director of the General Office, who asked Jiang to return them on the grounds that they were the 'precious property of the Party which no one can take away without permission'. Jiang refused and told Wang that it was Mao's secretary who had stolen them. Wang then informed Hua and both men were concerned that Jiang might falsify the record in some way, by destroying, hiding or 'tampering with' various texts. Consequently Hua telephoned Jiang and successfully demanded that they be returned. At which point, it was alleged, Hua and Wang discovered two texts had been tampered with. They said nothing about this, however, and on 21 September Hua ordered that the documents be sealed and locked away as there was 'no time for handling them' during the mourning period.

This incident provoked an emotional outburst from Jiang, who told Hua: 'You want to throw me out when Chairman Mao's body has not yet turned cold. Is this the way to show your gratitude for the kindness rendered to you by Chairman Mao who promoted you?' Hua replied:

I will never forget Chairman Mao's kindness. I asked you to return Chairman Mao's documents precisely because I want to repay Chairman Mao's kindness, to enable everybody to unite together and forever implement Chairman Mao's behests. As for trying to throw you out, I have no such intention. You live peacefully in your own house, so no-one will dare to drive you out.[25]

Jiang and her supporters were not willing, it would seem, to agree to Hua's suggestion that Mao's widow should withdraw into private life. On 12 September Yao Wenyuan, aided and abetted by Chi Qun and Xie Jingyi, arranged for people to send her 'oaths of fealty' and 'memorials appealing for accession to the throne'. Some called for Jiang to be made Party Chairman and for Zhang Chunqiao to become Chairman of the Party's Military Commission.

On 16 September the 'Gang' went further and published a joint editorial in the national newspapers and *Red Flag* which included Mao's supposed instruction 'Act according to the principles laid down'. Just after this an 'internal publication' described this slogan as a 'great call issued by Chairman Mao before he departed from us forever' and as an 'adjuration' given at 'the last moment of his life'. This article stated that Engels 'unswervingly kept to the principles laid down by Marx, and Lenin adhered to the principles laid down by Marx and Engels'.[26]

The instruction appeared on other occasions and, in early October, Yao Wenyuan prepared an editorial which was then published in *Guangming Daily* on 4 October. This read:

Tampering with the principles laid down by Chairman Mao means betraying Marxism, Socialism and the great theory of continuing the revolution under the dictatorship of the proletariat. No matter who practises revisionism, no matter which method he uses in doing so and no matter how violent an evil wind he blows, we should rebel against him . . . If any chieftain of revisionism dares to tamper with the principles laid down by Chairman Mao, he will absolutely come to no good end.[27]

These suggestions that someone was tampering with Mao's last wishes were accompanied by new moves to bolster Jiang Qing by commissioning articles on the Empress Lü of the

Western Han dynasty who had 'acted according to the principles laid down by Emperor Liu Bang'.

The significance of the slogan was, of course, that it differed from Mao's injunction to Hua on 30 April, that he should 'act according to past principles'. According to Hua's version Mao's note had been shown to a Politbureau meeting almost immediately, copies had been made, and these had been distributed quite widely among the leadership throughout China. If that were so there would have been little point in Jiang attempting to alter the slogan when she allegedly tampered with Mao's documents in September, even assuming that she had a skilled forger in her entourage. On the other hand it would have been perfectly possible for her to ignore the original slogan and publicise her own version for the Chinese public at large, who clearly remained in ignorance of Mao's utterance of 30 April until it was published as part of the campaign to discredit the 'Gang of Four'.

'Act according to past principles' can only be interpreted as an instruction to preserve continuity. 'Act according to the principles laid down', however, has a much more *specific* ring to it. It suggests that Mao could have left detailed instructions on what was to happen after his death. Jiang Qing may well have removed his documents from the General Office in order to acquire texts which would legitimise her claims to high office, as well as those of her supporters. As we have seen, Mao's behaviour in the last year of his life shows enough evidence of inconsistency to suggest that these might well have been forthcoming.

Indeed there is a possibility that Hua may have done some 'tampering' himself. To the best of this writer's knowledge, there is no evidence that Mao's 30 April note was known to exist before October. This conflicts strangely with the official claim that many leaders had seen copies: if so, why did news of it fail to circulate on the Chinese 'grapevine' or reach Taiwan intelligence, which has an excellent record of publicising material of a contentious and sensitive nature long before it has appeared in the Chinese press. An intriguing rumour on this aspect of the affair began to circulate in China at the time of Jiang's trial in 1980. According to this the 30 April note was genuine but it contained an added proviso. In encouraging Hua, Mao had mentioned that, if he needed advice, he should ask Jiang Qing!

If true, this would explain a great deal. It would account for Jiang Qing's otherwise foolish attempt to claim a major position in the leadership after her husband's death. Equally, it would explain why it was that Hua, and all those leaders who detested the 'Gang of Four', should have moved to silence them both by having them arrested and, thereafter, by raising accusations that they had been involved in forgery. Thus, even if rumours were to circulate giving a version of Mao's instructions more favourable to Jiang, these could easily be dismissed.

As mentioned earlier, there is no way that outsiders can confirm or deny Hua's version of the 30 April statement. All that can be said with certainty is that there undoubtedly was an attempt by the 'Gang' to claim Mao's last instructions were designed to give them a measure of legitimate power after his death, and that Hua and his supporters were equally determined to deny this.

The charge that the 'Gang' plotted an armed uprising in furtherance of their aims is even less amenable to satisfactory solution. It was alleged that, on different occasions in the 1970s, they bemoaned their lack of military strength, recognising that they possessed 'the pen but not the sword'. It was claimed that at varying times they sought to gain influence with the PLA but to little avail and, therefore, attempted to develop their own armed forces by the cultivation of militia organisations, most notably in Shanghai and Beijing.

There is some independent evidence to support this view. In September 1973 the first issue of *Study and Criticism* did carry an article on the Paris Commune of 1871 which spoke particularly favourably of the fact that it was defended by 'citizens under arms', and contained echoes of exceedingly radical statements made earlier in the Cultural Revolution to the effect that the armed masses were the best guarantee of the preservation of the revolution. Subsequently, in Shanghai particularly, attempts were made to build up the militia and, moreover, to ensure that it was under the control of the civil authorities and not the PLA. As mentioned in the last chapter, militias in Shanghai, Beijing and Liaoning were particularly active in hunting down 'counter-revolutionaries' in the wake of Tiananmen.

Whether the 'Gang' seriously contemplated some form of military uprising after Mao's death is, however, much more conjectural. Preparations to attack Hua were, allegedly, being made in Shanghai even before Mao died. In particular a compilation of material on 'Khrushchev's Rise to Power' was being prepared in this regard. This may have been designed to accompany some sort of armed action but there is no evidence for this. The same is true of the preparation of material comparing Hua with Beriya, Stalin's infamous Chief of Police.[28] (Interestingly, this charge was made only once, shortly after the 'Gang's' arrest, and was then dropped; possibly because it contained an element of truth.)

In fact, even the official charges do not really substantiate that the 'Gang' tried to move first. What appears to have happened was that, immediately after their arrest, supporters in Beijing telephoned Shanghai and said what had happened. Desperate meetings of the 'Gang's' followers there did discuss using the militia for an armed uprising in that city. This, it would seem, was only regarded as a bargaining counter. It was officially claimed that one or two enterprises and units were seized and it is possible that this was so. However, any action was so minimal that it passed unnoticed by the general populace of the city and various foreigners who were there throughout this period.

Thus, in reviewing the evidence offered, it is difficult to avoid the conclusion that it was Hua who struck first. In the summer of 1976 he had clearly strengthened his ties with various military leaders, including the venerable Marshal Ye Jianying and Wang Dongxing, Commander of the 8341 unit which carried out the arrests. He also had the support of Li Xiannian and many leading civilian cadres and, as events were to show, a considerable proportion of the general population. One rumour, common in Taiwan and Hong Kong, claims that Deng Xiaoping was the man behind the pre-emptive strike but this writer considers this most unlikely in view of Deng's long struggle thereafter to emerge into the limelight.[29]

In any event, the 'Gang' were imprisoned and were, apparently, allowed no contact with each other. Whatever the precise truth of the various explanations of their wrongdoings discussed in this chapter, these can all be subsumed in one short conclusion. The 'Gang' were hated by many millions of Chinese for their intolerant and sometimes brutal adherence to Leftist extremism. With the death of Mao they may have lost a critic; they certainly lost a protector. As the Chinese press was to put it, they 'overestimated themselves and underestimated our great people, our great army and our great Party. They underestimated Chairman Hua . . .' It is now high time to examine the career of the man who, at least in the short term, was undoubtedly 'in charge'.

Hua Guofeng

Hua did not grant a major interview to a foreign journalist until 1979 and, when he did, it was scarcely on a par with those given to Witke by Jiang Qing. Indeed it added little to what had by then emerged as the official record of his life. Although some twenty to thirty years younger than China's first generation of communist leaders, Hua remains, to some extent, far less well-known. Fortunately his own scanty autobiographical reminiscences have been supplemented, not only by hagiographic accounts published after 1976, but also by the painstaking work of various scholars outside of China who have mined numerous Chinese sources in their search for information.[30]

Hua was born in Shanxi province in 1920, apparently in humble circumstances. He graduated from primary school at the age of 13, worked briefly as a labourer, and then managed to spend some years attending a vocational school in his home county. Although his educational level was scarcely impressive by Western standards, it was relatively high by those of rural China. At the age of 17 he joined anti-Japanese guerrilla forces and also became a member of the Communist Party. He spent the next decade operating in various military and political capacities mainly in his home area.

In the spring of 1949, at the age of 29, he was transferred south to Hunan province, where he stayed for some twenty-two years. During this time he rose steadily and swiftly up the provincial Party hierarchy, beginning as Secretary of the

Party Committee in Xiangyin county, moving to more senior posts in Xiangtan prefecture, and eventually becoming First Secretary of the Hunan Party Committee in December 1970. *En route* he held different posts under the provincial government. In 1969 he was elected to membership of the ninth Central Committee but his work continued to focus on Hunan and it was only in 1971 that he was assigned to Beijing, reportedly at Mao Zedong's behest.

Thus Hua was very much a 'provincial' in the sense that his work experience from the time of liberation to 1971 was confined almost entirely to matters relating to Hunan, and he left the province only rarely, and for brief periods, in order to attend meetings in Beijing and elsewhere. But the use of the word 'provincial' can be misleading if it leads the reader to assume that he was nothing more than a 'local' politician. Hunan was a major province with a population comfortably exceeding that of many European states. It was also a province which had produced more than its fair share of communist leaders, including both Mao Zedong and Liu Shaoqi. And Hua's Hunan years gave him a superb general training in that he held posts in a variety of different functional arenas. His career may have been limited geographically, but it was not by any means narrow. And from a comparatively early stage he was in a position to meet, occasionally work with, and impress leaders of national importance.

Throughout his Hunan years Hua took a particular interest in, and demonstrated a considerable talent for, agricultural work. As a county-level cadre he was involved in implementing land reform and such practical measures as running a campaign to eradicate locusts. A few years later, when he had been promoted to prefectural level, he showed great enthusiasm for co-operativisation and, moreover, considerable organisational ability also. Under his leadership Xiangtan became a pace-setter for 'socialist transformation' in Hunan.

Moreover his skills in agricultural work did not go unnoticed. He was a firm believer in the value of carrying out 'on-the-spot' investigations which earned him a reputation for thoroughness. And, although personally somewhat self-effacing, he was an effective publicist. From his earliest days as a county Party secretary he published articles in the provincial press, usually on different aspects of agricultural policy, and these were sometimes outstanding enough to be reprinted for a wider audience. Unlike many cadres at his level he possessed sufficient education and political sophistication to 'combine theory with practice' in his writings. In 1955, when Hua clearly emerged as a strong proponent of 'socialist transformation' in the countryside, one of his articles appeared in the November issue of *Study*, the Party's theoretical journal which was the predecessor of *Red Flag*. As this issue also included Mao's own famous statement on the subject, together with reports by other national leaders, Hua was obviously attracting attention while still in his mid-thirties.

From then on Hua could be identified as someone who was 'sound' on agricultural policy. In the Great Leap Forward he gave general support to the establishment of the Communes while avoiding the error of excessive zeal. It is likely that, when Peng Dehuai attacked the Leap at Lushan, Hua was one of those who provided Mao with evidence which helped him defend it. Hua's career benefited accordingly, particularly because it contrasted with that of certain other Hunanese leaders. After the Leap Hua continued to be active in rural work.

In addition, however, he also gained valuable experience of other sectors. For a time he held major responsibilities for educational work in Hunan. These included running campaigns to eradicate illiteracy and to promote the use of the standard dialect of spoken Chinese (*Putonghua*). His office was also concerned with the multifarious tasks of expanding and administering the provincial school system and assigning its graduates to jobs. Hua was also involved with public health work, improving medical education and health facilities, and playing a part in a mass movement to attempt to eliminate schistosomiasis. He also spent a number of years in charge of finance and trade work in Hunan. This brought him into close contact with Li Xiannian, Finance Minister and Politbureau member, who was apparently impressed by Hua's competence. Hua also had some experience of military matters in that he held various posts as a political commissar.

In addition to acquiring and demonstrating organisational skills, Hua also developed a considerable aptitude for political survival. The steady and rapid progress of his career up to 1966 is evidence of this. But the ease with which he passed through the Cultural Revolution suggests political skills of a high order. Like so many 'bureaucrats' he was stripped of his powers early in 1967. However, his political recovery was exceptionally swift. In the summer of 1967 he became a 'leading member' of a preparatory group established to inaugurate the Hunan provincial Revolutionary Committee. Despite being attacked as a 'red capitalist' by 'Sheng Wu Lian', the particularly militant Red Guard organisation in Hunan, he was duly appointed as a Vice-Chairman of the Committee when it was set up in 1968.

Initially, real power in the Committee lay with two PLA veterans who were supporters of Lin Biao. However, Hua's election to the ninth Central Committee strengthened his position in Hunan. He became Acting Chairman of the Revolutionary Committee in the autumn of 1970 and was made First Secretary of the provincial Party Committee when it was re-established at the end of that year.

Hua suffered little in the upheavals of the Cultural Revolution, therefore, and emerged from them with greatly increased authority. It is possible that one reason for this was that he enjoyed the protection of Mao himself. For there is reason to believe that Hua had gone out of his way to demonstrate his loyalty to the Chairman. Mao, after all, had been born in the village of Shaoshan. This happened to be in Xiangtan where Hua had worked for many years. Hua would have been less than human had he not ensured that developments there were fully in accord with Mao's wishes and that the latter was kept fully informed of them.

In 1971 Hua was transferred in Beijing and assumed work of national importance. He played some part in investigating the Lin Biao affair and it is likely that in so doing he established a good working relationship with Ye Jianying who was to be instrumental in swinging the PLA behind Hua in 1976. His main responsibilities, however, were economic and related particularly to agriculture.

In 1973 he was elected to the Politbureau at the tenth Party Congress and, thereafter, assumed certain responsibilities in the field of science and technology. At the fourth National People's Congress in January 1975 he became the sixth ranking Vice-Premier, and concurrently Minister of Public Security. Interestingly, his ministerial post was one for which he appeared to have had no previous specialised experience. It is possible that he was given this extremely important and sensitive post precisely because he was widely regarded as politically 'neutral' in terms of the two major factional groupings within the élite.

Thus, although Hua's elevation in 1976 may have represented a compromise between Left and Right it is evident that he possessed impressive credentials. He may well have lacked Deng's acute intelligence and the 'Gang's' propaganda skills, but he had a massive organisational competence which had impressed his superiors at all stages of his career. As an agricultural specialist he possessed expertise in an area of absolutely fundamental importance but, as we have seen, his interests and experiences had ranged far beyond that sector. Of all the major policy areas the only one in which he appeared to be completely unqualified was that of foreign affairs.

Above all, he remained a consummate politician. In Beijing he successfully steered a course between the rival factions and could not be clearly identified with either. The image he presented was that of the diligent, moderate, modest and loyal follower of Mao. However, in 1976 if not earlier, he began to build up his own power base among both civil and military leaders. This was done unobtrusively and quietly, and with his characteristic efficiency. Inevitably he would have had no difficulty in gaining support from those who had suffered in the Cultural Revolution and thereafter at the hands of the Left. But Hua was also able to win over people like Wang Dongxing and Wu De, both of whom were widely regarded at the time as having Leftist sympathies and who were to fall from power at a later stage. Apart from the conspiratorial negotiations which must have taken place, Hua's ability to win friends in some unlikely quarters may have been due in part to his handling of the Tangshan disaster. Hua personally directed the massive relief operations and, by all accounts, did so superbly well. It is likely that his handling of the tragedy won him considerable prestige among leaders who may have differed from him on political grounds. When he chose to move against the 'Gang', he was not short of supporters.

5

Chairman Hua and the Return of Deng

'Wise Leader' Hua

Following the arrest of the 'Gang of Four', Hua moved swiftly to establish his claims to be top leader, and did so with such vigour that by the spring of 1977 a personality cult of considerable dimensions had developed. In the early stages there was much public repetition of Mao's 'with you in charge' note of 30 April 1976. This, however, was reinforced by reference to Hua's appointment as First Vice-Chairman on 7 April. It was emphasised that this was the first time in the Party's history that the post had existed and that, in creating it, Mao had 'explicitly designated' Hua as his successor. Moreover, it was claimed that Mao had produced an appropriate instruction to accompany Hua's appointment: 'It is necessary to do propaganda and give publicity to Comrade Hua Guofeng to make him known to the people of the whole country step by step.'[1]

On 20 December 1976, matters went further when Chen Yonggui delivered a report at the second National Conference — To Learn from Dazhai in Agriculture. As the semi-literate peasant whose devotion to principles of self-reliance had raised him from his humble role as leader of the Dazhai production brigade to Politbureau membership, Chen's endorsement was of inestimable value to anyone seeking to be identified as a loyal follower of Mao, and this was duly forthcoming. Mao, he said, had 'complete faith' in Hua. He had not only 'selected' him as his successor but also 'trained' him. The implication, then, was that there was nothing sudden about Hua's appointment; rather he had been 'groomed' for the succession for some time.

Chen went on to sing Hua's praises thus:

> Comrade Hua Guofeng is loyal to the Party and selfless, open and above-board, modest and prudent, democratic in his style of work, unassuming and approachable and good at uniting with comrades to work together. He has the ability to lead the whole Party and command the whole army and is an outstanding Marxist leader. The whole Party, the whole army and the people of all nationalities throughout the country take tremendous pride in once again having a wise leader of their own.[2]

In like manner another article praised Hua's 'magnificent contributions', his 'high proletarian mettle and political farsightedness', his 'rich experience in struggle' and his 'exceptional organisational talent'.

Hua's devotion to Mao was traced back to his days as a young guerrilla fighter in Shanxi province during the Sino-Japanese war. There, it was said, he was not only magnificently successful in prosecuting the struggle against the Japanese but also carried Mao's works in his knapsack and seized every opportunity to learn from them. Thus:

> If there were no oil lamps he used pine torches. He often studied late into the night and sometimes the soot from the torches darkened his face. When comrades teased him about this, Comrade Hua merely smiled.[3]

Nor did Hua ever lose the common touch despite his subsequent successes. In the early 1960s he visited a backward production brigade in Hunan where he lived in a poor peasant's house. His host recalled:

> When Chairman Hua lived in my house, he worked day and night for the Party. He never seemed to get tired. He ate what we ate and was never fastidious about his food and clothes. He took part in labour and often had heart-to-heart talks with the poor and lower-middle peasants as

well as chatting with the children. He never put on airs and was like a member of the family.[4]

Even his possible sycophancy was made the subject of favourable comment for it was noted that 'with profound proletarian feelings for Chairman Mao, Comrade Hua Guofeng paid great attention to socialist construction in Shaoshan, Chairman Mao's native village'. There it was Hua who had guided the building of the huge Shaoshan irrigation project. This scheme had involved constructing a trunk canal which was 240 kilometres long and which ran through mountains and across valleys and rivers. It had required 'tunnelling and building aqueducts and lateral branches several thousand kilometres long'. Work had begun in July 1965 and had been completed in ten months instead of the three years originally planned. Some 100,000 peasant-workers had taken part in building the project. Hua had also 'led the people' to build a railway line to Shaoshan so that people from all over China could go to pay homage at Mao's former home.[5]

Nothing was too trivial to be used to advantage. Thus one story told of how in 1971 he had visited a school attended by one of his children and had insisted on being treated like any other parent. A cartoon strip showed a cyclist falling off his bicycle and scattering his load of vegetables across the road. Who should help him pick them up but Chairman Hua.

Attempts were also made to identify him completely with Mao by Hua's assumption of his patron's style. On 9 May 1977 Ye Jianying asserted that Hua had 'carried on Chairman Mao's traditional style of work' and this was true in more senses than one. Like Mao, Hua began to provide inscriptions in his own calligraphy and these were reproduced in the press. Much use was also made of pictures and photographs. Thus an 'artist's representation' of the 'with you in charge' scene enjoyed considerable vogue. On 1 August 1977 the fiftieth anniversary of the founding of the PLA was marked by the publication of a photograph of Mao in soldier's uniform, and of Hua similarly attired. And Hua even modified his appearance. His original 'military' crew-cut was allowed to grow, and he began to sweep his hair back from the temples, giving him a definite resemblance to his predecessor.

Hua's lack of experience in foreign affairs also received attention in that he spent an inordinate amount of his time in receiving numerous foreign visitors. He also was able to bolster his credentials as a Marxist leader by having re-published certain articles he had written in his Hunan days and, most importantly, by authoring a study of the fifth volume of Mao's *Selected Works* which was published on 15 April 1977. Needless to say, Hua's article was extremely uncritical.[6] For, having sought to base his legitimacy on a claim to be the loyal follower of his predecessor, there was an obvious need to preserve Mao's image as far as possible. Thus, in January 1977, Hua had produced a slogan which subsequently became known as the 'two whatevers'. This originated in the draft of a speech he wrote which instructed: 'We must resolutely uphold whatever policy decisions Chairman Mao made and unswervingly carry out whatever Chairman Mao instructed.' This was openly published in the press the following month.[7]

In so far as it enabled Hua to reproduce carefully chosen passages from Mao's writings, which could be used to justify any desirable policy adjustments, there was nothing wrong with it. The difficulty, of course, lay in relating the slogans to Mao's activities and utterances in his later years, particularly in the Cultural Revolution decade.

What Hua hoped to do was to maintain that the Cultural Revolution had been fundamentally correct in conception but had been 'distorted' by the 'Gang of Four'. As we have seen in the last chapter, this stratagem involved producing 'evidence' to distance Mao from his wife and her supporters. It also required Hua to demonstrate that he had been a determined opponent of the 'Gang of Four'. This, however, raised the thorny question of Deng Xiaoping. Whatever Deng's faults and 'mistakes', everyone knew that he had been an outspoken critic of the 'Gang of Four' and had suffered the consequences in April 1976. What possible justification could there be for failing to restore him to office once the 'Gang ' were in disgrace?

The return of Deng Xiaoping

Hua himself could have had little wish to see Deng restored.

However innocent he may have been in the events surrounding the Tiananmen Incident, it was an inescapable fact that Hua's star had risen as Deng's had fallen and, as events were to show, it was obvious that Deng was his intellectual superior and possessed much greater experience of central politics. Deng was clearly a potential threat. The same held true for some other leaders, such as Wang Dongxing, Wu De and Chen Yonggui, who appeared to have offered little opposition to the 'Gang of Four' until after Mao's death and who had reason to fear Deng's vengeance.

Yet Deng had massive support. At Politbureau level he was backed by Generals Xu Shiyou and Wei Guoqing and his 'constituency' extended downwards to include many of those who had demonstrated during the Tiananmen Incident. Consequently, from October 1976 to July 1977 there was a lengthy debate and struggle, not so much over the question of whether Deng should be rehabilitated but, rather, when this should take place and how far it should go. In so far as Hua's actions during this time can be discerned, it seems that he wished to play for time in order to strengthen his own position and, moreover, to obtain from Deng certain assurances as to 'good behaviour'.

On the other hand, Deng's supporters sought to force Hua's hand in various ways. At the popular level, for example, there was a flurry of wallposters in January 1977, at the time of the first anniversary of Zhou Enlai's death, which called for Deng's rehabilitation. At a more senior and sophisticated level, heavy hints were dropped to foreign visitors by Chinese officials to the effect that Deng's return was imminent and, although it cannot be proven, it seems likely that a number of reports in the Hong Kong press were officially inspired. It was also strongly rumoured that some of Deng's most senior supporters resorted to a policy of non-co-operation, by refusing to attend top-level meetings in Beijing until the question of Deng was settled. It is significant in this respect that no Central Committee meeting could be held to ratify formally the momentous changes of October 1976, until the decision to restore Deng had been taken. Thereafter, it proved possible to expedite Party business and to convene a new National Party Congress without delay.

Deng himself facilitated his own return by adopting a

suitably humble demeanour. On 10 October 1976 he wrote to Hua, stating that he 'resolutely supported' him as Party Chairman and for his action in smashing the 'Gang of Four'. Deng stated that his own health was good and 'requested' that Hua should give him 'front-line work' to do.

Ultimately and, it would appear, with considerable reluctance, Hua gave way. In March 1977 he addressed a Central Work Conference in Beijing when he said that Deng had nothing to do with the Tiananmen Incident, that he had both achievements and mistakes on his record during the period when he was in charge in 1975, and that the Central Committee would give him an opportunity to work again. On 24 March Li Xiannian informed a distinguished British editor that Deng had served China well in the past and still had 'much to give the country'.

On 10 April Deng again wrote to Hua expressing his gratitude and promising to abide by whatever decision the Central Committee might make with regard to the time and the type of work he should be given. In his letters Deng expressed his deep grief at Mao's passing, admitted that he had made mistakes in 1975, and that he appreciated the help Mao had given him to correct his errors. He suggested that his letters be circulated among Party members and, possibly because of his apparent contrition, Hua agreed. This was done in May, and a formal Central Committee meeting could then be convened.[8]

The third plenum of the tenth Central Committee met from 16 to 21 July 1977, and carried out three major actions. First, it unanimously confirmed Hua's appointments as conferred by the Politbureau the previous October. Secondly, it restored Deng to all his posts, including Vice-Chairman of the Central Committee, Vice-Chairman of the Military Commission, Vice-Chairman of the State Council, and Chief of the General Staff of the PLA. Thirdly, the 'Gang of Four' were expelled from all posts both inside and outside the Party and, for good measure, to their long list of crimes was added the accusation that they had 'feverishly attacked and fabricated accusations against Comrade Deng Xiaoping'.[9] The leadership could now attempt to get down to the serious business of charting a new course for China.

The Party and state Congresses

The eleventh Party Congress convened in Beijing from 12–18 August 1977. As was befitting his rank, Hua delivered a 'Political Report' which lasted for more than four hours.[10] In it he paid fulsome tribute to Mao but it was interesting to note that he reserved the affectionate appellation 'esteemed and beloved' to describe Zhou Enlai and Zhu De, whose passing, along with that of other veterans was marked with a silent tribute. Hua also gave Deng's prestige a further boost by asserting that Mao himself had put him in charge of the day-to-day running of the Chinese state during Zhou Enlai's last illness. What is more he stated that Deng's criticisms of the 'Gang' had been in accordance with Mao's instructions. Already, it would appear, Deng's influence was being felt.

Much of Hua's report consisted of a very lengthy and thorough attack on the 'Gang'. This, however, was primarily of interest as a comprehensive and fully authoritative rehearsal of the case against them rather than as a source of new information, for Hua was able to add little or nothing to the countless articles published since their arrest.

Moving on to discuss the tasks facing the Party, Hua noted that 'the victorious conclusion of the first Great Proletarian Cultural Revolution [had] ushered in a new period of development in our country's socialist revolution and socialist construction'. This elliptical reference was of great significance. By referring to the 'first' Cultural Revolution it remained loyal to Mao's stated belief that many such movements would be required to safeguard the revolution. Equally, it was the most definitive statement to date that the Cultural Revolution was officially over, and later in his speech Hua was able to turn his attention (and China's) to questions of economic growth. Hua revived Mao's 1974 slogan on the need to 'push the national economy forward' and also invoked the late Chairman's invocation of the Great Leap Forward, by insisting that China must carry out the general line of 'going all out, aiming high and achieving greater, faster, better and more economical results in "building socialism"'. He hinted, however, that the extreme egalitarianism of the 'Gang of Four' was a thing of the past, and that those who had most to contribute would reap the greatest reward. For progress was to be on the basis of the socialist principle 'from each according to his ability, to each according to his work'. As Deng was to put it when his turn came to address the congress, what China needed was 'less empty talk and more hard work'.

In his report Hua insisted that the purge of the Leftists should be confined primarily to ringleaders who had joined the 'Gang's' 'factional set-up', that these were merely a 'handful', and that the larger group who had simply 'erred' and who were willing to repent should not suffer unduly. One reason for his moderation was, of course, the fact that the 'Gang's' principal supporters had, in many cases, already fallen from grace. This was made apparent with the publication of the names of the 201 full and 132 alternate members elected to the eleventh Central Committee. At the time, some 174 full members and 123 alternate members of the tenth Central Committee, elected three years previously, were still alive. Of these, 59 full members and 51 alternates failed to secure re-election to the eleventh Central Committee. Those cast into the wilderness included ex-ministers like Yu Huiyong (who had greatly assisted the 'Gang' to establish their stranglehold over cultural work), and many lesser figures who had held provincial-level appointments in Shanghai, Liaoning and other Leftist strongholds. Conversely, although the new Central Committee was based firmly on Party, state and army leaders who had been elected in 1973, it also contained a sizeable group of veteran cadres who had been disgraced in the Cultural Revolution and who had only just worked their way back to the centre of power. Perhaps the most prominent example of these rehabilitated cadres was Lo Ruiqing, a former Chief of the General Staff, who had broken both legs in a vain attempt to escape persecution by Red Guards in 1966.

At the highest levels of leadership the elections showed no surprises. The Standing Committee of the Politbureau consisted of Hua, Deng and the three leaders who had supported Hua against the 'Gang'. These were Ye Jianying, Li Xiannian, and Wang Dongxing.

On 18 August, the Congress adopted a new Party constitu-

tion. Its 'general programme' invoked the 'Four Modernisations', called for the strict observance of discipline and the
rejection of 'splittist' and factional activities. It also neatly
reversed a radical slogan of 1973, which the 'Gang' had used
as a justification for rejecting higher authority and encouraging
'anarchism'. Thus, instead of being encouraged to go 'against
the tide', Party members were told to go 'against any tide'
that ran counter to Mao's famous principles: 'Practise Marxism
and not revisionism; unite and don't split; be open and above-
board, and don't intrigue or conspire.'

By the time of the congress, Party membership stood at
35,000,000, half of whom had joined since the beginning of
the Cultural Revolution, including 7,000,000 since the tenth
Congress. Although in his speech Ye Jianying commented
that the 'overwhelming majority' were 'good or fairly good',
he admitted that 'a serious problem of impurity' existed. The
new constitution provided three means of dealing with this.
The first was the expulsion of 'proven renegades, enemy
agents, absolutely unrepentant persons in power taking the
capitalist-road, alien class elements, degenerates and new
bourgeois elements'. The second was to establish special
commissions for inspecting discipline at county level and
above, to police the Party as they had done before the
Cultural Revolution. The third was to tighten up admissions
procedures, so that no one could join a Party branch without
first being 'screened' by the Party Committee and the next
higher level. Clearly the days were over when callow in-
experienced youths could rise to the heights as 'helicopter
cadres', as Deng had called them.

The bases for the reorganisation of the Party having been
established, the next major task was to reform the state
framework, for which purpose the fifth National People's
Congress met in Beijing on 26 February 1978. In his 'Report
on the Work of the Government', Hua devoted less attention
to the crimes of the 'Gang' and concentrated rather on
economic construction plans for the period up to 1985.[11]
His speech echoed those of earlier reports by Zhou Enlai by
being more concerned with the nuts and bolts of practical
government than with theory. It made much of agricultural
mechanisation, increasing steel and grain production, en-

couraging foreign trade, and developing advanced science and technology. While a wide wage spread was to be avoided, Hua argued that 'the enthusiasm of the masses cannot be aroused if no distinction is made between those who do more work and those who do less, between those who do a good job and those who do a poor one'.

On 5 March the Congress adopted a new State Constitution to replace that of 1975. In its preamble it reaffirmed the commitment of the 'Four Modernisations' and claimed that China had now become a 'socialist country with the beginnings of prosperity'. Many of the constitution's provisions were similar or identical to those of 1975. Thus it repeated a clause asserting the Party's 'constitutional' right to exercise leadership over the state. It was, however, a lengthier document, much of the extra space being taken up with a detailed description of the functions of various state organs and the rights of citizens to participate in the management of state affairs.

Perhaps the most important changes were those relating to law and order. A common charge against the 'Gang' was that they had encouraged hooligan elements to indulge in orgies of 'beating, smashing and looting' and had replaced China's legal system with kangaroo courts and mob rule. Under their malign influence the police organs had been subverted and had ceased to work effectively. In the Cultural Revolution the tripartite division of labour between courts, Public Security and Procuratorate had ceased to have meaning, and the Procuratorate had actually vanished in the constitutin of 1975, its functions being taken over by the police. On 26 February Hua had said that it was 'essential to strengthen the socialist legal system if we are to bring about great order across the land', and the Procuratorate was re-established by the new constitution. This also laid down that 'no citizen may be arrested except by decision of a people's court or with the sanction of a people's procuratorate, and the arrest must be made by a public security organ'. The constitution also guaranteed various democratic freedoms.

At the same time the constitution continued to emphasise that the state would deal harshly with wrong-doers. It retained the concept of 'bad elements' which had existed throughout the history of the People's Republic. These included landlords, rich peasants and 'reactionary capitalists who have not yet been reformed', together with 'new-born bourgeois elements', a category conveniently general enough to cope with persons of impeccable class background who had, nevertheless, sold out to the 'Gang of Four'.

'Emancipating Our Minds'

Although Deng had acted with due humility in paving the way for his own return, once restored to office he began to act with characteristic vigour. As in 1975, he directed his efforts to restoring China's flagging economy, and he assumed special responsibilities for the development of science, education, and intellectual life generally. He again came forward to rally the academic and scientific community which was still somewhat wary of advocating a return to high standards for fear of again being condemned as élitist. With Deng's encouragement, however, intellectuals again began to speak up. A major indication of change came in the autumn of 1977, when it was decreed that competitive examinations for admission to university would once more be instituted.[12] The net was cast widely in that even school graduates of the pre-Cultural Revolution years were eligible to apply, the examinations were exceedingly tough and, at the beginning of 1978, China's universities admitted an intake of students which was quite outstanding in terms of academic ability.

Similarly there were official calls again to let 'one hundred flowers bloom' and a recognition that intellectual life could not flourish under too great a degree of ideological control. The contributions that intellectuals could make to China's development were once again the subject for praise, as they had been in the early 1960s, and a series of academic conferences was held. The greatest of these met from 18–31 March 1978. This was the National Science Conference and was the largest such gathering in Chinese history; nearly 6,000 delegates attended. Hua opened the proceedings but it was Deng's speech which was interrupted by 'prolonged applause'. For it could not have escaped notice that the themes of the conference repeated the views he had advanced in 1975. Moreover, in his speech Deng came dangerously close to equating dedication to one's professional work with political purity: the view which had contributed to his dismissal twice before, but which obviously went down extremely well with his intellectual audience. The major speech, however, was given by Fang Yi, the Vice-Premier directly responsible for scientific and technical work.[13]

Outlining a plan for 'high speed development' by 1985, Fang admitted that China was lagging fifteen to twenty-five years behind advanced world levels. He identified as key fields for development agriculture, energy, materials, electronic computers, space technology, high energy physics, genetic engineering and lasers. He also specified measures which were to be implemented in the interests of modernisation. It was necessary to build up a network of 'key' research institutions and to ensure that they were headed by experts. Large numbers of talented people were to be trained, particularly at postgraduate level, so that the number of professional scientific researchers would reach 800,000 by 1985. Scientific personnel were to enjoy sabbaticals, foreign travel and promotion on merit. 'Free contention' was to be encouraged and scientists were to publish their findings 'so long as they do not divulge state secrets or involve chicanery'. It was also necessary to learn from foreign countries and to increase international academic exchanges. Scientists were to be allowed to devote five-sixths of their time to scientific work and were to be provided with assistants to reduce their administrative and other chores. 'High priority' was to be given to refitting existing laboratories, to building new experimental installations and to the design and production of new instruments and equipment. Clearly, the age of the technocrats was at hand and, in the light of Fang Yi's remarks, the President of the Academy of Sciences could proclaim: 'The springtime of science is here.'

The following month, on 22 April, Deng addressed a National Educational Work Conference where he again stressed the need to raise standards:

Students must give first place to firm and correct political orientation, but this does not exclude the study of science and culture. On the contrary, the higher their political consciousness, the harder the efforts and the greater the voluntary efforts the students should make to learn science and culture for the revolution. Therefore the 'Gang of Four' were not only absurd in the extreme, but they were negating and betraying proletarian politics when they opposed what they termed 'putting intellectual education first' . . . [14]

He went on to call for the training of experts and also insisted that teachers be treated with respect not only by their students but 'by society as a whole'. 'Commendations and rewards' were to be 'extended with wide publicity to outstanding educational workers'.

In the same month the Academy of Social Sciences (which had been set up as an institution independent of the Academy of Sciences the previous year) publicised a forum which condemned the 'Gang of Four's' practice of 'cultural autocracy' which had resulted in many 'forbidden zones' in the studies of philosophy and social sciences. One area mentioned was the study of law. A leading jurist observed that China must make a 'big effort to institute laws including criminal law, a code of criminal procedure, civil law, a code relating to civil suits, and important laws concerning economic construction'. An historian discussed the 'Gang's' influence on his own subject where, he said, 'the appraisal of historical personages was once monopolised by the "Gang's" factional set up, and what they said was final'. As a result, some historical personages had been 'deified' while others were 'demonised'. Among those deified, he observed, was Qin Shi Huang. As pointed out in Chapter 2, Mao had chosen to identify with Qin Shi Huang and the 'Gang of Four' had followed suit. Hence the historian was coming dangerously close to saying that Mao had been deified and, he went on to assert, it was necessary to 'get rid of the bad habit of deception, break down metaphysical conventions and faithfully describe historical personages as they were during their lifetime and in the proper context, for such is the Marxist scientific approach'.[15]

The question of Mao was, of course, the crucial issue. Deng's determination to push China into a more technocratic mode of development in itself required a reinterpretation of Maoism which went further than Hua Guofeng's. In his letter to Hua of 10 April 1977 he had stated that 'we must forever apply *accurate and complete* Mao Zedong Thought to guide the whole Party, the whole army and the people of the whole country, and to push forward the cause of the Party and socialism'.[16] In 1981 it was to be claimed that this was evidence that he had opposed Hua's 'two what-evers' interpretation from the outset. Be that as it may, by the spring of 1978 Deng and his followers were certainly evolving their own distinctive approach.

Thus, on 9 May 1978, an article appeared entitled 'Prac-tice is the sole criterion for testing truth', a phrase of Mao's. This article was published in an internal publication of the Central Party School which was headed by Hu Yaobang, a leading supporter of Deng's, and the following day it was reprinted in *Guangming Daily*, the national newspaper primarily devoted to intellectual concerns. It reiterated a 'basic principle of the Marxist theory of cognition', namely, that 'only social practice can test whether a theory correctly reflects objective reality and is true'. It pointed out that 'we must dare to touch and to get clear the rights and wrongs' regarding the 'forbidden areas' set up by the 'Gang of Four'.[17]

On 2 June Deng himself provided a powerful statement when he addressed an all-army political work conference. In this he attacked un-named comrades who, he said:

... talk about Mao Zedong Thought every day, but often forget, abandon or even oppose Chairman Mao's funda-mental Marxist viewpoint and method of seeking truth from facts, proceeding from reality in doing everything and integrating theory and practice. Furthermore, some people even maintain that whoever persists in seeking truth from facts, proceeding from reality and integrating theory with practice is guilty of a heinous crime. In essence, their view is that one may only copy straight from Marx, Lenin and Chairman Mao, and should rest content with mechanical copying, transmitting and reproduction. They would insist that to do otherwise is to go against Marxism-Lenism-Mao Zedong Thought and the guidance coming from the Party Central Committee. What they raise is no minor issue. It involves the whole approach to Marxism-Leninism-Mao Zedong Thought.[18]

Deng went on to demonstrate that Mao himself had always sought truth from facts. He had, for example, 'firmly opposed the erroneous mentality of those who kept saying in discussions within the Communist Party, "show me where it's written in the book", as if whatever was written in a book was right'. Deng also reminded his listeners that Mao had said: 'When we say Marxism is correct, it is certainly not because Marx was a "prophet" but because his theory had been proved correct in our practice and in our struggle.'

There was much more in this vein and, as Deng said, 'concrete analysis of concrete conditions is the living soul of Marxism. Marxism-Leninism-Mao Zedong Thought would lose its vitality if it were not integrated with the actual conditions.' Indeed, as he cleverly observed, 'even if we paid lavish lip-service to Mao Zedong Thought, we would actually be running counter to it'. It was essential, therefore, to 'set things to rights and shatter spiritual fetters to effect a great emancipation of our minds'.

Deng's speech was reinforced on 1 July when, to mark the fifty-seventh anniversary of the founding of the Party, the press published a speech which Mao had made in January 1962. This had circulated in unofficial Red Guard compilations in the Cultural Revolution and was, therefore, known to be genuine but it had never been openly published before. The speech was significant for in it Mao himself made a spirited plea for tolerance, saying 'some of our comrades can't bear to hear any opinion contrary to their own and can't tolerate any criticism. That is very wrong'. But what was particularly important was that Mao himself admitted that he had made mistakes and was not above criticism. Referring to a meeting in June 1961, he said:

> ... I discussed my own shortcomings and mistakes. I asked the comrades to convey what I said to the provinces and localities. I found out later that many localities were not informed. It's as if my mistakes could or should be kept hidden. Comrades, they mustn't be kept hidden!

Of all the mistakes made by the Central Committee I am responsible for those directly related to me and I have a share of the responsibility for those not directly related to me, because I am its Chairman.

Later he condemned those who suppressed criticism, saying:

... forbidding people to speak out as if one were a tiger whose backside no-one dares touch — ten out of ten who adopt this attitude will fail. People will always speak out sooner or later. You think that people really won't dare to touch the backsides of tigers like you? They bloody well will![19]

Deng's attempt to 'shatter spiritual fetters' was opposed by Hua and, much more vigorously, by Wang Dongxing. As a security specialist Wang was one of the least known of China's leaders. He had, however, been Mao's personal bodyguard in the 1930s and since that time had been particularly devoted to him.[20] Despite his willingness to turn on Mao's widow in October 1976, he remained loyal to his leader's memory and, until official Chinese sources pointed out that Hua was responsible, was widely believed to be the originator of the 'two whatevers'. By his own subsequent admission, he had opposed the moves to restore Deng to power in the intra-Party debates of early 1977 and had delayed his return. His major concern, apparently, was that reversing the decision of 7 April 1976 would reflect badly on Mao and, therefore, 'should not be handled lightly'. Later, 'under the pressure of most comrades who insisted that justice should be done', he agreed to Deng's reinstatement. But he insisted that it should not be done 'with fanfare' and it should not be seen as a criticism of Mao's approval of Deng's original dismissal. He had also insisted, against the wishes of many colleagues, that there be no reversal of the verdict on the Tiananmen Incident.[21]

After the publication of 'Practice is the sole criterion for testing truth' Wang was, he later said, 'panic-stricken'. He ordered those in charge of propaganda work to prohibit *People's Daily*, *Guangming Daily* and *Liberation Army Daily* from publishing such articles, and he commissioned his supporters to write articles 'refuting' Deng's ideas in intra-Party journals. Wang also prevented the issue from being aired in the Party's major theoretical journal for several months. As he later confessed, 'I ordered the *Red Flag* magazine under my control not to publish articles discussing the criterion of truth and not to adopt lightly any kind of attitude so as to mislead people into believing that the discussion of the truth criterion was purely academic.'

He also tried to suppress the first issue of *China Youth* when it attempted to resume publication in September 1978, after twelve years of closure. The editors had apparently taken Deng's message to heart and the first issue was to contain articles speaking highly of the Tiananmen Incident, comparing the Mao cult with religious 'blind faith', and attacking the 'two whatevers' philosophy.[22] Wang justified his action on the grounds that publication would be 'detrimental to stability and unity'. However, it aroused the 'vehement opposition of the people' and Hua himself felt obliged to tell Wang that it was *his* 'way of doing things that was really unfavourable for stability and unity'. The journal was duly published.

In fact Deng was able to mobilise further support for his approach in the autumn of 1978. This was partly because of his popularity among 'the masses', but in the harsh world of Chinese politics their opinions were of only limited importance. What did matter was that the number of cadres in leading positions who shared his views was increasing dramatically. For the purge of the 'Gang of Four's' supporters at all levels of the Chinese leadership was naturally accompanied by a process of rehabilitation, in which Deng was simply the most prominent example. In a very thorough study of central and provincial leaders in the Party and state apparatus, David Goodman has demonstrated that there was a 65 per cent turnover of individuals between September 1976 and April 1978.[23] Although it would be misleading to assume that all those who lost high office in this period were dedicated Leftists, and that all those who assumed it were loyal to Deng, the trend was undoubtedly in that direction, and the burgeoning constituency of veteran cadres who had suffered in the Cultural Revolution undoubtedly strengthened Deng's hand. And this was a continuing process. In October 1977 Hu Yaobang had written a long article entitled 'Rectify the Rights and Wrongs in the Cadre Line That Were Reversed by the "Gang of Four" '. In this he called for 'rapidly and correctly solving the cadre problem and liberating large numbers of cadres who for various reasons had not been rehabilitated or assigned work'. Thereafter, Hu, as director of the Central Committee's Organisation Department, had been charged with the work of 'rehabilitating the victims of miscarriages of justice', and thereafter, it was later said, 'this work gathered pace'.[24]

Hence by late 1978 Deng was clearly in the ascendant and leaders like Hua and Wang Dongxing who had to a greater or lesser extent trimmed their sails to the Leftist winds of the Cultural Revolution were in a weaker position. This became apparent when a lengthy Central Work meeting was convened in November 1978, and was followed by the third plenum of the eleventh Central Committee which met in Beijing from 18–22 December. The third plenum was later to be described as 'a turning point of profound historic significance' in the history of the Party which 'put an end to the situation in which the Party's work had been stagnating since October 1976 and began to correct the Leftist mistakes committed before and during' the Cultural Revolution.[25]

At these two meetings there was considerable criticism of Mao. Some leaders obviously wished that it should be handled with discretion but were nevertheless open in acknowledging Mao's mistakes. Thus Ye Jianying argued that 'Mao Zedong Thought' should not be jettisoned, but that Mao had personally made 'many mistakes'. In particular he referred to Mao's disgrace of Peng Dehuai at the Lushan plenum of 1959 and regretted that he himself had not stood up to the Chairman on that occasion. General Xu Shiyou emphasized that he would be the first to oppose any attempt to 'imitate the way Khrushchev moved Stalin's corpse out of Red Square to feed dogs, degraded him, and aired personal hatred for a dead person without distinguishing right from wrong'. Xu asserted, however, that he had never hidden from Mao his distaste for the Cultural Revolution, and that Mao had 'ruled by the voice of one man alone, over-indulged Jiang Qing, and backed up the "Gang of Four" in recent years'.

Tan Zhenlin, a Central Committee member purged in the Cultural Revolution, directed his criticisms at Wang Dongxing:

> Who said that Chairman Mao is beyond reproach, that nothing must be done against him, that whosoever criticizes Chairman Mao's faults in history will risk decapitation, and that such criticisms would be tantamount to being disrespectful and deceptive to the emperor and the highest authorities as well as violation of Marxist-Leninist tenets. Then, wouldn't Chairman Mao be more deified than Jesus Christ, Sakyamuni and Mohammed, and more sacred and inviolable than the Jade Emperor, Marx and Lenin?[26]

Tan also attacked Wang for parroting Hua's words throughout the meeting. 'Are Chairman Hua's words necessarily right?', Tan asked, and continued to assert that Hua's 'two whatevers' formula had been wrong. Indeed, Hua was required to make a self-criticism in which he acknowledged his mistakes on the subject of Mao.

And 'seeking truth from facts' prevailed over the 'two whatevers' at the third plenum. Its communiqué declared: 'Comrade Mao Zedong was a great Marxist . . . It would not be Marxist to demand that a revolutionary leader be free of all shortcomings and errors. It also would not conform to Comrade Mao Zedong's consistent evaluation of himself.'[27] It went on to observe that Mao had initiated the Cultural Revolution 'primarily in the light of the fact that the Soviet Union had turned revisionist and for the purposes of opposing revisionism and preventing its occurrence'. The implication here appeared to be that Mao may have over-reacted, and the communiqué noted that the 'shortcomings and mistakes' of what it still called the 'Great' Cultural Revolution should be 'summed up at the appropriate time'. In fact the plenum did discuss 'some major political events' of the Cultural Revolution era. It stated that in 1975, 'when Comrade Deng Xiaoping was entrusted by Comrade Mao Zedong with the responsibility of presiding over the work of the Central Committee', there had been 'great achievements' and these should be recognised. The 'Gang of Four's' attack on them as a 'Right Deviationist Wind' was to be reversed. The communiqué also confirmed that the Tiananmen Incident was 'entirely revolutionary' (a decision reached the previous month and discussed in Chapter 6). It also announced that four veteran leaders who had suffered in the Cultural Revolution or earlier had been formally rehabilitated. Among them was the late Peng Dehuai. In a passage attacking 'false charges' and 'frame-ups' it condemned the past practice of setting up 'special case groups' to examine cadres without Party and mass supervision.

The plenum also decided that the time had come to switch attention from criticism of the 'Gang of Four', and devote China's efforts to 'socialist modernisation'. Carrying out the 'four modernisations' required great growth in the productive forces and that in turn required numerous changes in methods of management, action and thinking which stood in the way of such growth. It was made clear that the radicalism of the Great Leap Forward and later campaigns was not what was needed. The stress rather was on political stability and working 'according to objective economic law'. If these factors were ignored, it was said, experience showed that the economy developed slowly, or even stagnated and fell back.

In industry this was to amount to a new deal for management. The communiqué said that the Party was to stop substituting itself for the Government, and the Government was to stop making decisions that were best left to enterprise administrations. The responsibilities of managers were to be increased and a properly efficient system of rewards and punishments, and promotion and demotion, was to be introduced. In agriculture, the communiqué insisted that the material well-being of the peasants was to be protected and that the principle of 'to each according to his work' was to be properly implemented in order to overcome egalitarianism. It was forbidden to interfere with peasants' private plots, side-line occupations, and village fairs, and these elements of free enterprise were described as 'necessary adjuncts of the socialist economy'. Within the Communes it was emphasised that decentralisation was to be order of the day, so that the skilled and diligent should prosper.

Finally the plenum discussed the question of democracy and the legal system. The communiqué stated that there had been too little democracy in the past and that the constitutional rights of citizens must not be impinged upon. It was essential that the legal system be strengthened so that democracy was 'systematized and written into the law'.

The plenum also elected a number of Deng's supporters to key positions. Of these one of the most important was Chen Yun, a distinguished economist who had little time for Maoist ideas. He became a member of the Standing Committee of the Politbureau and also a Vice-Chairman of the Central Committee. He was also appointed to lead a new 100-member Central Commission for Inspecting Discipline which the plenum established 'to enforce Party rules and regulations'. Hu Yaobang and Wang Zhen, a foreign trade specialist, were also elevated to the Politbureau.

Thus 1978 was a year of momentous change in which China moved with speed from the Maoist era into something new. It was the year in which a search for a new sort of politics began to emerge. However, as we shall see in the next chapter, this did not usher in an era of harmony.

6

Breaking the Mould: In Search of a New Politics

The 'Democracy Movement'

In 1978 the Chinese leadership, under the increasing influence of Deng and his supporters, began to search for political arrangements which would mesh with, and support, the technocratic strategy of economic development to which they were committed. Just as they wished to replace the mobilisational style of development favoured by Mao with a more conservative and institutionalised one, so, too, they hoped to reform the political system into one in which changes should be implemented in an orderly manner, free from the arbitrary and often violent twists and turns which had characterised the political process from the Great Leap onwards, and especially since the Cultural Revolution began in 1966. To this end, therefore, they began to talk at length of 'socialist legality'. They also intended that the new arrangements should give more rights to 'the masses' and hence 'democracy' was a word that was much invoked. For the leadership it meant that the Party and government should be more responsive to public opinion, and that 'the masses' should be given institutionalised means by which they could supervise, criticize and, to a limited extent, choose their leaders. But as good Leninists, China's leaders intended that the Party should remain in full control, that the extension of freedoms should be gradual, and that there should be no decline into 'anarchism'. Their aim was to give Chinese socialism a 'human face', not to see it transmogrified into a 'bourgeois' democracy.

However, a number of ordinary Chinese either misread the

signs or were unwilling to proceed at a pace set by the leadership. The result was that a remarkable 'Democracy Movement' developed in which some citizens developed an alternative political style, the politics of protest. They claimed the right to criticize freely, not only official policies. but the leadership and, on occasions, the political system itself. Their style was characterised by the development of unofficial channels of communication, a high degree of spontaneity and, sometimes, an element of 'direct action'.

The element in this which aroused most attention in the West was the 'Democracy Wall' phenomenon. This reached its height in the spring of 1979 and by early 1980 it had virtually disappeared as a result of official repression. However, for a brief period, ordinary citizens did express themselves with considerable freedom, and, although a shocked leadership quickly reasserted its control, it may well have been influenced by what was said, and what happened, to push ahead with its own reforms. 'Democracy Wall' began in November 1978. In large measure it sprang up as a result of the continuing signs of increased liberalisation discussed in the last chapter. The promulgation of the new State Constitution, the encouragement given to the 'hundred flowers' policy and the science and education conferences, and the widespread popularity of Deng Xiaoping all played their part, as did the move to 'shatter spiritual fetters'. Moreover, as we have seen, the leadership was by this time also investigating the details of the Tiananmen Incident. It is not clear how widespread was the knowledge that a 'reversal of verdicts' was about to take place, but copies of the Tiananmen poems were circulating quite extensively and something of a cult began to develop.[1] This found tangible expression in November when an official rehabilitation of the Tiananmen Incident took place. On 15 November the Beijing Municipal Revolutionary Committee issued an official announcement to the effect that the Tiananmen Incident was 'completely revolutionary'.[2] It was also said that the Beijing Public Security Bureau had investigated the matter thoroughly and had 'proved' that not one of the 388 people arrested after the Incident was a counter-revolutionary.[3] Identical announcements were made in other cities where similar demonstrations had taken place.

Suddenly, therefore, 'Tiananmen' became fashionable. A volume of six hundred of the Tiananmen poems was officially published, with Hua Guofeng providing his calligraphy for the title. A play, 'Where the Silence Is', was set against the background to the Incident and enjoyed great success. Detailed descriptions of what 'really' happened appeared in the press and it was stressed that the events of 5 April 1976 were important in that they showed 'the masses' fighting against the 'Gang of Four'. Parallels were also drawn between '5 April' ('4.5' in Chinese) and '4 May' ('5.4'), the great cultural and nationalist resurgence of 1919 which had also begun in Tiananmen.

Thus, against a background of general liberalisation, the rehabilitation of Tiananmen gave encouragement to many ordinary Chinese who believed they now had the freedom and opportunity to make their views known. Wallposters began to appear in ever larger numbers and at Xidan, in central Beijing, a long wall conveniently situated on a major thoroughfare became a favourite spot for pasting up grievances. This was the original 'Democracy Wall' but other places in Beijing were also popular, and 'Democracy Walls' quickly sprang up in other major cities. These areas attracted large crowds and some developed into 'Speakers' Corners' where individuals and groups congregated to air their views and organise support. By December 1978, a number of unofficial publications had sprung up. Unlike the *samizdat* of the Soviet Union, these cheaply-produced Chinese journals were sold on the streets quite openly, with some vendors charging especially high rates to foreigners wishing to purchase them.

In addition to posters, publications and discussions, some activists began to organise marches and demonstrations. There was also a 'petitioning' movement whereby individuals and groups began to visit Party and government offices, together with organs responsible for legal work, to request redress of their grievances.

It should be emphasised that although the term 'Democracy Movement' was used in China to describe these phenomena, the term is somewhat misleading. There was a 'Democracy Movement' in that a small number of individuals and organisations did take this stand on what could be described as 'human rights' issues, and produced detailed critiques of the

Chinese political system which advocated fundamental reforms. But these activists were a tiny minority of those participating in a wide-ranging and amorphous expression of discontent.

In so far as 'Democracy Wall' was a 'Movement', it was essentially because it represented those members of Chinese society who had not only suffered as a result of the Cultural Revolution or earlier campaigns but, moreover, *had not been compensated thereafter.* This latter point is of the utmost importance for, by the end of 1978, many of the victims of the Mao era had had their good names restored and had been given responsible positions once more. Thus, in December 1978 the posthumous rehabilitation of Peng Dehuai[4] was but a spectacular example of what by then had become a common phenomenon of 'reversing the verdict' on veteran cadres purged in earlier campaigns. As discussed earlier, scientists, academics, writers, musicians, artists and managers had not only received the leadership's abject apologies but had been assured of good treatment, considerable freedom, and material rewards. A much more conciliatory line on 'Rightists' and those previously branded as being 'bad elements' was being implemented.[5] The 'no-nonsense' approach to the 'Four Modernisations' held out hope to all those who were prepared to work hard, who had skills or, in the case of the academically gifted, were intent on acquiring them.

Such people had experienced an improvement in their personal circumstances which they could scarcely have dreamed of before Mao's death, and they were obviously not inclined to protest. Thus a very significant feature of the 'Democracy Movement' was that it differed substantially from 'Dissident Movements' in the Soviet Union and Eastern Europe *precisely* because it did not include eminent scientific and literary figures. No Chinese Solzhenitsyn or Sakharov participated, and even university students were very thin on the ground.

It was, rather, a movement of 'little people' who felt they had been 'left out' of the post-Mao settlements. One of the most interesting of the elements involved here was drawn from the young people whose careers had suffered as a result of the Cultural Revolution. It will be recalled that a major reason for the launching of that movement was the belief that a 'new class' had formed which was using the educational system to ensure that its children would become members of the élite in due course. Consequently, the children of cadres, intellectuals and managers, who had been doing well under the previously existing élitism, not only found their education suddenly curtailed, but also suffered discrimination because of their background. In many cases their families had enough influence to prevent them from being sent down to remote Communes, but they were often assigned to menial jobs in the cities with little prospect of a 'good' career thereafter.

The renewed commitment to higher education, which began in 1977 with the restoration of entrance examinations, could not accommodate the massive 'backlog' of young people who had left school a decade earlier and who were now in direct competition for scarce places with their own younger siblings. They constituted, therefore, a particularly bitter group who had seen their hopes dashed and, moreover, who had matured in the highly-charged political atmosphere of the Cultural Revolution era. It is significant that a number of the best-known polemicists of 'Democracy Wall' belonged to this category, often having served their apprenticeship in the Red Guards.

Then there were the 'educated youths' in the countryside. The policy of 'sending down' urban youths had started in the late 1950s and had received a fillip ten years later when it became a convenient method of disposing of troublesome Red Guards. The system had always been extremely unpopular both because of the relative harshness of rural living conditions and, also, of the unfairness with which it operated. The post-Mao leadership was well aware of the difficulties it created but, faced with prospects of urban unemployment, could only offer modifications to the system and pious hopes that the problem would eventually be sorted out. Delegations of 'educated youths' therefore travelled to Beijing and other cities to demonstrate and petition against their treatment.[6]

Peasants, also, had grievances to air. It was admitted in 1977 and 1978 that there were considerable pockets of real poverty in rural China. Some areas sent representatives to Beijing to protest at their lot, and there were a number of well-publicized incidents where these spokesmen displayed their rags to foreign journalists and painted a picture of rural life far removed from the modest prosperity of the few hundred suburban Communes visited by tourists.[7]

Most protests, however, were narrowly focused on a single issue, often a highly personal one. Probably a majority of posters and petitions concerned a single case of injustice, mal-administration, bureaucratic inefficiency, or official dis-honesty. It was common to read accounts in which the writer claimed he, a relative, or a friend had been persecuted by a 'follower of the "Gang of Four" ' in his work unit or locality and, as a result, had been imprisoned, demoted, or lost his job. Such accounts regularly stated that appeals to local officials had either fallen on deaf ears or been 'suppressed', and that subsequent visits to bureaucratic agencies in Beijing or a provincial capital had been met with indifference or 'buck-passing'.

Others emphasised that, despite the massive switch in policy since the arrest of the 'Gang', many cadres were being slow to change their 'work style' and implement official directives. For example, in February a poster appeared in Beijing written by students and staff at *Renda* (People's University). This claimed that although a State Council directive had ordered the People's Liberation Army to hand back the educational buildings and other facilities they had expropriated for their own use during the Cultural Revolution, at *Renda* they were still refusing to do so. Others complained of police behaviour, including charges that some policemen were taking too close an interest in people who exercised their 'constitutional' right to put up posters.

Expressions of political opposition and discontent took many forms. A great number of them were simple *graffiti*. Thus, one poster on the 'Democracy Wall' in the 'People's Park' of Shanghai, simply read: 'I See the Chinese Press is Lying Again.' Another stated sarcastically: 'If the "Gang of Four" are Traitors, Jiang Jingguo (son of Chiang Kai-shek) is a Chinese Patriot!' Some attacked Mao, a common theme being 'Gang of Four or Gang of Five?' The Leftist leaders remaining in the hierarchy were also criticized, particularly Wang Dongxing. Even Hua Guofeng was not immune: 'Who

Was Minister of Public Security at the Time of Tiananmen?'

During the course of 1979 two particularly important events emerged which illustrated the extent of disaffection among some Chinese. The first concerned Wei Jingsheng, who quickly established himself as the best-known writer thrown up by the 'Democracy Movement'. The second was the case of 'educated youth' from Shanghai. In very different ways they reveal clearly various unresolved tensions remaining in Chinese society and are worth examining in some detail.

The case of Wei Jingsheng

Wei Jingsheng was approaching his thirtieth birthday when 'Democracy Wall' began. From a cadre's family, in the Cultural Revolution he had joined a Red Guard faction opposed to Jiang Qing. He was arrested for his 'reactionary' standpoint and, after his release, could only find employment as a humble electrician at Beijing Zoo. He was, therefore, entirely typical of the 'lost generation' in that his educational and career opportunities had been blighted by the Cultural Revolution. And, like many of his contemporaries, his sense of grievance must have deepened as he saw the new leadership introduce policies which made little attempt to compensate his reference group for the set-backs it had suffered.

In other respects, however, Wei was not typical. He was a particularly able writer who was not content to limit his output to short wallposters; he wrote lengthy articles. Moreover, he did not confine himself, as many others did, to making complaints about his own grievances or about specific abuses within the Chinese political system. Instead he wrote critiques of that system as a whole, and attacked not only the past leadership but the present one. And, at times he appeared to be arguing that Chinese Communism was not simply in need of reform but should be replaced.

Another feature distinguishing his protest was his involvement with foreigners. On 5 December 1978 he posted a lengthy article entitled 'Democracy is the Fifth Modernisation', on 'Democracy Wall'. This was one of the first major statements which could truly be regarded as 'dissident' and, as such, it aroused massive interest among foreign journalists in Beijing, who ensured that it was well-publicized through the international press.[8] Wei also began to edit an unofficial journal called *Exploration* (*Tansuo*). This first appeared in December, carrying his 'Democracy' article, and subsequent issues carried further articles continuing from this. In the eyes of foreign journalists Wei speedily became a 'leader' of the 'dissidents', an image which probably exaggerated his position and, undoubtedly, was inaccurate in suggesting that the 'Democracy Wall' movement was well-organised and united in its goals. However, Wei, through his writings, did claim to speak for vast numbers of ordinary Chinese, and was not averse to discussing his views with foreigners on a number of occasions in the early months of 1979.

His motives for doing so are not clear. He may have assumed that foreign contacts were now to be tolerated by the leadership. With the benefit of hindsight such a view was obviously naïve, but in the early months of 1979 such 'fraternisation' took place on an unprecedented scale with ordinary Chinese meeting foreigners in a wide range of social activities including eating out together, visiting foreigners in their apartments and, most unlikely of all, having 'mixed' dances. Alternatively, Wei may have felt that the interest of the foreign press was a valuable safeguard for the 'Democracy Movement'. It had, after all, afforded a measure of protection to some dissidents in the Soviet Union and it would not have been unreasonable to suppose that the Chinese leadership, out of an obvious desire to woo foreign governments and businessmen, might well have been reluctant to crack down on dissent under the watchful eyes of the foreign press corps. Or, he may simply not have cared about his own safety. In fact, as we shall see, Wei's foreign connections weakened his position and, ultimately, contributed to his arrest, trial and imprisonment.

What, then, were his opinions? The first issue of *Exploration* contained a statement of editorial policy which expressed these in general terms. The journal announced that it took as its guiding principle the freedoms of speech, press and assembly as provided under the constitution. It refused to recognise the 'absolute correctness' of any theory from any person. The editors saw themselves as being 'the spokesmen of the suffering people' and described their task as searching for the cause of China's 'social backwardness' by means of stimulating 'free discussions'.[9]

In his first article Wei argued that economic progress and human happiness could only be achieved through democracy. He made it clear that, in his opinion, there had been little of these under Mao and that, without fundamental changes, the new leadership was unlikely to be much of an improvement. Promises had always been made but, as old Chinese maxims put it, these simply boiled down to asking the masses to appease hunger by looking at a picture of a cake or looking at plums to quench one's thirst.

He observed that promises to create a democratic society had never been honoured. He noted that the people's desire for democracy had enabled the Communists to defeat the Nationalists. Thereafter a 'People's Democratic Dictatorship' had been established but, of course, this had speedily given way to the much narrower conception of the 'Dictatorship of the Proletariat'. This in turn was soon replaced by the 'autocracy' of Mao, whom Wei referred to ironically by his Cultural Revolution title of the 'Great Helmsman'. And, at this stage, a new promise was made: 'Because the leader is great, implicit faith in such a leader, rather than democracy, will bring more happiness to the people.' People had believed this but, Wei asked:

... are they any happier? Are they richer or more prosperous? Unconcealable facts show that they are poorer, more miserable and more backward. Why? This is the first question to be considered. And what to do now? That is the second question. There is no need now to determine the ratio of Mao Zedong's merits and shortcomings ... People should now think for a while and see if, without Mao Zedong's autocracy, China could be in its present backward state. Are Chinese people stupid, or lazy, or unwilling to enjoy wealth? Are they expecting too much? Quite the opposite. Then why? The answer is quite obvious. Chinese people should not have taken this road. Then why did they take it? Only because they were led by that self-exalting autocrat.[10]

The road taken was the 'socialist road'. Wei reminded his readers that in Marxist theory socialism meant that the people were their own masters. But, he sarcastically asked, what rights did they enjoy? He catalogued the low living standards of the population both in absolute terms and relative to those enjoyed in capitalist states. He pointed out that since 1949 the Chinese had produced considerable wealth through their own unremitting efforts but had little to show for it. Some had been creamed off by the rulers for their own benefit. Some had been 'thrown away' in foreign aid. He was particularly scathing about Mao's willingness to give handouts to Albania and Vietnam while many Chinese had too little to eat and there were beggars on the streets. The trouble was, he said, that China had suffered 'feudal socialism' or 'socialist autocracy', and he went on to draw parallels not only with the Soviet Union but even with the 'National Socialism' of Hitler.

Wei insisted that the system must be democratised for various reasons. The first was that this was what the people wanted and he emphasised the rights and needs of the individual in relation to the collective interest. But he also claimed that democracy was a prerequisite for a high level of economic development. He specifically rejected leadership views that democracy would produce 'disorder' which would be economically harmful. On the contrary, he asserted, it was autocracy which created instability. Autocratic systems could only function on the basis of conspiracy, violence and power struggles that brought great social upheaval and caused immense damage to production and living conditions. Wei also repudiated the official line that democracy in the West was simply a sham, emphasising that 'from what we can witness, the human rights of Western people . . . are safeguarded; their thinking is free, and their material life far surpasses what is possible under the "advanced socialist relations of production".' His rejoinder to the oft-repeated claims that the capitalist world suffered from such evils as slums and prostitution was to point out that China was not free of these either.

In his articles Wei did not spell out in detail what he meant by democracy. It is not entirely clear whether he was actually calling for the complete destruction of the Communist system or simply its radical modification. He did, however, insist that the people should be able to control or supervise their leaders and he noted approvingly that in Western systems the people could get rid of leaders like Nixon and Tanaka if they wished.

On 25 March 1979 Wei published an article entitled 'Democracy or a New Dictatorship' in which he expanded on earlier themes and also focused his attack particularly on Deng Xiaoping, for the events of the preceding months had caused increasing concern among some leaders who advocated a measure of suppression.

Initially, Deng had been relatively tolerant of 'Democracy Wall' and had discussed it with an American journalist on 27 November 1978. At that time he had defended Mao to the extent of saying that without him 'there would have been no New China', but went on to affirm that it was a constitutional right to put up posters, noting that 'if the masses feel some dissatisfaction, we must let them express it ... That is nothing to be afraid of'.[11] On 16 March 1979, however, he made a speech to senior cadres in which he appears to have moved somewhat from his earlier stance. Although he spoke out against dissolving the human rights organisations and closing down 'Democracy Wall' he equivocated to the extent of saying he would go along with the majority opinion if his senior colleagues felt otherwise. Wei immediately took up his pen.

This criticism began with a claim that the campaign for democracy was 'not limited to a few individuals' but was a 'trend in the development of Chinese society'. Wei insisted that those who understood this and agreed to strive for this goal were standing at the forefront of the historic trend. Those who opposed or hindered it were traitors to history. And those who suppressed this 'genuine popular movement' would be tried and punished.

Turning to Deng Xiaoping, Wei attacked his speech of 16 March claiming that in it Deng had 'foisted all kinds of charges on the Democratic Movement, attempting to blame it for the failure of Hua and Deng's policies to salvage China's economy and productivity. Once again, the people were the scapegoat for the failure of their policies'.

Wei's view was that no political leader was entitled to the

people's confidence unless he practised policies beneficial to them, and if the people were opposed 'all authorities must bow their heads'. Deng, he said, refused to do this. Thus:

> When the people universally demand an enquiry into the reasons for China's backwardness over the past thirty years and into Mao Zedong's crimes against the Chinese people, he always jumps up and says: 'Without Mao Zedong there could not be a New China.' Furthermore, not only did he stubbornly reiterate that in his 16 March speech, but he also explicitly upheld Mao Zedong's thought as the banner of the Chinese nation, stressing that Mao Zedong's short-comings were trivial matters hardly worth mentioning.[12]

Deng, in fact, did not want democracy. Like the 'Gang of Four' using the pretext that some people burned cars in order to suppress the Tiananmen demonstrations, Deng used the excuse that the Democracy Movement posed a threat to social order. It was necessary, therefore, for the people to beware of the possibility of Deng's 'metamorphosis into a dictator'. He was, said Wei, 'no longer worthy of the people's trust and support'. Like many leaders in Chinese history he had won the people's confidence and was now on 'the road to dictator-ship'. He ended by again insisting on the need for democracy:

> If the people wish to reform the government and its leaders into servants of the people, they must first place firmly in their own hands the power to delegate and to supervise while ensuring that the rights and procedures to elect and to recall are protected. Only on the basis of an honest universal election by the people is it possible to organise a government and a group of leaders who will serve the interests of the electors. When the government and its leaders are really delegates and supervised by the people, it will also be possible to cure the coercion and megalo-mania of the leaders.[13]

In Beijing the most important form of protest was the proliferation of unofficial journals in which writers expressed their discontent, although few of them went as far as Wei had done. In Shanghai, however, the 'Democracy Movement' had a somewhat different focus.

'Educated Youths' and the Shanghai Demonstrations

'Educated youths' played some part in the unofficial political life of the capital in the early months of 1979. But it was fairly limited and, moreover, those involved were not necessarily natives of Beijing, but simply went there because it was the centre of power. Thus in December 1978 protests were organised by representatives of young people who had been sent down to Yunnan where, it was claimed, conditions were so bad that a prolonged strike had taken place. These people received little comfort. Wang Zhen, a deputy premier, told them to go back to Yunnan and 'feed the pigs well'. He recommended that they 'get married and start a career there, regard Yunnan as your home and create a paradise'. More prosaically he suggested that they should grow more vegetables in order to improve their diet. Although some demonstrations took place, these were relatively minor affairs, and the 'educated youths' concerned seem to have returned to Yunnan without making much trouble. In February it was reported that the strike was over.[14]

In Shanghai, where protests by 'educated youths' had started as early as 25 November 1978, the problem was not solved so easily, for in China's most industrialised city it was particularly acute. The Cultural Revolution had severely disrupted the local economy and had exacerbated the perennial problem the municipal authorities faced in finding jobs for its youthful population. The response had been to apply the 'sending down' policy with greater vigour. About 2 million youths had been assigned to the countryside since 1966 and, although some were subsequently able to return to the city, about 1 million remained in the villages in 1978. Of these, some 600,000 had been sent down in 1968 when Mao had urged permanent rural resettlement, partly as a means of curbing Red Guard excesses. Consequently, the number of Shanghai families affected was disproportionately high.[15]

Moreover, young Shanghainese found the countryside more uncongenial than most. For not only were they exiled from the city with the best amenities in the whole of China, but they were also often sent to provinces which, like Anhui and Gansu, were desperately poor or, like Xinjiang and Heilongjiang, were distant frontier regions. Hence their representatives were quick to express their grievances and, unlike Beijing where the leadership of the 'Democracy Movement' came largely from urban-based young people, those with a background of compulsory rural service were active in directing it.

A prominent figure in the early stages was Teng Husheng, who had been sent to the countryside after graduating from technical middle school in 1968. His family had subsequently fallen into difficulties and his elderly father was reduced to selling old clothes on the streets in order to make ends meet. Teng married in 1970 but was forced to live apart from his wife as she lived in Shanghai. Separation, financial problems and a sick baby imposed considerable marital suffering.

Understandably embittered, he wrote wallposters which somewhat resembled the writings of Wei Jingsheng in that they were highly critical of Mao. For example, one dated 27 November 1978 observed:

> In his late years Mao Zedong became a tyrant and dictator! The so-called Great Proletarian Cultural Revolution, which went against the tide of history, instigated by Chairman Mao Zedong, opened a bloody page in the history of Chinese feudalism . . . He incited and utilised naïve and immature 'Red Guards' to get rid of our country's good chairman, Liu Shaoqi . . . This was done for his own throne and for those following him, he didn't care if the people lived or died!

In a further poster he claimed that 'Mao put the entire people of the country into a mental asylum and shot them with sedatives'.

Most 'educated youths', however, concentrated on their specific problems. A common complaint was that their earnings in the countryside were so low that they had to rely on handouts from their parents and were never able to acquire the financial independence which would enable them to marry. Others complained that they were treated as 'hirelings or slaves' and not given full political rights on the Communes. One poster vividly portrayed the plight of a youth who had been sent down, quite willingly, to Fengyang county in Anhui in 1968. From the outset he did a full adult work load, labouring seven days a week on a diet consisting almost entirely of rice. Yet, as he was only 17 he was paid at the 'junior' rate of five cents a day. His family had to send him ten *yuan* a month which he spent on necessities, yet at the end of his first year his production team claimed that he actually owed it six *yuan*. Only after seven years was he paid at the adult rate of ten cents a day. Eventually he was permitted to return to Shanghai because of ill-health.

There were many accounts of this nature, detailing economic hardship, political and social discrimination, and health problems. And the depressing feature of all of them was their familiarity. They repeated numerous accusations made by an earlier generation of 'educated youths' in the Red Guard tabloids and wallposters of 1967—8. Clearly, despite promises made in the Cultural Revolution that the policy would be applied more humanely, little had actually changed. The young man quoted above no doubt reflected the resentment of many when he wrote:

Every day I would think, my family and the the state have spent so much money on sending me down to the countryside. I don't speak of the losses I personally suffered. I also increased the burden on the peasants. I don't know what the advantage of it all was. By day I worked and at night I thought. Now it's all clear to me ... I hate myself for having been deceived.

On 10 December a rally of 'educated youths' took place in Shanghai. Hundreds of demonstrators marched from 'People's Park' to the muncipal Party headquarters on the Bund, blocking traffic and sitting down in the street. At the headquarters they chanted such slogans as 'We want work!', 'We want food!', and 'Going to the mountains and villages is reactionary!'. Wang Yiping, a member of the Party committee, urged the crowd to disperse and await the publication of a report on rustication which a Work Conference of the Central Committee was then preparing. According to a poster put up by Teng Husheng, the rally then broke up peacefully. A few days later he was secretly arrested.

This development produced a spirited public reaction. Some posters gave Teng whole-hearted support and endorsed his views. Others were more critical but argued that his errors should be discussed and refuted through public debate. As a result of this popular outcry he was released from prison in early January when (according to rumour) he was given a job on the condition that he remained silent.

Although this display of leniency may have gone some way towards defusing a tense situation, the publication of the Work Conference's report on rustication on 15 December did little to meet the demands of 'educated youths'. For the report recognised that it was simply impossible to end the policy of 'sending down' or, for that matter, to find urban employment speedily for those who, it acknowledged, had already done a lengthy stint in the villages. Reform measures were introduced both at national and local level, but it was obvious that these could have only limited effect in alleviating difficulties, at least in the short term.

Consequently, as Chinese New Year approached in late January, the Shanghai authorities became increasingly anxious about the likely reactions of the large numbers of 'educated youths' who would be returning to visit their families during China's only annual holiday of any significance. Official attempts were made to organise light entertainment for them, but they were not to be fobbed off with such palliatives, In fact some were particularly annoyed to be greeted on arrival with detailed instructions on when and how they should return to the villages — not the warmest of welcomes.[16] They responded by holding a series of rallies, marches and demonstrations in the last week of January and the first week of February. On occasion the marchers seized traffic police pavilions and angry crowds gathered outside Party headquarters.

Matters came to a head on 5 February when a large crowd marched to Party headquarters and called on the Shanghai leadership to appear. After two hours of unproductive shout-

ing the crowd marched to the main railway station where
some of them lay down on the tracks, disrupting rail communications for twelve hours. A 'Telephone Directive' from
the State Council in Beijing urged the crowd to leave the
station and warned them that all offenders would be dealt
with severly. Police used magaphones to order the crowd to
leave. When they failed to do so a large number of police,
supported by militia, surrounded the crowd, made a number
of arrests and forced them to disperse.

Badly shaken by these events, the Shanghai authorities
began to crack down.[17] Official slogans were posted all over
the city urging obedience to the State Council's instructions,
warning people not to damage public property, pound on the
doors of government offices, abuse cadres and hold up the
traffic. Something of a smear campaign began in the local
press directed at such unseemly phenomena as the circulation
of 'yellow' (i.e., pornographic) photos, the singing of lewd
songs and idle youth with dyed, permed hair. These were
linked with those who created disturbances, pounded on the
doors of government organs and disrupted traffic.

Much more ominous was the fact that protest through
wallposters also come under fire. On 16 February one Shanghai
paper commented:

> Shanghai is an important port and a city of international
> repute. We should pay great attention to the tidiness of the
> city, its good appearance and civilised air ... Take Nanjing
> Road, for example, there are crude scrawls all over the
> place, these make one feel uncomfortable when passing by
> ... Some people consider that putting up big character
> posters of the kind, 'we strongly call for ...' or writing a
> few slogans can gain public sympathy and put pressure on
> the leaders. This kind of thinking is totally wrong.

By the beginning of March newspaper articles and 'readers'
letters' were defining an official view of democracy along the
following lines:

> [the majority of cadres and the masses have livened up
> their thinking and lifted the mental cangue imposed by the
> 'Gang of Four'] ... but we cannot but notice that in the

area of ideology bourgeois thought has a certain currency. This kind of individualistic thought which places one's own interest higher than everything else, this kind of variegated 'New Wave of Thought' which raises such slogans as, 'We want human rights', 'Return to our homes', and so on, and also the bourgeois life-styles which are emerging in some corners, these are all part of the sidestream which must not be ignored.

On 6 March a notice from the Public Security Bureau was displayed all over the city, and a local newspaper subsequently expanded on its contents. Except for a few defined places (which were not specified) it was no longer permitted to put up posters. Marches were not to obstruct traffic and participants were to submit to police instructions. It was forbidden to rally outside Party or government buildings, to smash public property or to abuse the police and cadres. Inciting crowds to cause disturbances, and slander and defamation were absolutely impermissible. A week later only the posters in 'People's Park' remained.

The drive for 'Socialist Legality'

A factor stimulating the 'Democracy Movement' in Beijing, Shanghai and other cities at this time was the knowledge that the Chinese leadership was paying considerable attention to the need to establish 'Socialist Legality' as a means of ensuring that the arbitrary use of power which had so marked the Cultural Revolution could never happen again. To some extent this reflected an official desire to return to the 'good old days' before the Cultural Revolution when China had possessed a legal system which, although harsh in its treatment of transgressors, was not completely arbitrary.

There was, for example, a considerable corpus of law. In the decade following the promulgation of the State Constitution of 1954 more than 1,100 important laws and decrees had been enacted[18] to add to the handful of very wide-ranging statutes which had provided a loose framework for the administration of a decidedly rough justice in the consolidation period (1949–53). Moreover, there were recognisable institutions charged with the task of law enforcement. Theoretically, the Public Security (police) organs were responsible for the maintenance of public order; the investigation, arrest and detention of suspects; and the administration of the prisons and 'Reform Through Labour' camps. The offices of the Procuratorate decided who should be prosecuted and provided the personnel, and the court network tried offenders.

In practice, however, it was the police who dominated in all matters of law enforcement. *They* decided who to prosecute and the Procuratorate usually rubber-stamped their decisions and got on with the job. The police also decided who was guilty and what sentences should be given; the courts functioned mainly as educational institutions which publicised the offenders' guilt as a lesson to others. Indeed the police had the power to imprison without trial in certain cases and, as prison sentences were virtually open-ended in that they could be shortened or lengthened in the light of a prisoner's willingness to 'reform', the police had considerable discretion to recommend parole or an extension of sentence. Even after release, ex-offenders were subjected to a more-or-less permanent system of probation under public supervision.

Furthermore, the police exercised fairly tight control over the lives of all citizens. Each household was required to keep a registration book of those domiciled within, travel was exceedingly difficult without police permission, and itinerants had to register with the local police on arrival at their destination. Use was also made of the old Chinese system of mutual surveillance. A network of residents' committees, Youth League branches and other mass organisations made it their business to keep a watchful eye on unlawful or unseemly behaviour on the part of their members, privacy being a commodity accorded little respect in Chinese society.

It is not surprising, therefore, that China was an orderly society with little crime in the normal sense. Nevertheless, in many respects the system contained a great measure of predictability. The government devoted considerable attention, through its highly efficient propaganda network, to telling its citizens how to behave. And, in terms of ordinary crime the police did not act in an arbitrary manner. Many of them took their job seriously, spent a great deal of time amassing evidence, and usually arrested someone only after they had built up a solid case. Importance was paid to following the 'proper procedures'. Similarly, penalties could be reduced if the offender manifested a desire to reform, which could best be done by making a full confession or through 'achieving merit' by turning 'State's Evidence'.

More informally, ordinary citizens could adjust their actions in the light of such 'case law' as had been built up over the years. People of 'bad' class backgrounds, together with Party and State cadres in 'positions of trust', were aware that their sins would be punished more severely then those of 'the masses'. Timing, too, was important. By 1966 the Chinese political system had settled into a pattern of phases of mobilisation alternating with periods of relaxation and routinisation, and appropriate codes of behaviour had developed for each.

In the area of *political* crime, however, predictability was often lacking. Here fragile legal structures and procedures could easily be by-passed by the waves of mass campaigns which played a major part in the political system. And, moreover, a new element could enter the legal equation in the shape of the *secret* police. For in addition to the *State* legal organs discussed above, there were *Party* organs charged with security work. Until recently little was known of the activities of such bodies, but in November 1978 they were discussed in some detail by Hu Yaobang. In a speech attacking Kang Sheng, the life-long crony of Jiang Qing who had presided over the secret police until his death in 1975, Hu revealed that:

[In May 1951] . . . the Central Committee held a meeting to study the problems of suppression of counter-revolutionaries and of a new organisation and system of public security. From the present perspective the meeting adopted a/wrong resolution: division of the security system into two and integration of the Soviet model into the public security system. Henceforth, there emerged in China a security department which coexists with, and even dominates, the Ministry of Public Security, and stays above the control of any state administrative department. Later it became the Social Department, the Central Investigation Department, or the Central Security Bureau [of the Party]. Like the Soviet Union, there is a secret committee for suppression of counter-revolutionaries, besides an open police force. When it was established it rested on good will. But the mysterious line it followed made it possible for the knife of the organisation to fall on our own head rather than on the enemy's when its powers were concentrated in the hands of an evil man.[19]

As early as 1951 Kang Sheng followed an 'erroneous Stalinist line' creating a number of framed-up cases and killing a number of comrades. Thereafter,

He manipulated secret and security departments, established a wide network of intelligence action groups, imposed lynch law, unscrupulously obtained confessions by compulsion and gave them credence, and brought under his supervision old-generation proletarian revolutionaries and Party leaders, including Chairman Mao and Premier Zhou.[20]

The Cultural Revolution increased Kang Sheng's power and also severely damaged the State legal organs, which were early victims of the Left's determination to drag out 'capitalist-roaders'. In 1967 the Leftist factions 'seized power' by invading and ransacking police stations and court buildings and by beating, torturing or imprisoning police and legal officials who, by the very nature of their work, tended to be on the side of established authority and therefore easy targets for the 'rebels'. In one province alone it was later claimed that 281 police stations were sacked, and over 100,000 dossiers were stolen, as were large quantities of guns and ammunition.[21]

Throughout 1967 and 1968 legal institutions virtually ceased to function and mob-rule was the order of the day throughout most of urban China. Rival factions battled for supremacy, sought revenge for real or imagined grievances, and acted with massive violence. Hundreds of thousands of cadres from Liu Shaoqi downwards were paraded before

rallies of Red Guard activists where they were abused, tor-
mented and sometimes tortured as a prelude to being thrown
into prison or labour camp where some of them remained
until, finally, rehabilitation had to be posthumous, as the sad
and sorry stream of memorial meetings to honour dead comrades, held from 1977 onwards, testified.

In some cases factions even set up their own private prisons.
For example, in the Tianjin Soda Works a secret prison was
established by the 'responsible person' there, where his
'ruffians' used torture to extract confessions from 'leading
cadres and the broad masses', and held them in custody for
long periods. In 1970 when outrage was mounting, the
'responsible person' found a masterly way of suppressing it.
He issued a directive making it an offence to comment on the
prison's existence.[22]

The long-term existence of such institutions is further
attested by a case in Beijing. Here, after the Public Security
Bureau was taken over by the Leftists, fifty-six children of
senior government officials were arrested and put in what was
euphemistically called a 'study class' but was, in fact, an
unofficial prison. 70 per cent of them were under 20, one
was only 14, and some were held there for five years. They
were worked hard, ill-treated and forced to write lengthy
reports on their parents' alleged crimes.[23]

Although the worst of the violence was over by 1969, Kang
Sheng's secret police remained active, and Kang himself was
reportedly used by Lin Biao who said: 'Lenin needed Feliks
E. Djerzhinski [founder of CHEKA, the first Soviet police
organ]; Stalin needed Laurenti P. Beria; Wladuslaw Gomulka,
worrying about his life, also needed Moczar [head of the
Polish secret police]; so we also needed such a man as Kang
Sheng to use the knife in his hands to behead others.'[24]

It is claimed that Kang not only organised 'spy cases' but
that he may have been involved in the assassination of various
leaders who died during this period.

Hence by 1976 there was a real fear in China of the 'knock
on the door' and the leadership drive to end this situation
was strengthened by the fact that high-ranking cadres had
been at least as likely to be the victims as ordinary citizens.
Three measures were adopted to put matters right. The first

of these we have already noted: the campaign to rehabilitate victims unjustly accused, which began in 1977, swelled in 1978, and culminated early in 1980 with the reversal of verdicts on Liu Shaoqi and public promises that such tragedies would never be allowed to recur.[25]

The second was less public, consisting of decisions within the Party leadership to curb the powers of the secret police. In his speech of November 1978, Hu Yaobang announced that the Central Committee intended to abolish 'organisations for special cases' and to recruit a better class of person into security work. It also resolved to rid the security organs of unsuitable personnel, defined as:

> ... those who are pushy but illiterate, wavering but preju-
> diced, credulous simpletons who deem themselves wise.
> Those who indulge in catching at shadows, who are foolish
> and stupid, easy-going, inept or who fumble things, do
> their work carelessly, and lack drive. They may do other
> jobs but not security work.

He also stated that, in future, it would be expressly forbidden when launching campaigns to fix a target for the number to be sentenced.

The third measure, and the one to receive most publicity, was to hold open discussions on the need to reform the *State* legal system. An early sign of this came in the State Constitution promulgated in March 1978. Whereas its prede-cessor of 1975 had reflected the real power of the police by announcing that henceforth they would exercise procura-torial functions, it was now announced that the Procuratorate had been re-established as a separate entity. Later in the year the official press published statements made in 1957 (a high point in earlier attempts to establish 'socialist legality') by Dong Biwu, a veteran Communist who was then President of the Supreme People's Court, in which he had argued that a well-developed legal system was the hallmark of a modern state and that China still had a long way to go.[26] Thereafter, the Commission for Legal Affairs of the Standing Committee of the National People's Congress was re-established and, in June 1979, the drafts of seven new laws were presented to the second session of the fifth National People's Congress for implementation as of 1 January 1980.

Naturally enough those active in the 'Democracy Movement' were encouraged by these developments, and made their own contributions to the debate. Indeed, Chinese dissenters had pointed to the legal inadequacies of the Chinese state long before the post-Mao leadership took up the cause. In November 1974, for example, a group of youths in Guangzhou, writing under the collective name of 'Li Yizhe', had produced a massive wallposter making the link between 'Socialist Democracy and Legality' in which they complained bitterly of the injustices of the 'Lin Biao system', arguing that it had survived his death.[27] For their pains the authors were imprisoned but were released in 1979. The need for 'Socialist Legality' was a common theme in the posters and unofficial journals of 1978–9. As the journal *Renmin Zhisheng* (*Voice of the People*) neatly put it, it was essential to perfect the legal system so as to 'free the Motherland from nightmares'.[28]

These activists, however, were naïve in assuming that the leadership's desire to establish 'Socialist Legality' would protect their 'democratic rights' in the Western sense. For, at the very time official moves were being made to improve the legal system, steps were being taken to suppress the 'Democracy Movement'.

The fall of 'Democracy Wall'

The clamp-down in Shanghai, already alluded to, was accompanied by even more serious suppression in Beijing. In the early months of 1979 reports began to circulate that the police were taking a keen interest in certain 'democracy' activists and that one of them had been arrested. She was Fu Yuehua, a young municipal worker who had involved herself in assisting out-of-town petitioners to find shelter and food during their sometimes lengthy and unprofitable sojourns in Beijing. Wei Jingsheng's journal, *Exploration*, raised her case and, moreover, touched on another sensitive subject by publishing an account of conditions in a maximum security prison near Beijing (where, it was rumoured, Jiang Qing was being held), which referred to it as a 'Chinese Bastille'. These articles, together with his attacks on the leadership past and present, contributed to Wei's own arrest on 29 March.

At that time the Beijing authorities published a circular to rein in the 'Democracy Movement'. This stated that 'all slogans, posters, books, journals . . . and other publications which oppose socialism, the dictatorship of the proletariat, the leadership of the Chinese Communist Party, Marxism-Leninism-Mao Zedong Thought . . . are prohibited'. On 5 April, the third anniversary of Tiananmen, *People's Daily* warned that no one should make 'revolution' without official leadership, and Tiananmen was well-patrolled by police to ensure that there were no untoward demonstrations. Police read out new regulations forbidding the placing of posters in the square and promptly tore down from the Martyrs' Memorial a poetic eulogy to Zhou Enlai. Leaflets reporting the arrest of Ren Wanding, another dissenter, were confiscated.[29]

In the weeks that followed, reports of other arrests circulated, including that of Yang Kuang, the deputy editor of *Exploration*. Then, in June, the Beijing authorities tightened restrictions on unauthorised contacts with foreigners. Unless on official business, Chinese were expressly forbidden to have meals with foreigners, visit them in their homes or give them their addresses.[30] 'Fraternisation' was officially over and from then on the 'Democracy Movement' was severely weakened, and the unofficial journals ceased regular publication, although *Exploration* did issue a statement in May urging foreign governments to press for the release of those detained.[31]

Throughout the summer of 1979 there were signs that the leadership was divided on how best to handle the 'Democracy Movement'. On 8 September, for example, the *Guangming Daily* published an article urging that free exchange of opinions was the best way to arrive at the truth and that debates should be allowed to run their full course. The September issue of *Red Flag* admitted that it had made errors of political line and attitude in 1978 by being too dogmatic and refusing to test the canons of Maoism against actual conditions. There was also speculation that Hua Guofeng's impending visit to

Western Europe might be accompanied by a 'goodwill' gesture of releasing the dissenters.

In October, however, it became clear that a decision to take a hard line had prevailed: Wei Jingsheng was brought to trial. Foreign journalists together with some of his friends and relatives were excluded from the courtroom, and the trial took place before an 'invited' audience. Two hours before the verdict was given, the *Xinhua News Agency* referred to Wei as a 'counter-revolutionary'.[32]

The charges against him were 'disseminating counter-revolutionary propaganda' and 'disclosing military intelligence to foreigners'. The latter charge related to conversations Wei had had with French and British journalists at the time of China's invasion of Vietnam in February. In his defence statement Wei admitted to the conversations but asserted that he had possessed no secret information. Everything he knew came from reading the newspapers and from what he had gleaned from the 'grapevine'. If, he argued, he had inadvertently picked up secrets from the media, were they not equally guilty of disseminating military intelligence? In reply to a prosecution claim that he had failed to observe the 'rules for safeguarding state secrets' he observed that no one had ever told him what these were. Emphasising that at no time had he had access to confidential government documents he ridiculed the court for regarding the trivial information at his disposal as being of importance to national security. Thus he said: 'I talked about the name of our commanding general at the front. Who has ever heard that one side has won a battle because it kept the name of its commander secret?'[33]

The prosecution was not impressed. It pointed out that regulations had been introduced in 1951 on the maintenance of national security and that the matters discussed by Wei were covered by these. The fact that Wei claimed to have received his information through the grapevine was of no consequence, as this did not prevent its being classified. Wei's counter-revolutionary intent was also relevant.

On the charge of disseminating counter-revolutionary propaganda, Wei defended himself on the grounds that the Constitution guaranteed freedom of speech and this meant that he had the right to criticize both Marxism and the leadership. But the prosecution responded by arguing that the Constitution laid down that the nation's guiding ideology was Marxism-Leninism-Mao Zedong Thought and that the national system was socialist. Any 'slanders' against either were, therefore, counter-revolutionary acts:

> Our Constitution stipulates that you have freedom of belief, and that you may believe or disbelieve Marxism-Leninism-Mao Zedong Thought, but it also states that you are definitely forbidden to oppose it — for opposition is a violation of the Constitution, and violation of the Constitution lays you open to legal sanctions.[34]

On 16 October Wei was found guilty and was sentenced to fifteen years' imprisonment, to be followed by a further three years' deprivation of political rights. The harshness of his sentence was probably due to three factors. The first was the decision to make an example of him in order to deter others; the second was his willingness to publicise discontent before the foreign press corps; the third (and probably the major reason) was his insistence on maintaining his innocence. Had he confessed his 'errors' and expressed contrition, as other dissenters were later reported to have done, he may well have escaped much more lightly.

From then on the 'Democracy Movement' withered away. A few issues of unofficial journals appeared in subsequent months but most had disappeared by March 1980. The 'Democracy Wall' at Xidan was also scrubbed clean and a greatly inferior substitute was provided in the form of a small, enclosed park, where *signed* posters could be put up under the watchful eye of the police. Finally, the constitutional provisions permitting the expression of discontent were repealed. For in February 1980 the fifth plenum of the eleventh Central Committee issued a communiqué which declared:

> The Plenary Session holds that it is our Party's unswerving policy to carry forward socialist democracy and perfect the socialist legal system and to guarantee that the masses have the full right and opportunity to express their views

on state affairs and make suggestions to and criticize Party and government leaders. But experience shows that the practices of 'speaking out freely, airing views fully, holding great debates and writing big-character posters' are not a good way to achieve this. These practices, taken as a whole, never played a positive role in safeguarding the people's democratic rights but, on the contrary, hampered the people in the normal exercise of their democratic rights. To help eliminate factors causing instability . . .[the plenum] proposes to the National People's Congress that this section be deleted from the Constitution.[35]

'Socialist Legality' revisited

The depressing fate of Wei Jingsheng and his fellow-campaigners might seem to suggest that official concern for 'Socialist Legality' consisted solely of platitudes and that those in power were continuing to bend the law as they saw fit. However, it would not be fair to assume that the post-Mao leadership was simply acting with cynicism and duplicity in first tolerating and later suppressing dissent. It is evident that a real debate on the limits of tolerance did take place in 1978–9, that this was reflected in the official media, and that a measure of ambiguity resulted. It is also likely that some leaders, initially sympathetic to liberalisation, were scandalised by some of the events which followed. Leaders *were* sometimes unjustly slandered in posters and journals, and demonstrators sometimes *did*, as in Shanghai, go beyond the bounds of legitimate protest as defined in liberal-democratic societies. The new freedom also had its seedy side: 'dirty' photographs did circulate and there were cases of Chinese girls prostituting themselves for foreigners. Overseas Chinese and, more rarely, foreigners did contribute to a black market in Western consumer goods.

Moreover, ambiguities aside, official statements on 'Legality' were always prefaced by the term 'Socialist' and this fact was sometimes ignored by the dissenters. If we look at the laws introduced in 1979 it is abundantly clear that the state remained consistent on the need to suppress *political* crime.

Nevertheless, on all other matters the legal reforms constituted a major step forward.

Consider, for example, the *Criminal Law*, introduced in June 1979.[36] Based on drafts produced before the Cultural Revolution, this gave China its first Criminal Code since 1949. In some respects it remained vague and sweeping in its provisions, particularly with regard to political offences. Thus twenty-four articles dealt with 'counter-revolutionary' crimes. These included such standard offences as plotting to overthrow the government, leading armed rebellions, seducing soldiers to turn traitor, and destroying military installations. But it also echoed earlier enactments by making it an offence to use 'counter-revolutionary slogans . . . to spread propaganda inciting the overthrow of the political power of the dictatorship of the proletariat and the socialist system' — a phrase which could mean just about anything.

That aside, the *Criminal Law* had the great merit of bringing together in one relatively short document the major categories of criminal offence and the range of penalties they were likely to attract. Eleven articles dealt with 'violations of public security' and related primarily to crimes of arson and sabotage likely to endanger life, limb and public property. 'Acts against the socialist economic order' were the subject of fifteen articles dealing with smuggling, forgery, profiteering and speculation; damage to the environment was also covered.

Nineteen articles dealt with acts against citizens' personal and democratic rights. These included such 'ordinary' crimes as murder, manslaughter, rape, assault and battery, but also made special mention of offences which had become common in the Cultural Revolution. Thus penalties were laid down for extracting confessions by torture; gathering a crowd for 'beating, smashing and looting'; bringing false charges; unlawfully incarcerating a person; and 'seriously insulting' him or her by any means, including the use of wallposters to spread libel.

Seven articles on 'Encroachments on property' covered the theft of public and private property, and embezzlement. The *Law* then gave attention to 'acts against public order', with twenty-two articles covering a splendid diversity of offences. These included obstructing an official in the performance of his duties; impersonating an official; 'practising witchcraft for the purpose of spreading rumours or swindling people'; being a professional gambler or organiser of gambling; selling obscene books or pictures 'for profit'; manufacturing or selling narcotics; and assembling a crowd to disturb public order in public places. Interestingly, illegal emigration only merited one year's imprisonment and those organising the traffic were to receive no more than five years.

'Acts against marriage and the family' were covered in six articles. These included forcing people to marry against their will, committing bigamy and (an interesting footnote on the influence of the People's Liberation Army in Chinese politics) cohabiting with the spouse of a soldier. 'Vile cases' of failing to look after elderly or sick family members were also criminal offences. Finally, the *Law* laid down penalties for state functionaries who abused their positions by taking bribes, showing favouritism and practising nepotism; as well as those who opened other people's mail 'without permission'.

In all cases the appropriate penalties were stipulated. In ascending order of degrees of severity these were:

Surveillance — essentially a form of probation, not to exceed two years.

Detention — imprisonment by the local police for not more than six months, during which time the offender was allowed to return home for two days a month, and was to be paid for work done under police supervision.

Fixed term or life imprisonment — to be served in prison or labour camps.

Death penalty — by firing squad. Here the *Law* followed earlier statutes by insisting that this should only be used for the most heinous offences *and*, moreover, that the penalty should often be deferred for two years, during which time the offender would be imprisoned and given the opportunity to show if he or she had 'reformed', in which case the sentence was to be commuted to imprisonment for life or a shorter period. (The Chinese have always claimed, *pace* Dr Johnson, that this was a splendid device for concentrating the mind!)

The *Law* also provided for 'supplementary' penalties, most notable of which are confiscation of property, fines and deprivation of political rights. It also echoed earlier enactments (and, indeed, ancient Chinese ideas on legal matters) by stressing that mercy should be shown to those who were contrite. Voluntary surrender, confession, and the achievement of merit by implicating fellow offenders were to be rewarded by reduced punishment. And even in gaol not all was lost — 'good behaviour' could result in early parole.

The *Law*, then, gave the citizen a reasonably clear picture as to what was forbidden, and the penalties the transgressor was likely to incur. On most of the criminal offences of a 'universal' nature (i.e., murder, theft, rape, arson, etc.), it was fairly specific. To be sure, it continued the principle of 'crime by analogy' laid down in earlier enactments in that a person might be punished for an offence not specified in the *Law*, which 'approximated' to one which was. But in such cases, the Supreme People's Court was to pronounce on the desirability or otherwise of such a move. For the most part, then, it constituted a 'Good Citizen's Guide to Keeping Out of Trouble', and it was reinforced by a *Law on Criminal Procedure*, adopted at the same time.[37] Indeed, this *Law* was of especial importance in that it made meticulous arrangements for the handling of criminal cases, and carefully defined the rights and responsibilities of the legal organs and those accused.

Thus it distinguished between the functions of the three branches of the legal *apparat*. The police were to investigate and detain suspects. The Procuratorate was to approve arrests, check on police investigations and, where appropriate, institute prosecution. The People's Courts were to try cases. 'No other government organ, institution, organisation or person has the right to exercise such powers.' It was laid down that in minor cases, where a private individual filed a suit, a court could handle the matter on its own initiative; in cases of corruption or 'dereliction of duty' the Procuratorate could choose to prosecute independently; otherwise the police were to initiate proceedings. The *Law* carefully specified the sort of cases which were to be tried at different levels, and laid down stipulations as to when legal officials must withdraw from a case (interested parties, relatives involved, etc.).

It spelled out that the accused was entitled to a defence by him or herself, a lawyer, someone appointed by a mass organisation or work unit, a relative or a guardian. The court 'might' appoint an advocate for someone who had failed to do so.

The accused or his or her advocate had the right to see the material pertaining to the case, witnesses had to be available for examination and (shades of confessions extracted by torture), no one could be convicted on the basis of a 'statement' unsupported by other evidence.

The *Law* also made careful provision for those who might help the police with their enquiries. Criminals caught in, before or immediately after the act, together with 'major suspects' could be put under arrest by anyone, as could escaped prisoners and those on 'wanted lists'. Otherwise the police had to produce a warrant from the Procuratorate. After arrest, a detainee's family were normally to be informed within twenty-four hours. Moreover, the police were required to ask the Procuratorate to examine and approve the arrest within 3 days. The *Law* also stipulated the time in which the accused should normally be brought to trial, and laid down detailed regulations governing delays in so doing. It also stipulated that trials should be public (except where state secrets were involved or where the innocent might suffer unnecessary embarrassment), and that there were to be proper appeal procedures.

Further laws were also enacted in 1979 governing, inter alia, the organisation of the courts and the Procuratorate.[38] Taken together, and in conjunction with editorials urging legal personnel to apply them conscientiously, it is evident that a serious attempt was being made to give Chinese citizens real rights. As we have seen, these stopped short of the rights enjoyed in liberal-democracies. But they did offer something which had been missing for many years, and which is widely regarded as a major function of good government: predictability. This, in essence, was what Deng and other leaders were trying to achieve. Although they would have disliked the comparison, they were in some respects echoing the philosophy of Han Fei, the 'Legalist', who had asserted that the Prince might legislate as he pleased, but he had the duty to ensure that his laws were clear and readily understood.

7

1981: The Year of the Verdicts

Prelude: preparing the ground

On 18 June 1979 Hua delivered his 'Report on the Work of the Government' to the second session of the fifth National People's Congress in which he emphasised that the leadership was indeed attempting to create a fairer and more constitutional framework for the Chinese political system. Then he dwelt on the fact that class-based divisions and 'labels' of the Maoist era were no longer appropriate. Landlords, rich peasants and capitalists had ceased to exist as separate classes, he said, and he also noted that 'the work of removing the Rightist label from those designated as such has been completed, and most of those who were wrongly labelled have been rehabilitated'.

He also acknowledged that 'the masses' should be allowed to 'criticize and supervise leading bodies and leading cadres', so as to 'overcome bureaucracy and conservatism, promptly expose political degenerates, grafters and embezzlers, counter-revolutionaries and criminals and consolidate the socialist cause and the socialist state'. He claimed that the leadership was striving to 'take heed' of popular opinion, and that suggestions and criticisms were to be given due publicity in the press. He urged that greater attention be paid to the wishes and needs of groups which had been disadvantaged, particularly national minorities, women and youth.

Because of China's 'long feudal tradition' and because the country was 'relatively backward economically and culturally' there were problems of 'autocracy, bureaucracy, love of privilege, the patriarchical style of work, and anarchism'. These, he suggested, should be solved through institutional

means. The elective principle was to be extended at the grass-
roots and 'people's deputies' were to be given the facilities to
allow them to act effectively. He warned, however, and presumably with the danger of 'anarchism' in mind, that 'all
conspiracies and acts of sabotage by anti-socialist elements
must be resolutely suppressed'.[1]

The themes in Hua's speech were repeated and enlarged
upon throughout 1980, as China continued to move away
from the patterns of the Maoist era. What is not clear is
whether Hua sincerely believed that such changes were necessary or was merely attempting to safeguard his position by
falling into line with the views of the 'reformers' round Deng.
In the event, Hua was skilled and experienced enough to delay
his fall and, perhaps, to 'cushion' it when it eventually came.
But he was either unwilling or unable to hang on to the power
he had obtained in October 1976.

For Deng and his supporters were able to increase their
strength and impose still further their technocratic and non-
Maoist strategies, creating an atmosphere in which Hua's
position as the 'chosen successor' became ultimately unten-
able. Thus, at the fourth plenum of the eleventh Central
Committee, which met in Beijing from 25 to 28 September
1979, a number of new appointments were made which
added to Deng's support. Thus Peng Zhen, whose attempts
to impede the development of the Cultural Revolution were
noted in Chapter 1, was elected to the Politbureau. So, too,
was Zhao Ziyang.[2] In the Cultural Revolution Zhao had been
purged from his post as First Party Secretary in the major
province of Guangdong and, although he re-emerged in 1971
he was then relegated to a post in Inner Mongolia, a very
clear demotion. He returned to Guangdong again in 1974 and
the following year was posted to Sichuan, China's most popu-
lous province. There he was successful in restoring the provincial economy after the devastation of the Cultural Revolution
and became known for his un-Maoist approach to economic
matters.

When the fifth plenum met in Beijing, from 23 to 29
February 1980, the power of the 'reformers' grew still further.
In particular, the post of General Secretary (which had been
in abeyance since the start of the Cultural Revolution) was

revived, and Hu Yaobang was appointed. Hu was an experienced veteran who had been on the Long March and, before the Cultural Revolution, had held key posts in youth work and provincial administration. Purged in the Cultural Revolution, he had survived the fall of the 'Gang of Four' to become Head of the Organisation and Propaganda Department of the Central Committee. At the fifth plenum Hu was elected to the Standing Committee of the Politbureau, as was Zhao Ziyang.[3]

The plenum also removed from all their Party and state posts, four leaders who were regarded as having been too close to the 'Gang of Four' and too unwilling to accommodate themselves to changes brought in since 1976. In fact all four had been severely criticized in private at the time of the third plenum in 1978. But it was a sign of the new insistence on observing the proprieties that the fifth plenum refrained from openly discussing their 'crimes' or 'errors' and simply 'approved the requests to resign' which the four were supposed to have made. Among them were Wang Dongxing and Wu De.

Deng's faction was then in a position both to impose more measures in the direction of constitutionalism and to deprive Hua of yet more of his power. On 18 August 1980 Deng gave a major speech at a Politbureau meeting, in the course of which he dealt with matters to be raised at the third session of the fifth National People's Congress which was about to be convened. In the course of this he gave a very clear view of what he thought was wrong with China, and what should be done to put it right.

First, he said that it was necessary to move away from that excessive concentration of power which had hindered 'the full exercise of collective wisdom' and resulted in 'individual arbitrariness'. Secondly, it was not to be permitted to 'hold too many concurrent posts and deputised positions'. An individual's knowledge, experience and energy were limited, and holding too many posts made it impossible to work effectively. Thirdly, it was necessary to begin to separate Party and governmental affairs, and to stop using the Party as a substitute for the government. Fourthly, it was time for China's gerontocrats to step down: 'Let the younger comrades go to the first line while the older comrades act well as advisers to support them.' He particularly stressed the need to promote young people with good qualifications and, on the other hand, condemned the system of 'lifelong tenure for leadership positions'.

In a blistering attack on bureaucracy, Deng observed that it existed throughout the political spheres of both Party and state. He described its principal manifestations as:

> . . . holding forth in high positions, abusive usage of authority, isolation from reality, keeping aloof from the masses, fondness of keeping up appearances, fondness of empty talk, ossified thinking, sticking to conventions, bloated organisations, having more people than there is work for them, stalling and dragging in work, no emphasis on efficiency, irresponsibility, breaking promises, issuance of needless official papers, mutual dodging of responsibility, excessive bureaucratic airs, constantly dressing down other people, retaliation for personal grudges, suppressing democracy, deceiving the superiors and deluding the subordinates, imperiousness and despotism, favouritism and bribery, taking bribes and bending the law . . . [4]

All these, he said, had reached 'intolerable proportions'. Partly, they were the result of feudal attitudes such as the 'patriarchal mentality'. Thus, during the Cultural Revolution, when one man became an official even 'his chickens and dogs ascended to heaven'; when one man was down and out, 'even his remotest relatives were persecuted'.

But, Deng asserted, part of the problem was the way in which socialism had developed in China. He observed that bureaucracy had

> . . . a close association with our long-standing belief that socialism and planned management must have systems highly characterised by concentrated power over economics, politics, culture and society. *Our leadership organs at various levels have customarily managed a great number of matters that they should not manage, cannot manage and must not*

manage at all. So long as there are regulations and rules, these matters can be handled with much ease by the lower-level enterprises, businesses, and social units . . . [5]

Deng's speech had an immediate impact which went far beyond the confines of the Politbureau. On 28 August, as the third session of the fifth National People's Congress convened, the press echoed certain of his remarks in a thinly veiled criticism of Hua. Thus, it was stated that: 'The patriarchal system of lifetime tenure *and the system of designating successors by the "patriarch"* cannot make the "patriarch" and his designated successor wiser.'[6] On 7 September Hua addressed the Congress and repeated, in somewhat diluted form, many of the points made by Deng. He announced that he had proposed to the Central Committee that he should surrender the premiership; this had been accepted, and Zhao Ziyang had been appointed to replace him. Hua also announced that a number of veteran cadres, including Deng and Li Xiannian, had given up their posts as Vice-Premiers because they were 'advanced in age'.[7]

The session was, in fact, the most lively in the history of the People's Republic. It reverted to a pre-Cultural Revolution practice of deliberating in public, with foreigners in the press gallery, and there was genuine and lively debate in which individual deputies put forward the opinions (often conflicting) of different sections of society. The deputies themselves had been properly elected. Although it would be fanciful to compare it with a liberal-democratic legislature, it was a vast improvement on the fourth National People's Congress held in January 1975 which, although serving as the platform for Zhou Enlai's launching of the 'Four Modernisations', had been characterised by much 'unanimous acceptance' and 'prolonged applause', and which appears to have been attended by deputies who had not been 'elected' in any meaningful sense.[8] The event, therefore, was a further step in the Long March away from the Cultural Revolution. And it was followed by the delivery of formal verdicts on three 'matters arising'. These were: the fate of the 'Gang of Four', the position of Hua, and the legacy of Mao.

The trial of the 'Gang'

The formal decision to establish a special court to prosecute the 'Gang of Four' (and the surviving members of Lin Biao's 'counter-revolutionary clique') was taken by the Standing Committee of the fifth National People's Congress on 27 September 1980.[9] In fact, various pre-trial hearings had already taken place.[10] The final indictment named ten defendants as well as listing malefactors now dead, such as Lin Biao and Kang Sheng. Those who actually faced the court when proceedings began on 20 November were Jiang Qing, Zhang Chunqiao, Yao Wenyuan, Wang Hongwen, Huang Yongsheng, Wu Faxian, Li Zuopeng, Qiu Huizuo, Jiang Tengjiao and, to complete the list, the 76 year old Chen Boda. Forty-eight charges were laid against the defendants but these could loosely be subsumed, in the words of the indictment, under the general accusation that the defendants were all 'principal culprits of the Lin Biao and Jiang Qing counter-revolutionary cliques' who:

> ... acted in collusion during the 'great Cultural Revolution' and, taking advantage of their positions and the power at their disposal, framed and persecuted Communist Party and state leaders in a premeditated way in an attempt to usurp Party leadership and state power and overthrow the political power of the dictatorship of the proletariat. They did this by resorting to all kinds of intrigues and using every possible means, legal or illegal, overt or covert, by pen or by gun.[11]

The 'cliques' were obviously tried at the same time so that one would suffer by identification with the other, and the prosecution regularly sought to establish linkages between individual members of each when handling specific charges in the indictment. However, the court established two tribunals, the first of which dealt with the 'civilian' 'Gang of Four' and Chen Boda, while the second heard the case against the five military men. As Chen Boda and the soldiers had ceased to play any part in Chinese politics by late 1971, the fol-

lowing discussion will restrict itself largely to a considera-
tion of the trial as it affected the 'Gang of Four'.

The trial did not take place 'in open court' in any meaningful sense. Foreign observers were banned and there was only
a specially-invited and rotating audience of Chinese. Many of
them were victims and their relatives. Moreover, although the
trial was given massive coverage on television and in the press,
this was partial and highly selective. No full transcript of the
proceedings was published. Altogether both tribunals 'held
forty-two sessions for investigation and debate, during which
forty-nine witnesses and victims appeared in court to testify,
and 873 pieces of evidence were examined'.[12]

The demeanour of the accused varied considerably. Yao
Wenyuan was the only one of the 'Four' to exercise his
right to legal representation and, although insisting that he
had committed 'mistakes' rather than 'crimes', was generally
co-operative. Evidently well-rehearsed, on one occasion he
had to spend a full minute flicking through a thick bundle
of notes when asked a question apparently out of turn. Wang
Hongwen, a pathetic shadow of his former self, confirmed
his guilt and implicated his colleagues. Zhang Chunqiao,
evidently convinced that he had nothing to lose, treated the
court with open contempt, refusing to say a word.

But it was Jiang Qing who lived up to her role as principal
villain of the piece. On her first appearance, she entered the
courtroom with head held high and an expression of haughty
disdain on her face. She responded to questions with replies
that she 'couldn't remember' and a general air of boredom.
On at least two occasions, however, she rounded angrily
on her accusers and was forcibly removed from the courtroom for 'disrupting order'.

If Jiang was making full use of her gifts as an actress, her
behaviour was entirely appropriate. For as one foreign
observer in Beijing pointed out at the time, the trial was 'a
piece of theatre that rivets the entire country to radios and
televisions each evening as the episodes unfold'. He continued:

An utterly Chinese pageant, this trial-as-theatre solves one
mystery, only to create two or three more. Each conspiracy
is shown to envelop several others. The most innocent acts

are seen by the audience to have ulterior motives as the culprits plot to purge their rivals, seize power and even murder Mao.

Ordinary Chinese, brought up on tales of the ancient imperial courts and their intrigues, a literary genre here, are suddenly admitted to those of the Mao court.

They eavesdrop on the top leaders, including the conspirators, all of whose conversations have been carefully tape-recorded and transcribed, complete with expletives. They hear about their leaders meeting late into the night, their secret trips around the country by special planes, their tangled alliances, their nicknames for each other, their sharp infighting . . . And they get glimpses of their leaders' private lives, luxurious state guest houses, sumptuous meals, private limousines – a world unimaginable to most Chinese.[13]

And such traditional Chinese themes as usurpation of power and the machinations of corrupt officials were ultimately brought to a happy ending by finding the accused guilty. Space does not permit a full description of their crimes, but a few examples may be given of their multifarious 'counter-revolutionary' offences. Jiang Qing's included having 'framed and persecuted' Liu Shaoqi. In order to do this she had been responsible for the arrest, interrogation and torture of people she believed could supply evidence against him. Liu's own death and that of certain 'witnesses' against him were attributed to her.

On one occasion in 1968 it was claimed that she had 'worked hand in glove' with Kang Sheng 'to cook up false charges against no fewer than eighty-eight members and alternate members of the eighth Central Committee'. As a result of false charges she had made against the Minister of the Coal Industry in December 1968, he had been illegally incarcerated and beaten up, and later died of his wounds. She had also used the Cultural Revolution to seek to destroy evidence of her early days in Shanghai when, it was implied, her behaviour had been no better than one might expect from an actress of progressive leanings. Thus she had ordered the homes of five persons who had known her at that time to be ransacked in search of old letters, and the people concerned had been 'persecuted physically'. As late as 1976 she had worked with her three Shanghai cronies 'to create new disturbances across the country'. Finally, the court declared, 'she bore direct or indirect responsibilities for all the offences committed during the decade of turmoil by the counter-revolutionary clique she organised and led, of endangering the People's Republic of China, working to overthrow the Government and tyrannising the people'.[14]

Zhang Chunqiao, inter alia, was accused of having instigated Kuai Dafu, a radical Red Guard leader, to organize the first demonstration calling for the overthrow of Liu Shaoqi. Other crimes included engineering violent incidents in Shanghai and elsewhere during the Cultural Revolution, and having leading Shanghai cadres labelled as 'renegades', 'enemy agents' and 'counter-revolutionaries'. In collusion with Wang Hongwen he had built up the Shanghai militia and plotted an armed rebellion.

Yao Wenyuan was also found guilty of vilifying and framing cadres at various levels, and of having used his control of the media to conduct propaganda and agitation for counter-revolutionary ends over long periods. His role in branding Deng Xiaoping as the 'chief boss behind the counter-revolutionary political incident at Tiananmen Square' was specifically noted.

Wang Hongwen's particular claim to fame was that he had participated directly in acts of violence. In one particularly brutal incident in August 1967 he had organised an attack on the Shanghai diesel engine plant in which 650 people were imprisoned, wounded or maimed.

The judgement of the court, delivered on 23 January 1981, prescribed severe punishment. Jiang Qing and Zhang Chunqiao were both sentenced to death, subject to a two-year reprieve. This form of sentence was common in Chinese law, as noted earlier, and was normally intended to give the prisoner an opportunity to manifest repentance. Jiang's immediate reaction was unpromising. As the death sentence was pronounced Beijing television viewers saw — but did not hear — her shout slogans as she was handcuffed, and she was unceremoniously ejected from the court.[15]

Yao Wenyuan was sentenced to twenty years' imprisonment and Wang Hongwen was gaoled for life. In view of Wang's willingness to confess, his sentence was surprisingly harsh. It may have reflected the fact that he, more than the others, had been personally involved in violent acts including, perhaps, a willingness to consider using the militia. Or it may simply have been because he was, at 45, the youngest defendant on trial and a limited sentence might not have sufficed to ensure that he would never again return to freedom. The other six defendants received sentences of sixteen to eighteen years. As their ages ranged from 61 to 76, there was little likelihood that any would ever complete them.

For foreign observers the decision to hold a trial appeared superfluous as the 'Gang' had already been condemned many times over. As we have noted earlier, the Central Committee had published lengthy documents cataloguing their numerous 'crimes' in considerable detail. The mass media had provided readers, listeners and viewers with saturation coverage from late October 1976 onwards. A trial might provide additional detail but could add little to the general picture. It also appeared to be a retrograde step. Many foreigners (and some Chinese) were bound to see the event as a ghoulish re-enactment of Stalin's show trials, and this at a time when the post-Mao leadership was proclaiming its commitment to 'Socialist Legality'. Then there was the range of problems presented by reliving the turmoil of the Cultural Revolution decade and the danger that mud would stick to present leaders and that the memory of certain dead ones would be sullied also.

Deng and his colleagues, however, saw matters in a different light. As was pointed out at the time, Chinese law did not presuppose the innocence of the accused until proven guilty. In this respect the torrent of adverse publicity, which made Western jurists shudder, was irrelevant. What did matter, in terms of 'Socialist Legality' was that 'proper procedure' be observed. The analogy with Nuremberg has been noted by various commentators and is not entirely fanciful. The 'Gang of Four' were deemed to have committed horrendous crimes and it was essential to bring them to trial both to prove their guilt beyond question and, symbolically, to purge the system of evil. Although not a 'fair trial' in the Western sense, the semi-public proceedings in Peking were at least a great improvement upon the happenings of the Cultural Revolution when thousands of luckless victims were beaten, tortured, harassed by kangaroo courts, or simply 'disappeared'.

Furthermore, the potential political embarrassment of the trial could be limited by judicious management and selective reporting. Where defendants admitted their guilt, well and good. Where they did not, their 'defiance' could also be presented as proof of their 'crimes'. The press fastened on Jiang Qing's arrogant behaviour from the moment she stepped into the courtroom.

And to some extent the trial was of value to Deng's faction precisely because it touched on sensitive issues. It was almost impossible for anyone to hear or read the harrowing evidence without concluding that the Cultural Revolution was completely devoid of redeeming features. It thus served to legitimate the new policies Deng was bent on pursuing. Equally it helped to pave the way for a new, and in many ways unflattering, appraisal of Mao which was already being prepared, and which is discussed later in this chapter.

And it assisted Deng's faction in its drive against Hua Guofeng. Hua's legitimacy rested largely on his claim to be Mao's successor, not only in the sense of having been 'appointed' by him but also in the sense of Hua maintaining continuity in policy terms. By denting the old chairman's image the trial dented the new one's also.

The fall of Hua Guofeng

With the convening of the 'Gang of Four' trial the pressure increased to remove Hua from his posts of Party Chairman and Chairman of the Military Commission. Reports reaching Hong Kong journals with a reputation for receiving 'inside information' indicated that the trial had been used to induce him to go quietly. It was claimed that the decision to drop from the indictment charges relating to the Tiananmen Incident, which inevitably would have raised ugly questions about Hua's role as Minister of Public Security at the time, was taken as a quid pro quo for Hua retiring gracefully. In view of the significance of that incident in focusing hatred of the 'Gang of Four', it is difficult to explain the trial's failure to exploit it to the full except in these terms.

In any event Hua was severely criticized at a Politbureau meeting which began on 13 November 1980. The Politbureau met for nine days in all, but sessions were interrupted by problems associated with the management of the trial and the meeting did not formally conclude until 5 December. Many Politbureau members attacked him for committing 'grave mistakes' in political and economic policy since Mao's death. These included showing an 'unclear attitude' on questions of 'rehabilitation'. It was said that he had deliberately delayed the return to power of Deng Xiaoping and Chen Yun, and had opposed the posthumous rehabilitation of Peng Dehuai. He had also disagreed with the decision to 'reverse verdicts' on the Tiananmen Incident. Ideologically, he had advanced the 'two whatevers' slogan and had been reluctant to support the alternative advanced by Deng, that 'practice is the sole criterion of truth'. It was claimed that he had not opposed the latter outright but had been 'reluctant to show his opinion on the issue' and had instructed certain provincial leaders, including those from Hunan and Hebei, not to express their views either. Furthermore, he had fostered his own personality cult by use of such phrases as 'Great Leader Chairman Hua', by having his portrait put alongside Mao's, by having his calligraphy posted everywhere, and by permitting excessive praising of himself. He had failed to propose any action for the 'liberation of thought' or the rectification of the economy, and had set excessively high targets.[16]

The Politbureau did affirm his achievements in fighting the 'Gang of Four' but considered him unfit for the high offices he held, and Hua offered to resign. It was agreed that his resignation should be offered to the sixth plenum of the eleventh Central Committee, and that that body should be asked to appoint Hu Yaobang as Party Chairman and Deng as Chairman of the Military Commission. In the interim Hu and Deng would assume these responsibilities informally, but Hua would be permitted to retain his 'ceremonial' functions by receiving foreign guests. It was also proposed that the sixth plenum should appoint Hua as a Vice-Chairman of the Central Committee.

It was assumed at the time that the sixth plenum would convene relatively quickly, but it did not do so. One reason was that it took longer than anticipated to reach an official consensus on the question of Mao, which the plenum was also expected to adopt. Another was that Hua apparently had second thoughts about surrendering power and failed to co-operate in his own political demise.

In fact Hua showed his displeasure less than a month after the 'nine-day meeting'.[17] On New Year's Day 1981, the Party leaders gave a celebratory tea party in the Great Hall of the People, and it was expected that Hua should attend in the interests of Party unity. When he failed to appear Hu Yaobang personally went to his house to request that he come. He discovered Hua resting 'in easy clothes' in a rear courtyard. 'Smiling wryly', Hua told Hu that he was ill and could not attend.

Hua's very 'Chinese' demonstration of distaste for the way he had been treated by making this 'withdrawal' from public life resulted in a postponement of the sixth plenum. Instead, in March, a further Politbureau meeting was held. On this occasion Hua's manner was much tougher than it had been earlier. Deng was apparently conciliatory and said that he hoped Hua would be appointed a Vice-Chairman of the Central Committee and member of the Standing Committee of the Politbureau once he had resigned his higher office. Hua showed his displeasure by giving two opinions of his own. First, he asserted that 'mine is the greatest merit in overthrowing the "Gang of Four" '. Secondly, that if it was felt that he was lacking in leadership ability he did not see how he could function as a Party Vice-Chairman either.

Hua's stubbornness was apparently due to a mood of sympathy for him which had developed after the 'nine-day meeting'. He still retained some powerful support, particularly in the PLA. In addition some leaders felt that his role in overthrowing the 'Gang of Four' was an outstanding achievement for which he was now receiving too little credit, and that his mistakes, although undoubted, were not inexcusable in the context of the very difficult situation prevailing in the years immediately following Mao's death. There was also the question of Hua's successor, Hu Yaobang. Not all of those who accepted that Hua had his limitations were convinced that Hu Yaobang's record demonstrated any manifest superiority.

Furthermore, Hua enjoyed reasonable popularity among the masses. It was perhaps ironic that his personality cult should have made so much of Hua's alleged modesty and humility. There was, nevertheless, a widespread feeling that he had not abused his position by amassing the special privileges of which so many senior cadres were fond. For example, it is known that one of the greatest perquisites available to the Chinese élite in recent years has been the ability to provide their children with access to superior education. Deng Xiaoping and many other cadres had sent their children abroad to study in foreign universities; Hua was not known to have done so.

In the spring there were two indications that matters remained unsettled. On 19 April, Li Xiannian received David Steel, leader of the British Liberal Party. He told him that the sixth plenum would probably be held in May or June 1981, but might have to be postponed still further.[18] Then, on May Day, an evening party attended by 15,000 guests was held in Beijing. Hua's arrival was greeted by a round of enthusiastic applause which lasted for more than ten minutes.

In June a preparatory meeting for the sixth plenum was held, at which Hua's supporters sought to minimise his fall by having him appointed a 'First' or 'Second' Vice-Chairman of the Central Committee. Debate raged for over ten days, and it was unofficially reported that two stories harmful to Hua were disseminated in Beijing. One of these was to the effect that Hua avidly pursued privilege after all. It was said that he had insisted on moving into a 'mysterious luxury official residence' previously occupied by Mao. The other concerned the famous utterance, 'with you in charge, I'm at ease'. There had, of course, always been considerable scepticism within China as to the veracity of this statement and to its context. Indeed, on the streets of Beijing it had been transformed into several exceedingly vulgar puns. The latest story claimed that the original note had been examined by doctors who had concluded that as Mao was suffering from Parkinson's disease he would have been physically incapable of writing or, at least, would not have been able to write characters which were recognisable. It was also pointed out that Mao's alleged note was not addressed to anyone nor was it dated or signed. In the circumstances it could scarcely be regarded as 'an imperial edict for assigning Hua Guofeng to the throne'.[19]

It is possible that these tales were the product of a 'dirty tricks' organisation seeking to undermine Hua but it seems far more likely that they signified popular recognition of the fact that Hua had at last lost. This was confirmed when the sixth plenum eventually met in Beijing from 27 to 29 June. It was attended by 195 members and 114 alternates, and 53 individuals identified only as 'non-voting participants' were also present, for reasons which remain unclear. The meeting finally brought to a close the era of Maoist influence by formally removing from power his 'chosen successor, by confirming the power of Deng Xiaoping's faction, and by issuing a weighty pronouncement on Mao which put the erstwhile Chairman in his place in more senses than one.

Technically, of course, Hua was not dismissed. The official communiqué of the plenum confirmed in skeletal outline some of the main points of the 'nine-day meeting' discussed above. Thus it acknowledged his 'contribution' to the overthrow of the 'Gang of Four' but carefully failed to recognise his major role. It also referred to the 'useful work' he had done thereafter. The communiqué itself was somewhat reticent in discussing his mistakes. But the 'Resolution on certain questions', discussed below, was more forthcoming, and declared:

... he promoted the erroneous 'two-whatevers' policy, that is, 'we firmly uphold whatever policy decisions Chairman Mao made, and we unswervingly adhere to whatever instructions Chairman Mao gave', and he took a long time to rectify the error. He tried to suppress the discussions on the criterion of truth unfolded in the country in 1978, which were very significant in setting things right. He procrastinated and obstructed the work of reinstating veteran cadres in their posts and redressing the injustices left over from the past (including the case of the 'Tiananmen

Incident' of 1976). He accepted and fostered the personality cult around himself while continuing the personality cult of the past.[20]

It was also said that Hua 'also had his share of responsibility for impetuously seeking quick results in economic work and for continuing certain other "Left policies" '.

As expected, Deng replaced Hua as Chairman of the Military Commission and Hu Yaobang became Party Chairman. Zhao Ziyang was elected as a Vice-Chairman. There was no mention of a replacement for Hu Yaobang as General Secretary, and it was not clear if he had, therefore, relinquished that power-ful post. However the plenum did elect Xi Zhongxun to the Secretariat of the Central Committee. A Party member since 1928, Xi had played an active revolutionary role in north-west China before liberation. From 1952 to 1962 he had worked in the State Council and had since been identified as a fol-lower of Deng's. It is possible that his appointment to the Secretariat was intended to groom him for the post of General Secretary. In any event it meant that Deng had suc-ceeded in moving yet another supporter into a key position.

Hua Guofeng was elected as an 'ordinary' Vice-Chairman, his supporters having lost the battle to accord him a prominent status at that level. His retention was justified:

> . . . as a return to the traditional way advocated by Mao Zedong, that is, allowing people to make mistakes and to correct them instead of using a club against them. Party history shows that knocking out a comrade once he commits some mistake would make people overcautious and prevent them from speaking their minds freely. This would damage democracy.[21]

Any suggestion these words may have conveyed to the effect that Hua's humiliation had now ended were negated only three weeks after the plenum. On 20 July 1981 a *People's Daily* article listed him along with Lin Biao as one of those responsible for building up the cult of Mao. Being placed in such company was hardly a good omen. The following day the paper repeated the charge that Hua had opposed until

March 1977 the return of Deng Xiaoping. It also said that he had authorised the arrests of an unspecified number of people in April 1977, on the first anniversary of Tiananmen.

Therefore, at the time of writing (July 1981) it would be foolhardy to predict whether the Chinese political system has developed to a stage where top leaders can be removed without being condemned to the dustbin of history. All that can be said is that the sixth plenum itself acted with an apparent moderation which contrasted markedly with the ways in which the losers had been treated in the struggles of the late Maoist era.

Thus as a Vice-Chairman Hua was also a member of the seven-man Standing Committee of the Politbureau, China's supreme inner leadership. So, too, was the aged and infirm Marshal Ye Jianying, whose support within the PLA and general prestige enabled him to ignore suggestions that the elderly should make way for younger men. The other five members, however, were all Deng's men. They were Deng himself; his protégés Hu Yaobang and Zhao Ziyang; and Li Xiannian and Chen Yun, the economics specialists who broadly shared Deng's views on the correct strategy for China's modernisation.

The 'Tragedy' of Mao

In addition to instituting leadership changes the plenum also adopted a 'Resolution on certain questions in the history of our Party since the founding of the People's Republic of China'. With an appropriate sense of history this was published on 30 June, the eve of the sixtieth anniversary of the Party. Despite its bland title this lengthy text was of the greatest importance, constituting as it did the leadership's attempt to bring to a close the agonising and divisive argument on Mao's role, so that the Chinese polity might devote its full attention to the tasks ahead.

The debate on Mao had raged with particular intensity since 1978 and had produced numerous interpretations from the pens of Party members, intellectuals and, as we have seen, participants in the 'Democracy Wall' movement. The writing of an 'official' resolution on the matter was raised by Marshal

Ye Jianying in his speech on the occasion of the thirtieth anniversary of the People's Republic in 1979. Drafting of the resolution started in March the following year under the direct guidance of the Standing Committee of the Politbureau and the Secretariat of the Central Committee. Members of the Party's top leadership 'took up the matter/personally by defining the contents and structure of the document, attending briefings, making concrete suggestions and revising the rough draft'.

In October 1980, 4,000 senior Party leaders discussed the first draft for twenty days and revised it. It then went 'through the hands' of some fifty senior Party leaders. In May 1981, the Politbureau held an enlarged session lasting twelve days and attended by 76 people, and made further revisions. Finally, between 22 and 25 June, 130 leading members of China's democratic parties and non-Party democrats were asked for their comments and suggestions.[22] The aim, then, was obviously to reach as wide a consensus as possible. The resolution went through six major revisions in all and must surely rank as one of the most carefully polished statements ever produced by a ruling Communist Party. During its lengthy gestation a number of articles on Mao appeared in newspapers and journals, and were presumably designed both to test popular reactions to particular theses and also to prepare the public to 'endorse' the final product. One of the most interesting of these was published on 10 April 1981, and was written by Huang Kecheng. Although Huang had been purged along with Peng Dehuai in 1959, he expressed concern that Mao was being defamed in certain quarters and praised Mao's 'immortal deeds'. He did, however, criticize Mao for mistakes made in his later years. Mao had, he wrote, been far too impatient over the pace of socialist construction. He had also exaggerated class struggle. Although he acknowledged 'profound historical and social reasons' as a source of Mao's mistakes, he also came very close to suggesting that Mao had become somewhat unstable mentally:

> Our comrades should know that Chairman Mao worked intensely and racked his brains for the cause of the people throughout his life ... he started racking his brains to

think about problems day and night. When I had the chance of being with him in 1958, I felt he had overtaxed his brain. When a person overtaxes his brain he is apt to make mistakes.

As a member of the Central Committee and Permanent Secretary of the Central Discipline Inspection Commission, the body which 'policed' the behaviour of Party members, Huang was one of the few people powerful enough to put such a suggestion in print. It was not, however, taken up in the resolution of 30 June.

Predictably, the resolution was severely critical of Mao's role in Chinese politics from the late 1950s onwards. It asserted that the Great Leap Forward had given rise to 'Left' errors, characterised by 'excessively high targets, the issuing of arbitrary directives, boastfulness, and the stirring up of a "communist wind" '. This was because Mao, together with other 'leading comrades' who were un-named, had 'become smug about their successes, were impatient for quick results and overestimated the role of Man's subjective will and efforts'. Mao was also deemed to have erred in attacking Peng Dehuai at Lushan in 1959.

Although the resolution went on to say that Mao had joined with senior colleagues in 1960 in attempting to rectify the mistakes of the Leap, this assertion was somewhat negated by the fact that it immediately credited Liu Shaoqi, Zhou Enlai, Chen Yun and Deng Xiaoping with implementing the 'correct policies' introduced to achieve that end. It noted, moreover, that 'Left' errors 'actually grew' between 1962 and 1966 precisely because of Mao's increasing intolerance and consequent tendency to see the world in highly polarised terms. In the jargon of the resolution, he had 'widened and absolutised the class struggle' during these years; his mistakes became more and more serious, his 'personal arbitrariness gradually undermined democratic centralism in Party life, and his personality cult grew graver and graver'. Because the Central Committee had failed to act speedily to correct these faults, Lin Biao and Jiang Qing were able to manipulate matters to their own advantage, so contributing to the launching of the 'cultural revolution'.

The illegitimacy of that movement was confirmed by the fact that the resolution referred to the term 'cultural revolution' [sic] in quotation marks throughout. It was deemed to have lasted from May 1966 to October 1976, and to have been 'responsible for the most severe setbacks and the heaviest losses suffered ... since the founding of the People's Republic'. It had been 'initiated and led' by Mao for reasons which the resolution completely rejected as conforming 'neither to Marxism-Leninism nor to Chinese reality'.

The Maoist thesis that the movement constituted 'a struggle against the revisionist line or the capitalist road' was flatly dismissed: 'There were no grounds at all for this definition.' Many things denounced as capitalist or revisionist during this decade were actually Marxist, socialist and correct. The 'cultural revolution' had confused 'the people' with 'the enemies of the people'. The 'capitalist-roaders' thrown out were, in fact, 'the core force of the socialist cause'. Moreover, although nominally conducted by relying on the masses, in reality many ordinary folk had been attacked and the movement had provided openings for 'opportunists, careerists and conspirators' to advance themselves. Practice had shown that the 'cultural revolution' was in no sense a revolution or social progress: 'It was we and not the enemy at all who were thrown into disorder.' Under socialism there was no justification for such a destructive upheaval. History had shown that the movement, 'initiated by a leader labouring under a misapprehension and capitalised on by counter-revolutionary cliques, led to domestic turmoil and brought catastrophe'.

The resolution produced a periodisation which divided the 'cultural revolution' into three stages. The first stage was from May 1966 to the ninth Party Congress in April 1969. During this phase, collective leadership was replaced with Mao's personal leadership, which was characterised by 'Left' errors. The cult of personality was pushed to extremes and there was nothing to redeem Mao's behaviour.

The second phase lasted from the ninth Party Congress to the tenth in August 1973, and the assessment of Mao's role here was not entirely negative. He had, it was claimed, acted with Zhou Enlai to thwart the Lin Biao plot and had subsequently supported the Premier when he took charge of the work of the Central Committee. However, he had continued mistakenly to fear the influence of ultra-Rightism and, due to his support, the 'Gang of Four' had gained considerable power at the tenth Party Congress and thereafter.

The third stage lasted from the tenth Congress until Mao's death in September 1976. The resolution acknowledged that he had eventually recognised the threat posed by the 'Gang of Four' and had criticized them. But it attacked him for having again fallen into error by turning on Deng Xiaoping in 1975–6. At that time, it said, Mao 'could not bear to accept systematic correction of the errors of the "cultural revolution" by Comrade Deng Xiaoping and triggered the movement to "criticize Deng and counter the Right Deviationist trend to reverse correct verdicts", once again plunging the nation into turmoil'. Along with the Politbureau, Mao 'wrongly assessed the nature of the Tiananmen Incident'.

Thus the resolution came down firmly on the side of Mao's severest critics in holding him personally responsible for the 'cultural revolution' and branding that movement as an unmitigated disaster. At the same time it went to considerable lengths to ameliorate the harshness of this judgement, and there were obvious reasons for so doing.

Hence Mao was presented as a tragic hero. His 'cultural revolution' was indeed 'an error comprehensive in magnitude and protracted in duration' but 'it was the error of a great proletarian revolutionary'. Mao had acted from the highest motives, out of a concern to safeguard the revolution to which he had devoted his life. Unhappily, his analysis of the situation was incorrect: 'Herein lies his tragedy.' The resolution emphasized that 'the history of the socialist movement is not long and that of the socialist countries even shorter'. The Chinese Communist Party had 'long existed in circumstances of war and fierce class struggle' and, it was suggested, modes of thought and behaviour appropriate to such an environment had tended to become ingrained and had endured into an era when they were no longer appropriate. Furthermore there was in China 'the evil ideological and political influence of centuries of feudal autocracy'. The resolution observed:

... for various historical reasons, we failed to institutionalise and legalise inner-Party democracy and democracy in the political and social life of the country, or we drew up the relevant laws but they lacked due authority. This meant that conditions were present for the over-concentration of Party power in individuals and for the development of arbitrary individual rule and the personality cult in the Party. Thus, it was hard for the Party and state to prevent the initiation of the 'cultural revolution' or check its development.

Besides, the resolution made clear, Mao's mistakes in his later years should not be allowed to outweigh his enormous achievements earlier. Rather ingeniously it was suggested that the ability of the Party, state, PLA, and socialist economy to weather the storms of the cultural revolution was in no small measure due to Mao's earlier work in creating and strengthening them. The resolution dealt at length with Mao's role up to 1957, and particularly up to 1949. Mao was acknowledged as 'the most prominent' of the 'many out-standing leaders of the Party'. He had 'more than once' saved the revolution from disaster.

Considerable attention was devoted to 'Mao Zedong Thought', defined as the 'valuable spiritual asset of our Party'. On the one hand, Mao was credited with having made numerous and lasting ideological contributions in the years up to 1957. On the other, the resolution made it absolutely clear that 'Mao Zedong Thought' was not to be confused with the sum total of Mao Zedong's thinking. His 'Thought' consisted of those ideas which had been tested in practice and found to be valuable and correct. Hence the resolution could state that in the 'cultural revolution' the chairman had actually gone against the 'Thought' which bore his name. And in one particularly telling passage it was made clear that Mao's achievements, in ideology as in everything else, could not be separated from those of the Party as a collective entity:

Victory in the Chinese revolution was, won under the guidance of Marxism-Leninism. Our Party had creatively applied the basic tenets of Marxism-Leninism and integrated them with the concrete practice of the Chinese revolution.

In this way the great system of Mao Zedong thought came into being and the correct path to victory for the Chinese revolution was charted. This is a major contribution to the development of Marxism-Leninism.

In other words *the Party* asserted its claim to decide what 'Mao Zedong Thought' should be. And the resolution also contained a suggestion that it was again to be regarded as something separate from (if not inferior to) the eternal truths of the founding fathers of Marxism. Whereas the late 1960s had seen the appearance of the formulation 'Marxism-Leninism-Mao Zedong Thought', accompanied by the assertion that the latter was the 'highest form' of the former, there was now a return to the less controversial 'Marxism-Leninism and Mao Zedong Thought'.

'Lessons Learned'

The resolution concluded by reviewing the Party's experience since the founding of the People's Republic and listing the lessons it had learned from both 'negative as well as positive experience'. It acknowledged that it had not responded adequately enough to the need to improve the people's material and cultural wants, and that the 'central task' must be economic construction. This, however, was to be based firmly on systematic and carefully staged measures. There was to be no return to 'Left' mistakes which had earlier caused the Party to depart from realities and to try to exceed actual capabilities. Within the planned economy it was necessary to give some play to market forces and, indeed, individual enterprise.

It recognised that class struggle was no longer the principal contradiction as the exploiters had been eliminated as classes, and it acknowledged that there were 'diverse contradictions in Chinese society which do not fall within the scope of class struggle'. Nevertheless, while suggesting that there would be tolerance of diversity for those whose basic commitment to socialism was accepted, the resolution reaffirmed that those who thought like Wei Jingsheng would continue to receive harsh treatment: 'It is imperative to maintain a high level of vigilance and conduct effective struggle against all those who are hostile to socialism and try to sabotage it in the political, economic, ideological and cultural fields and in community life.'

The creation of a 'highly democratic socialist political system' was described as a 'fundamental task' and the failure to do so after 1949 was a 'grievous lesson' from which the Party had to learn. The resolution insisted that state organs be made more democratic, that there should be a gradual move towards 'direct popular participation in the democratic process at the grass roots' and that special attention should be given to stressing democratic management in enterprises. The socialist legal system was to become 'a powerful instrument for protecting the rights of the people', and the 'chaotic situation' of the 'cultural revolution' must 'never be allowed to happen in any sphere'.

As for Party leadership, the resolution insisted that there must be no personality cult in any form. It was important to uphold the prestige of Party leaders but at the same time demand that their activities be supervised by the Party and the people.

8

Conclusion

In the summer of 1981 the People's Republic of China has reached a crucial stage in its development. In the space of less than five years changes have been introduced which are remarkable in their scope and, potentially, in terms of their long-term impact on the political life of a nation of 1,000 million people. At this juncture China's political system gives the appearance of resembling the more 'mature' industrialized states in the socialist world. It would be foolish to write of 'the end of ideology', but in China 'Marxism-Leninism and Mao Zedong Thought' is now being 'creatively applied'. The political process is far more open than it was, and is much more institutionalized. The leading bodies of both Party and state meet frequently, and their deliberations are given considerably more publicity in the offficial press. The days when the late Mary Wright, the distinguished sinologist, described the People's Republic as 'a journalist's paradise and a scholar's nightmare' may at last be ending. And the introduction of more regularized procedures has important implications for leadership change. In the immediate aftermath of Mao's death, the 'Gang of Four' and many others were unceremoniously removed from office with scant regard for even constitutional niceties. More recently, however, there appears to have been a genuine attempt to observe the 'proper procedures' at least, and most notably in the case of Hua Guofeng. Whether there is more to it, only time will tell. It may be that Hua will be the first of many top leaders to be dismissed peacefully, with some dignity, and with the chance to return to a senior position on subsequent occasions. On the other hand, the events of June 1981 may simply presage a return to the dismal process of vilification, dishonour, and worse, which has, unfortunately, provided the subject matter for much of this book. Friends of China will fervently hope that the first alternative proves to be the case.

Notes and References

Introduction

1. S. Bialer, *Stalin's Successors*, (London: Cambridge University Press, 1980).
2. There are exceptions, as the case of Kampuchea shows. After the collapse of the Lon Nol regime in April 1975, the Khmer Rouge established a brutal dictatorship which endured until the end of 1978. During this period much use was made of the term 'Angkar' which means 'organisation', rather than use of the names and titles of actual leaders. One authority described it thus: '. . . the anonymous Angkar is a new divinity to which the people are to devote themselves body and soul . . . Everything in Kampuchea is done "under the very intelligent, very enlightened and very just leadership of the revolutionary Angkar". Criticism of the Angkar is sacrilege, which under this new Institution can be punished only by death.' (François Ponchaud, *Cambodia Year Zero*, (Harmondsworth: Penguin Books, 1977), pp. 107–8.) Kampuchea illustrates another problem in identifying the top leader, following the Vietnamese invasion which set up the Heng Samrin regime in January 1979. Even if it is assumed that Heng Samrin is the leading Kampuchean, (itself a matter for conjecture), it can be argued in view of his 'puppet' status that the real top leader of Kampuchea is Vietnamese!
3. R. Garside, *Coming Alive! China After Mao*, (London: André Deutsch, 1981).
4. S. Bialer, *op. cit*, pp. 65–6.
5. M. Rush, *How Communist States Change Their Leaders*, (London: Cornell University Press, 1974), pp. 13–14.
6. On 16 September 1979 it was announced in Kabul and Moscow that Nur Mohammed Taraki, top leader of Afghanistan, had asked to be relieved of his post because of health problems and mental unfitness. His successor was Hafizullah Amin. On 9 October Kabul Radio announced that Taraki had died after a 'severe and prolonged illness'. On 25–26 December 1979 Soviet forces invaded Afghanistan. By 27 December Amin was dead, and had been succeeded by Babrak Kamal.

Chapter 1

1. M. Rush, *How Communist States Change Their Leaders* (London: Cornell University Press, 1974), p. 253.
2. *Ibid.*, p. 252.
3. *RF*, 16 April 1981, in *FE*/6725.
4. L. Dittmer, *Liu Shao-ch'i and the Chinese Cultural Revolution: The Politics of Mass Criticism* (London: University of California Press, 1974), p. 26.
5. *Ibid.*, p. 27.
6. J. Gray and P. Cavendish, *Chinese Communism in Crisis: Maoism and the Cultural Revolution* (London: Pall Mall Press, 1968), p. 155.
7. *PR*, 7 July 1978, p. 18 (my emphasis).
8. S. R. Schram, 'Introduction: The Cultural Revolution in Historical Perspective', in S. R. Schram (ed.), *Authority, Participation and Cultural Change in China* (London: Cambridge University Press, 1973), p. 73.
9. For a convenient survey of Lin's attempts to 'revolutionise' the Army, see E. Joffe, *Party and Army: Professionalism and the Chinese Officer Corps* (Cambridge, Mass.: Harvard University Press, 1965).
10. *Training Successors for the Revolution is the Party's Strategic Task* (Beijing: Foreign Languages Press, 1965), pp. 46–7.
11. A. C. Miller and Chung Hua-min, *Madame Mao: A Profile of Chiang Ch'ing* (Hong Kong: Union Research Institute, 1968), p. 62.
12. Dittmer, *op. cit.*, p. 93.
13. Decision of the Central Committee of the Chinese Communist Party Concerning the Great Proletarian Cultural Revolution (Beijing: Foreign Languages Press, 1966).
14. Dittmer, *op. cit.*, p. 100.
15. *Xinhua News Agency*, 3 December 1980, in *FE*/6593.
16. For an excellent discussion of recent material concerning the fall and miserable death of Liu see L. Dittmer, 'Death and transfiguration: Liu Shaoqi's Rehabilitation and Contemporary Chinese Politics', *Journal of Asian Studies*, May 1981, pp. 455–79.
17. For an interesting study of the Cultural Revolution, see A. P. L. Liu, *Political Culture and Group Conflict in Communist China* (Oxford: Clio Books, 1976).

Chapter 2

1. Lin's *Report* is reprinted in M. Y. M. Kau (ed.), *The Lin Piao Affair: Power Politics and Military Coup* (New York: International

Arts and Sciences Press, Inc., White Plains, 1975), pp. 518—62. This quotation is to be found on pp. 523—4. Kau's excellent compilation draws together virtually all the key documents relating to the Lin Biao affair published before Lin's fellow conspirators were put on trial in November 1980, and I have relied heavily on it.

2. For a particularly hagiographic pamphlet commemorating Lin's elevation, see *Chairman Mao's Successor — Deputy Supreme Commander Lin Piao* (June 1969) in American Consulate General (Hong Kong), *Current Background*, 27 October 1969.

3. S. R. Schram, 'The Party in Chinese Communist Ideology', in *CQ*, April—June 1969, p. 24.

4. E. Joffe, 'The Chinese Army After the Cultural Revolution: The Effects of Intervention', in *CQ*, July—September 1973, p. 457.

5. *Ibid.*, p. 456.

6. Interestingly, the attacks on Lin after his death accused him of both Leftist and Rightist errors.

7. P. H. Chang, *Power and Policy in China* (London: Pennsylvania State University Press, 1978), p. 198.

8. P. Bridgham, 'The Fall of Lin Piao', in *CQ*, July—September 1973, p. 432.

9. *Ibid.*, p. 431.

10. For the relevant text, see Kau, *op. cit.*, p. 93.

11. *Ibid.*, p. 107

12. *Ibid.*, p. 61.

13. *Xinhua News Agency*, 23 November 1980, in *FE*/6585. This lengthy article adds valuable detail to the documents in Kau, *op. cit.*

14. Kau, *op. cit.*, p. 72

15. E. Snow, *The Long Revolution* (London: Hutchinson 1973), pp. 168—70.

16. Kau, *op. cit.*, p. 62.

17. Chang, *op. cit.*, pp. 198—9.

18. *Mao Zedong Sixiang Wansui, (Long Live Mao Zedong Thought)*, (1969), p. 195.

19. This important speech is reprinted in Kau, *op. cit.*, pp. 326—45; this quotation is to be found on p. 328 (my emphasis).

20. *Xinhua News Agency*, 23 November 1980.

21. *Ibid.*

22. *Ibid.*

23. Kau, *op. cit.*, p. 92.

24. *Ibid.*, p. 89.

25. *Xinhua News Agency*, 23 November 1980.

26. Kau, *op. cit.*, p. 65.

27. *Ibid.*, p. 62.

28. *Xinhua News Agency*, 23 November 1980.

29. *Ibid.*
30. *Ibid.*
31. *Ibid.*
32. Kau, *op. cit.*, p. 70.
33. It was subsequently rumoured that Lin Doudou had been assassinated. The November 1980 version of events makes no mention of her.
34. *Free China Weekly*, 12 April 1973, cited in Kau, *op. cit.*, p. xlvii.
35. Kau, *op. cit.*, pp. 118–23.
36. *Ibid.*, pp. 202–21. This quotation is to be found on pp. 208–9.
37. *Ibid.*, p. xlvii.

Chapter 3

1. E. Rice, 'The Second Rise and Fall of Teng Hsiao-p'ing', in *CQ*, September 1976, pp. 494–5.
2. *PR*, 26 August 1977, p. 26.
3. Rice, *op. cit.*, p. 496.
4. 'Deng Xiaoping Shi Da Zui Zhuang', ('Ten Great Crimes of Deng Xiaoping'), in Ting Wang (ed.), *Zhong Gong Wenhua Da Geming Ziliao Huibian, (Compendium of Chinese Communist Documents on the Great Cultural Revolution)*, Hong Kong, 1967, p. 487.
5. American Consulate General (Hong Kong), *Current Background* 891, p. 71.
6. Schram (ed.), *Mao Tse-tung Unrehearsed*, (Harmondsworth: Penguin Books 1974), p. 265.
7. Rice, *op. cit.*, p. 496.
8. According to Deng's memorial oration on 15 January 1976.
9. *PR*, 24 January 1975, p. 21.
10. These texts are translated in Chi Hsin, *The Case of the Gang of Four*, (Hong Kong: Cosmos Books, 1977), pp. 201–95.
11. For example, the 'Gang of Four' were to be accused of 'reviling' as a programme for 'capitalist restoration' a 'Central Committee Document (1975), no. 9', dealing with Railways policy and, it may be assumed, advocating the sort of measures mentioned in the texts under discussion. To the best of my knowledge the actual document has never been published.
12. Quoted in Chi Hsin, *op. cit.*, p. 209.
13. *Ibid.*, p. 227.
14. *Ibid.*, p. 289.
15. D. Zweig, 'The Peita Debate on Education and the fall of Teng Hsiao-p'ing', in *CQ*, March 1973, pp. 141–59. Zweig was a student at Beijing University in 1976 and witnessed a number of the events discussed in this chapter. He also visited Hangzhou in 1976.

16. For an account of the chaos in Hangzhou, see *PR*, 30 September 1977, pp. 34–7.
17. *PR*, 26 August 1977, pp. 27–8.
18. Chinese leaders have generally been reluctant to discuss the state of Mao's health before the summer of 1976.
19. *PR*, 21 January 1977, pp. 14–17.
20. Zweig, *op. cit.*, p. 150.
21. *Wenhui Bao*, 18 November 1978, in *FE/5970*.
22. *PD*, 21 and 22 November 1978, in *FE/5977*. This very long account is the most detailed official report on the events surrounding the Tiananmen Incident.
23. Zweig, *op. cit.*, pp. 154–8.
24. *PD*, 21 and 22 November 1978.
25. *Ibid.*
26. *Ibid.*
27. Zweig, *op. cit.*, p. 158.
28. *PD*, 21 and 22 November 1978.
29. *PR*, 9 April 1976, p. 4.
30. Personal observation by the author.
31. Among those who believe there was co-ordination is J. Domes; see his 'The "Gang of Four" and Hua Kuo-feng: Analysis of Political Events in 1975–76', in *CQ*, September 1977, p. 492.
32. *PR*, 9 April 1976.
33. *PD*, 21 and 22 November 1978.
34. *Ibid.*
35. *Study and Criticism*, April 1976, pp. 11–33.
36. *Zhengzhou Radio*, 4 May 1976, in *FE/5202*.
37. *PD*, 21 and 22 November 1978.
38. For example, a correspondent reporting for the *Far Eastern Economic Review*, 30 April 1976, stated that he spent several hours in Tiananmen but did not hear Deng's name once.
39. *I & S*, July 1978, p. 92.
40. *Ibid.*, pp. 94–5.
41. *Zhengzhou Radio*, 27 April 1976, in *FE/5199*.
42. *Study and Criticism*, September 1976, pp. 10–13.
43. Personal observation by the author.
44. *I & S*, July 1978, p. 100.
45. *Shenyang Radio*, 18 June 1976, in *FE/5243*.
46. *I & S*, July 1978, p. 101.
47. *Ibid.*, p. 96.
48. Zhang's speech is translated in *I & S*, December 1976, pp. 94–107.
49. Domes, *op. cit.*, p. 491.
50. *I & S*, July 1978, p. 100.
51. *I & S*, November 1978, pp. 102–10.

Chapter 4

1. *The Times*, 16 June 1976.
2. *South China Morning Post*, 5 January 1977.
3. *PR*, 13 September 1976, p. 7.
4. For a thorough account of the circumstances surrounding the arrest of the 'Gang' see Andres Onate, 'Hua Guofeng and the arrest of the "Gang of Four" ', *CQ*, March 1978, pp. 540—65.
5. The importance of ideology was dramatically illustrated by the fact that on 8 October, just one day after the arrests, it was officially decided that Volume V of Mao's *Selected Works* should be published at the soonest possible date.
6. A detailed account of these reports was given in *Ming Bao*, a Hong Kong newspaper with an excellent reputation for obtaining information from China, in a series of articles published from 26—31 October 1976.
7. Handwritten copy, in author's possession.
8. Most of these Central Committee materials were subsequently translated in *I & S*, and I have simply cited them by reference to that journal.
9. *Ming Bao*, 22 October 1976.
10. *Ming Bao*, 27 October 1976.
11. R. Witke, *Comrade Chiang Ch'ing*, (London: Weidenfeld & Nicolson, 1977), pp. 12—14. This remarkable book is by far the most detailed study of Jiang Qing.
12. *Ibid.*, p. 4.
13. *Ibid.*, pp. 5—6.
14. *I & S*, September 1977, pp. 89—91.
15. *Ming Bao*, 29 October 1976.
16. *I & S*, February 1979, p. 95.
17. *I & S*, September 1977, pp. 99—100.
18. J. Domes, 'The "Gang of Four" and Hua Kuo-feng: Analysis of Political Events in 1975—76', in *CQ*, September 1977, p. 480.
19. *I & S*, February 1979, pp. 95—6, (my emphasis).
20. *Ming Bao*, 27 October 1976.
21. *Ming Bao*, 29 October 1976.
22. *Ming Bao*, 28 October 1976.
23. *I & S*, October 1977, p. 87.
24. *I & S*, October 1977, p. 99.
25. The role of this journal is discussed in some detail in J. Gardner, "Study and Criticism": The Voice of Shanghai Radicalism' in C. Howe (ed.), *Shanghai: Revolution and Development in an Asian Metropolis* (Cambridge: Cambridge University Press, 1981), pp. 326—47.

26. *Ming Bao*, 28 October 1978.

27. *PD*, 17 December 1976, in *FE*/5394.

28. *Shanghai Radio*, 13 November 1976, in *FE*/5368.

29. There is a little evidence that Deng may have given general encouragement but it is not strong and certainly does not suggest that he played an active part. See R. Garside, *Coming Alive! China After Mao*, (London: André Deutsch, 1981), pp. 140—41.

30. The interview was with Felix Greene and is available in *NOW!*, 12—18 October 1979, pp. 68—75. The most detailed studies of Hua, on which the following account is based, are: M. Oksenburg and Sai-cheung Yeung, 'Hua Kuo-feng's Pre-Cultural Revolution Hunan Years, 1949—66: The Making of a Political Generalist', in *CQ*, March 1977, pp. 3—53; Ting Wang, *Chairman Hua* (London: C. Hurst, 1980). My account of Hua's career up to 1976 draws heavily on these works.

Chapter 5

1. *PR*, 7 January 1977, p. 31.

2. *Ibid.*, p. 6.

3. *PR*, 8 April 1977, p. 9.

4. *PR*, 25 February 1977, p. 7.

5. *Ibid.*, p. 9.

6. *PR*, 6 May 1977, p. 15.

7. *PD*, 21 July 1981, in *FE*/6683.

8. Deng's letters to Hua have never been officially published although their existence has always been officially acknowledged. This discussion is based mainly on Chi Hsin, *Teng Hsiao-p'ing — A Political Biography*, (Hong Kong: Cosmos Books, 1978), pp. 135—7; and R. Garside, *Coming Alive! China After Mao*, (London: André Deutsch, 1981), pp. 174—82. Both authors draw on well-informed Hong Kong sources.

9. The communiqué of the third plenum of the tenth Central Committee is to be found in *PR*, 29 July 1977, pp. 3—8.

10. For all the documents of the eleventh National Party Congress see *PR*, 26 August 1977.

11. For the documents of the fifth National People's Congress see *PR*, 15 March 1978.

12. *Xinhua News Agency*, 20 October 1978, in *FE*/5648.

13. Fang Yi's speech is in *Xinhua News Agency*, 28 March 1978, in *FE*/5776.

14. *PR*, 5 May 1978, p. 7.

15. *Ibid.*, 12 May 1978, p. 17.

16. *PD*, 21 July 1981, in *FE*/6783. My emphasis.
17. *Ibid.*
18. *PR*, 23 June 1978, p. 15.
19. *PR*, 7 July 1978, p. 11.
20. A useful study of Wang is P. H. Chang, 'The Rise of Wang Tung-hsing: Head of China's Security Apparatus', *CQ*, March 1978, pp. 122–37.
21. This discussion of Wang is based primarily on a self-criticism he made on 19 September 1979. The full text is reprinted in *I & S*, October 1980, pp. 90–96.
22. Garside, *op. cit.*, pp. 196–7.
23. D. S. G. Goodman, 'Changes in Leadership Personnel After September 1976', in J. Domes, (ed.), *Chinese Politics After Mao*, (Cardiff: University College Cardiff Press, 1979), pp. 37–69.
24. *PD*, 21 July 1981, in *FE*/6783.
25. *Ibid.*
26. These criticisms are translated in *I & S*.
27. For the text of the communiqué see *PR*, 29 December 1978, pp. 6–16. An excellent survey of the background to the plenum, based on 'leaks' in the Hong Kong press, is given in Garside, *op. cit.*, pp. 202–9.

Chapter 6

1. For an excellent study of the role of poetry in the 'Democracy Movement' itself, see D. S. G. Goodman's, *Beijing Street Voices: The Poetry and Politics of China's Democracy Movement*, (London: Marion Boyars, 1981).
2. *PR*, 24 November 1978, p. 6.
3. *Ibid.* This very low figure presumably refers to arrests made *immediately* after the incident as opposed to the massive roundup of 'counter-revolutionaries' thereafter, discussed in Chapter 3.
4. On 24 December 1978 Deng Xiaoping addressed a memorial meeting for Peng at which he praised him for his 'honesty and integrity', and 'selflessness', *PR*, 29 December 1978, p. 4.
5. In November 1978 it was announced that the 'Rightist' label had been removed from those so classified and that they were being assigned to jobs again. *PR*, 24 November 1978, p. 3. In 1979 steps were taken to allow other 'bad elements' to rejoin the ranks of 'the people'.
6. *The Guardian*, 21 March 1979.
7. *The Daily Telegraph*, 15 January 1979.
8. See, for example, the lengthy summary of his poster in *The Sunday Telegraph*, 17 December 1978.

9. Joint Publications Research Service, *Translations on People's Republic of China*, no. 534, (26 June 1979), p. 6.
10. *Ibid.*, pp. 9–10.
11. *PR*, 1 December 1978, p. 3.
12. Wei's article is translated in *I & S*, June 1979, pp. 106–11. This quotation appears on p. 108.
13. *Ibid.*, pp. 110–11.
14. *The Guardian*, 14 March 1979.
15. Unless otherwise indicated, this account of the Shanghai protests and the quotations from Teng Husheng's posters are taken from Anne McLaren's excellent article, 'The Educated Youth Return', in the *Australian Journal of Chinese Affairs*, July 1979. The author was a student in Shanghai at the time.
16. Information from a colleague who was able to talk to some 'educated youths' during the course of these events.
17. When I visited Shanghai almost one month later, a pronounced police presence was still evident in and around the railway station, to ensure that there was no possibility of a repeat performance.
18. *Xinhua News Agency*, 19 October 1978.
19. To the best of my knowledge Hu's speech on Kang Sheng is the fullest official acknowledgement that a *secret* police, displaying the classic Stalinist features, has existed since the early days of the People's Republic. The speech is translated in *I & S*, June 1980, pp. 74–100. This quotation appears on p. 78.
20. *Ibid.*, p. 95.
21. *Shaanxi Radio*, 3 September 1978, in *FE/5911*.
22. *Tianjin Radio*, 14 August 1978, in *FE/5895*.
23. *Xinhua News Agency*, 13 September 1978, in *FE/5918*.
24. *I & S*, June 1980, p. 95.
25. The decision to re-investigate Liu's case was taken at the third plenum of the eleventh Central Committee in December 1978, and Hu Yaobang was one of those charged with leading it. On 16 September 1979 Deng Xiaoping made a speech in which he claimed that the investigation had 'clearly established that Kang Sheng was the Chief Conspirator who had framed Comrade Shaoqi', *I & S*, October 1980, p. 81. The full text of Liu's formal rehabilitation by the fifth plenum of the eleventh Central Committee (adopted on 29 February 1980) is translated in *I & S*, November 1980, pp. 75–93.
26. *Xinhua News Agency*, 24 October 1978, in *FE/5950*.
27. For a succinct discussion of the Li Yizhe poster, see R. Garside, *Coming Alive! China After Mao* (London: André Deutsch, 1981), pp. 102–8.
28. Joint Publications Research Service, *op. cit.*, p. 5.

29. *The Daily Telegraph*, 6 April 1979.
30. *Ibid.*, 4 June 1979.
31. *Ibid.*, 21 May 1979.
32. *Ibid.*, 17 October 1979.
33. Wei's defence statement is translated in *I & S*, March 1980, pp. 101–8. This quotation appears on p. 103.
34. A transcript of the prosecution's statement was acquired and translated by John Scott, and published in *Harpers and Queen* Magazine, May 1980. This quotation appears on p. 60.
35. *BR*, 10 March 1980, p. 10.
36. *PD*, 7 July 1979, in *FE/6172*.
37. *Xinhua News Agency*, 7 July 1979, in *FE/6167*.
38. For a discussion of the new legislation see Peng Zhen's explanation in *BR*, 6 July 1979, pp. 32–6.

Chapter 7

1. For the full text of Hua's speech, see *BR*, 6 July 1979, pp. 5–31.
2. *BR*, 5 October 1979, p. 33. For a useful biography of Zhao Ziyang, see Ch'en Yung-sheng, 'Chao Tzu-yang: His Rise to Premiership', in *I & S*, December 1980, pp. 25–37.
3. *BR*, 10 March 1980, p. 3.
4. Deng's speech is translated in *I & S*, March 1981, pp. 78–103. This quotation appears on p. 88.
5. *Ibid.*, p. 88. My emphasis.
6. *Xinhua News Agency*, 28 March 1980, *FE/6514*. My emphasis.
7. For the full text of Hua's speech see *BR*, 22 September 1980, pp. 12–29.
8. For a detailed study of the role of the National People's Congress, see D. Gaspar, 'The Chinese National People's Congress', in D. Nelson and S. White, (ed.), *Communist Legislatures in Comparative Perspective*, (London: Macmillan, 1982).
9. *BR*, 6 October 1980, p. 3.
10. Lin Nan, 'Lin Biao Sirenbang Liang Jituan Yushen Xiaoji', ('The Pre-trial of the Lin Biao and Gang of Four Cliques'), *Zhengming*, (*Contend*), October 1980, pp. 48–9.
11. *Xinhua News Agency*, 20 November 1980, in *FE/6582*.
12. *Ibid.*, 25 January 1981, in *FE/6633*.
13. M. Parks in *International Herald Tribune*, 1 December 1980.
14. *Xinhua News Agency*, 25 January 1981, in *FE/6633*.
15. *Ibid.*
16. Lo Bing, 'Zhonggong Hexin Gaizu Ji' ('Reorganization of the Core

of the Chinese Communist Party'), in *Zhengming*, (*Contend*), February 1981, pp. 48–9.

17. *Zhengming Daily*, 5, 6, 7, 9, 10, and 21 July 1981, in *FE*/6778.
18. *The Daily Telegraph*, 21 April 1981.
19. *Zhengming Daily*, *loc. cit.*
20. The full text of this exceedingly important resolution is in *Xinhua News Agency*, 30 June 1981, in *FE*/6764.
21. *Ibid.*, 29 June 1981, in *FE*/6762.
22. *Xinhua News Agency*, 15 July 1981, in *FE*/6778.

Select Bibliography
of English-language Sources

Books

S. Bialer, *Stalin's Successors*, (London: Cambridge University Press, 1980).

P. H. Chang, *Power and Policy in China*, (London: Pennsylvania State University Press, 1978).

Chi Hsin, *Teng Hsiao-p'ing – A Political Biography*, (Hong Kong: Cosmos Books, 1978).

L. Dittmer, *Liu Shao-ch'i and the Cultural Revolution: The Politics of Mass Criticism*, (London: University of California Press, 1974).

J. Domes, (ed.), *Chinese Politics After Mao*, (Cardiff: University College Cardiff Press, 1979).

R. Garside, *Coming Alive! China After Mao*, (London: André Deutsch, 1981).

D. S. G. Goodman, *Beijing Street Voices: The Poetry and Politics of China's Democracy Movement*, (London: Marion Boyars, 1981).

M. Y. M. Kau, (ed.), *The Lin Piao Affair: Power Politics and Military Coup*, (White Plains, New York: International Arts and Sciences Press, Inc., 1975).

A. P. L. Liu, *Political Culture and Group Conflict in Communist China*, (Oxford: Clio Books, 1976).

L. Pye, *Mao Tse-tung, The Man in the Leader*, (New York: Basic Books, 1976).

M. Rush, *How Communist States Change Their Leaders*, (London: Cornell University Press, 1974).

S. R. Schram, *Mao Tse-tung*, (Harmondsworth: Penguin Books, 1970).

S. R. Schram, (ed.), *Mao Tse-tung Unrehearsed*, (Harmondsworth: Penguin Books 1974).

R. H. Solomon, *Mao's Revolution and the Chinese Political Culture*, (London: University of California Press, 1971).

Ting Wang, *Chairman Hua*, (London: C. Hurst, 1980).

D. Wilson, (ed.), *Mao Tse-tung in the Scales of History*, (Cambridge: Cambridge University Press, 1978).

R. Witke, *Comrade Chiang Ch'ing*, (London: Weidenfeld & Nicolson, 1977).

Articles

J. Domes, 'The "Gang of Four" and Hua Kuo-feng: Analysis of Political Events in 1975—76', in *CQ*, September 1977, pp. 473—97.

H. Harding, 'China After Mao', in *Problems of Communism*, March—April, 1977, pp. 1—18.

M. Oksenberg, 'The Exit Pattern From Chinese Politics and its Implications', in *CQ*, September 1976, pp. 501—18.

M. Oksenberg and Sai-cheung Yeung, 'Hua Kuo-feng's Pre-Cultural Revolution Hunan Years, 1949—66: The Making of a Political Generalist', in *CQ*, March 1977, pp. 3—53.

E. E. Rice, 'The Second Rise and Fall of Teng Hsiao-p'ing', in *CQ*, September 1976, pp. 494—500.

Documents

Many important directives, resolutions, speeches and reports of major meetings are translated in *Beijing Review* (formerly *Peking Review*). The BBC, *Summary of World Broadcasts, Part 3: The Far East*, carries translations of broadcasts from local radio stations as well as material issued by *Xinhua News Agency*.

Index